**FOR PRESS INFORMATION ABOUT THE AUTHOR
PLEASE CONTACT:**

Sallie Olmsted
Rogers & Cowan Los Angeles
1-310-854-8124
solmsted@rogersandcowan.com

POINT OF CONTACT (POC)

A Memoir

By Robert H. Remmert

I have recreated events, locales, and conversations from my memories of them. In some instances I have changed individuals' names, in order to maintain their anonymity.

Copyright © 2014 by Robert H. Remmert

All rights reserved. No parts of this work may be reproduced or used in any form or by any means—graphic, electronic, or mechanical, including photocopying or information storage or retrieval system—without written permission from the publisher. The scanning, uploading and distribution of this book or any part thereof via the Internet or via any other means without express permission of the publisher is illegal and punishable by law.

Robert H. Remmert
POINT OF CONTACT (POC) 1-855651711

Live a good life.
In the end, it is not the years in a life,
but the life in the years
—Abraham Lincoln

The empires of the future
are the empires of the mind.
—Winston Churchill

If the camel once gets his nose in a
tent, the body will soon follow.
—middle eastern proverb

H. M. YACHT BRITANNIA

At Sea.   19th May. 1991.

Dear Mr. ,

Lady Airlie and I hope you will accept this small memento.

We would like to thank you for always being there and for looking after us so well. Umbrellas at the ready etc. It has been a really memorable visit and I hope one day I can return & see all the sights in a leisurely way.

Contents

1. Boss of the Wild Bunch 1
2. Proof I Was Here 3
3. Marigold Magic 9
4. Mobbed 11
5. An Electrifying Encounter 16
6. On the Lam(b) 18
7. One Scared Cop 21
8. The Last Laugh 23
9. Let Sleeping Sharks Lie! 25
10. Flying High with a Nine Year Old 29
11. The Misplaced Rolls 33
12. The Holy Grail 38
13. Mr. Syriana 42
14. Field of Dreams 46
15. Oops: Lending a Movie Star a Hand 50
16. Slovakian Humor 52
17. Ego Alley 55
18. Richie Rich 62
19. Skipping School 64
20. Celebrity Sightings 66
21. Gigi Saves the Day 68
22. Contagious 71
23. Chicken Little 73
24. Partying with the First President 75
25. Airborne 78
26. Get Around, Get Around, I Get Around 84
27. Blowing Bridges 87
28. Heaven Sent 88
29. A Coppola Birthday Party 90
30. A Close Call with the Soviet Military 92
31. Speeding to Las Vegas in a Purple Haze 94
32. Going to the Prom in Style 98
33. And You Thought This Was a Safe Neighborhood 100

34. Dropped by a Drink	102
35. The Curious Guest Saves the King	104
36. Crete, Armed and Dangerous	108
37. Clandestine Candelabra	113
38. Quality, not Quantity	115
39. Welcome to the Rockies	116
40. Babysitting the Family Jewels	119
41. College and the Caribbean Cartel	121
42. Everyone Remembers their First Time	124
43. Hotel Oasis	127
44. Timing is Everything	129
45. Sushi	130
46. Spring Break 1976	131
47. Paying in Cash	139
48. Defensive Moves for the Federal Government	141
49. Waiting for War in the Alps	144
50. The Midas Touch	148
51. On a Wing and a Voodoo Prayer	152
52. Soybeans	156
53. The Price of Admission	159
54. Tunnel Vision	161
55. Meant to Be	166
56. Someone to Watch Over Her	168
57. Weaponized	171
58. A World Cup Win	174
59. The Prince and Chauffeur	178
60. Banana Bikes	180
61. The Race	182
62. Inauguration Day in the Land of the Free	186
63. Graduation Party	192
64. Shielded from Harm	195
65. Saudi Arabian Customs	199
66. Celebrating My Birthday with Lincoln	202
67. All-Day Duty	204

68. The Queen Mother 207
69. Twentieth High School Reunion 209
70. The Hidden City 210
71. In the Money: the Best Summer Job a Guy Could Have 214
72. Memories of El Salvador 217
73. Thai Chicken 221
74. Broccoli Goes to the Movies 223
75. It Wasn't Me: A Brush with the Law Between Brussels and Paris 225
76. Breaking (In) Bad 227
77. Fine Wine 231
78. 9/11 232
79. Saying Goodbye 236
80. New School: A Survival Strategy 241
81. Table for Three (Two Rock Stars and Me) 242
82. The Fourteenth Street Bridge 244
83. Mermaid Tales 247
84. VIPs Converge 249
85. After You: Good Manners Save the Day 250
86. Chance Encounters 252
87. Paris by Night 254
88. A Deer in the Headlights 256
89. Shark Bait 259
90. Night Owls 261
91. Here Comes the Bride 263
92. Cadillacs 264
93. The Five Elements 267

The White House Ambassador Credentialing Ceremony

U.S. Department of State

Russian president's security detail at the White House

POINT OF CONTACT (POC)

1
Boss of the Wild Bunch

Owning a company with a limousine division, a security division, and a travel / hotel / private jet division involved a lot of different personalities and situations. We never owned the jets but rented them as needed—mostly Gulfstreams, Challengers, Lears and the occasional big jet. The limousine drivers, all long-term employees, were one breed I found fairly easy to deal with. But the security people were a whole different breed; they kept me awake at night waiting for the next crisis.

They were a wild bunch, more demanding to deal with than anyone I worked with. Three incidents stand out. The first involved a security detail in Beverly Hills with a princess and her entourage at a five-star hotel. I was in my office in Washington, D.C. and I got a call reporting that one ex-Navy Seal and a moonlighting police officer had gone out and had a good time while they were off duty. When they returned to the hotel, one of them had accidentally shot the bed in their room.

I said, "You could have shot through the wall and killed the princess or a hotel guest!" They went out and bought new sheets for the bed and got rid of the bullet-ridden ones. No one ever found out about it but I knew I should start thinking about shutting the company down.

The next incident happened when I had to let one of the security people go. He got to be too much to handle and wanted me to falsify some bank documents for him and other things well beyond the law that I just wasn't going to do. My desk was always bugged with a voice-activated device, and I always recorded uncomfortable partings with employees, just in case. I knew that he'd been an ex-mercenary in Central America and Africa, which was intimidating enough. He tried to back me into a corner and I absolutely was not going to sign off on what he wanted me to do, but we both knew it was the end. He came in and pulled out a notebook of pictures to show me before our meeting started. The photos were of all these different animals he'd killed. As he turned the pages, I expected people to appear in the pictures, but they never did.

He closed the notebook and said, "So what did you want to talk to me about?" He was clearly trying to intimidate me so I'd change my mind, but I stuck to my decision.

The last incident took place one night when I had a Gulfstream jet stop at Teterboro to drop off some members of a group going into New York City. Then it was to fly to Washington, D.C. to drop off the remainder of the group and return to its base in the Midwest. The lead security agent, once in New York, called to tell me that he forgot his gun on the jet that was now on its way to D.C. He was security and he forgot his gun! I said, "Okay, I'll take care of it. I'll have a car meet the jet and drive your gun back to you in NYC." I knew this would cost about $600. But the agent called me back and said not to worry about it; he'd figured out a solution and insisted I cancel the car, that everything was fine.

I said, "Are you sure? It's no big deal," even though it was. He said, "Yes, all is okay; don't worry about it."

The next day I found out he'd called the jet and had them fly back to NYC to drop off his gun after they delivered the guests in D.C. The cost? A mere $16,000 dollars.

2
Proof I Was Here

The limousine company I worked for in college had a contract with the State Department Protocol Office to supply limousines for Heads of State visits. This meant USSS motorcades, presidential delegations heading overseas out of Andrews Air Force Base (AAFB), and new ambassadors presenting their credentials to the president. All of it was great fun especially since I was in the center of all the action at the White House.

The Heads of State visits were the best, and it didn't matter if it was a king or a prime minister. I'd get the chance to drive like a bat out of hell all over Washington, D.C. for three days behind Park Police Harleys clearing the way with lights and sirens. We'd race up one way streets the wrong way, take the wrong side of two way streets, any route that would keep us moving until we reached our destination. The

Secret Service supplied two armored limousines, one for the VIP and one as a backup, and Suburbans with CAT teams (counter assault teams) as well. We were included with the rest of the limousines. In high security cases, a helicopter flew over us just above treetop level as an added precaution. Of course our motorcade bubble was heavily protected on the ground. Traffic would be stopped and we'd follow the leader, limousine after limousine, flying through the city, trying not to crash into the limousine directly in front of the one we were driving, since we were required to travel very close behind one another. It was like being

a race car driver with a license to speed. The tail car was always a D.C. police car with lights and sirens going full blast. Any time I was driving the limousine directly in front of the tail car I had to fight the instinct to pull over.

A master schedule for the visit listed all departures and destinations with timed precision, allowing only five or ten minutes to reach the other side of the city—trips that would normally take almost a half hour. These visits usually started on 17th Street next to the reflecting pool between the Lincoln and Washington Monuments, now the World War II Memorial. In bad weather, these trips started at Andrews AFB.

We'd stage the motorcade with press people, fire trucks, soldiers, and a red carpet on the sidewalk facing the Lincoln Memorial. We'd then wait as military bomb dogs sniffed all of the cars and soldiers checked the engines for anything suspicious.

The president's guest stayed at Blair House, which is actually not a house, but a series of connected townhouses across the street from the White House. The two short sidewalks to nowhere actually had a purpose: providing a landing site for the giant green and white topped presidential helicopters from Andrews AFB. As passengers arrived, we picked them up and rocketed to Blair House. The next day there would be a very patriotic arrival ceremony on the south side or in the rear of the White House with a review of the troops, bugles and drums, and a speech by the president, followed by a speech by the Head of State. Lunch in the White House followed, and then miscellaneous appointments around D.C.

POINT OF CONTACT (POC)

The official state dinner would be held that night in the State Dining Room. More appointments would follow the next day with lunch at the Capitol then a dinner hosted by the ambassador. On the last day of the visit, it was back to the helicopters and goodbye.

Even though I was only twenty-two at the time, I'd done so many of these that I was completely comfortable with the routine. Part of the fun was that I had the opportunity to work with my boss's bodyguard who liked doing these Heads of State visits too. He was a 6' 3", good looking German who'd attended Georgetown University. His name was Carl, or Garliff, but his nickname was Lurch, from *The Addams Family* television show because he was so big. He was great fun to watch in action, and to just hang around because he had absolutely no regard for authority and knew how to get away with anything. The son of a diplomat, he looked like one himself, but that's where the similarity ended. Carl was quick to punch anyone who offended him in the face.

Once we dropped the passengers at the North Portico for the state dinner, the usual routine was to sit there with the motorcade in front of the White House for the next five hours until the end of dinner, then we shuttled people across the street to Blair House. Except for the main VIP, guests normally wanted to walk back, so we were then dismissed until the next day.

To dispel the boredom of a long wait, Carl came up with a great thing to do every time we ended up in this situation. We'd walk out of the White House compound and have dinner and a bunch of drinks at Old Ebbitt Grill next to the Treasury. He was famous there and knew everybody in D.C. bars, so the food and drinks were often complimentary. In the summer we would sit on the roof of the Hotel Washington next door, now the W, and have a drink after dinner and look into the White House. Occasionally, Carl would smoke a doobie before returning. I didn't have

the nerve knowing I'd have to talk to all the Secret Service agents on the way in, but he just didn't care. If Carl wasn't assigned to the same visit, I sat in the back of the limousine to study or do homework. Only a few people can say they studied for college classes in the front driveway of the White House.

It was always fun driving in and out of the White House just because it was the White House. One night, at the end of the dinner, we motorcaded the Head of State across the street. Our Protocol contact only wanted two limousines to run shuttles, so while everybody else went home, Carl and I made a couple of runs, and the rest of the guests walked.

Carl and I normally parked right by the foot of the steps of the North Portico. When our contact came out, I'd walk to the top of the steps to meet the passenger or obtain an update on how soon the next person would be ready. The Protocol Officer had been there forever. He was always immaculately dressed in black tie and primarily looked after the First Ladies. That night, each time he came out with a party guest I could tell he'd been progressively indulging in cocktails a little more.

Carl and I always tried to one up each other or make each other laugh just to get through the day. So on this occasion, since I had a little liquid courage in me, I decided to do something over the top to entertain Carl.

Two marine guards in dress uniform always stood at attention all night at either side of the entrance so they saw me walking up and down the steps of the North Portico for instructions all evening, but I knew they were far enough away that they couldn't hear what was being said.

Carl was leaning against the front grill of his limousine, and I was standing at the bottom of the steps when the Protocol Officer came out of the front door with a woman from the State Department so I knew that we were about to be dismissed. An idea sprang to mind. I turned quickly to Carl and said, "Watch this." I waited as far away from the guards as I could, forcing the Protocol Officer and the woman from the State Department to come over to me. Sure enough, they'd come out to thank us and tell us to come back in the morning. I engaged the Protocol Officer in a small conversation about how the party was going and asked if he was having a good time, nodding my head a bit for the benefit of the guard, who had a direct view of us. When the Protocol Officer and the woman turned to go back into the White House, I followed right behind, just close enough to make the guard think I'd been told to come in. I figured that if the guard stopped me I'd say I had a question for the Protocol Officer. If I was caught by the Protocol Officer, I'd ask him if he wanted me to pick him up in the morning (which was absolutely forbidden). Once I crossed the threshold into the White House, neither story would help and, if caught, I'd be arrested.

POINT OF CONTACT (POC)

I made it past the marine guards, and I was now inside, but I needed to peel away from the Protocol Officer without being spotted. A string quartet played to my right, but the minute I entered the White House unauthorized, the theme from the James Bond movies began playing in the back of my head. There was the famous staircase on my left and people milling about everywhere. I was dressed in a nice suit, white shirt, and tie and had a security pin, while everyone else was in black tie. Only Secret Service would know that my security pin identified me as a limousine driver, yet here I was, inside the White House. Definitely risky business. The Protocol Officer turned to the left, and I walked straight ahead across the entrance and across the hall under the seal of the president, right into the Blue Room.

There were so many guests, I had to be careful not to bump into anyone, including the president. I saw a few famous people, politicians, and some of the president's Cabinet as I walked into the Blue Room, but once in, I went directly to the window to see the view. I received a few curious looks from Cabinet members but stayed cool and took in the view of the Washington Monument and Jefferson Memorial. I knew that all of the presidents in our history had stood on this spot at one time or another, looking at the same view. After a few minutes, I meandered casually back out into the hallway knowing I had to get out of there. I was really pushing my luck. There were enough people socializing that I could get lost in the crowd. I almost left, but then it occurred to me that I needed a souvenir, something to prove I'd been inside. So I started looking for something small and found myself in the State Dining Room. Nothing. I watched a butler go through a door and on impulse, followed him into what turned out to be a pantry.

"No one will believe I was here," I said when he turned around. "Do you have any type of souvenir?" He was a laid back older African American who seemed a little surprised that a guest was in the pantry, but without hesitation, he reached in his pocket and gave me a white pack of matches with the President's Seal on one side and a relief drawing of the White House with Jimmy Carter beneath it on the cover.

"How's this?" he asked.

I was thrilled. It was perfect!

I thanked him and he gave me a perplexed smile. Now I had to cross what seemed to be a hundred miles to the front door, all the time expecting that dreaded hand on the shoulder. Hyperaware of everyone, and with the cool sophistication of James Bond, I made my way down the cross hall, across the entrance hall, and outside to the freedom of the North Portico! Never looking back, I walked directly to the safety of my limousine. Carl looked stunned.

I said, "Don't say anything. Let's get out of here!"

We went to Chadwick's in Georgetown, the hangout of Aldrich Ames, the Soviet mole in the CIA. I showed Carl the matchbook.

"How are you going to top that?" I asked.

"Easy," he said. "When they leave, I'll be on one of the helicopters."

3
Marigold Magic

It was the summer of 1968, and we lived in a house that my father had built on a picturesque lake in Stamford, Connecticut. The memory stays with me since I was only 10 years old, and it was the summer of the Martin Luther King and Robert Kennedy assassinations *and* the white marigold contest.

We had so much fun living on the lake—swimming in the summer and ice skating in the winter. I thought I had perfected the technique of walking past my parents soaking wet from falling into the lake and fooling them, but of course they were never fooled. We had a great group of neighborhood kids that we all played with on the short street we lived on.

This particular summer, my older sister, who was 11, and several of the neighborhood kids got involved in The Burpee Seed Company's nationwide contest to grow a white marigold and win a $10,000 prize. It was just a big gimmick to sell marigold seeds and virtually impossible to do, but my sister and the other kids took it very seriously, concocting all kinds of different potions to produce a white marigold.

My sister had one nemesis, Roger, who lived a couple of houses away and who was determined to beat my sister and her team. Of course he was competing with her and talking smack because he had a crush on her.

The seeds were planted in everyone's yards and the contest began. My sister had picked a sunny spot along a stone wall next to the basement door we used to go out to the lake. There was also a window in the living room that looked out at the lake from which we could see the marigolds. My sister used that window to regularly check on them, waiting for the coveted white marigold to appear.

The marigolds grew throughout the summer in everyone's gardens and my sister's confidence slowly faded. Not one of the beautiful marigolds in the row looked even faintly white. She was beginning to feel defeated, and her nemesis Roger taunted her, claiming that he'd grown a white flower but didn't want to show it to anyone.

I was always building plastic models and other things on my project desk in the basement in front of a huge window that looked over the lake. To my left was the glass panel basement door where I could see the rows of marigolds growing. I knew my sister was getting sad that summer was now coming to a close, and she hadn't succeeded in producing her white trophy flower. One day, as I sat there painting one of my little model airplanes, I decided to take control of the situation and paint one of her marigolds bright white with my model paint.

I was very careful not to get any paint on the ones next to the beauty I picked out. It was the biggest flower, located in the middle of the whole row. Once it was white, an airplane could have spotted it. I told my mother what I'd done and she loved it because it wasn't a trick on my sister, but a trick on smug Roger. My mother called my sister downstairs and casually asked her if she'd look out the window for our collie Blaze, who was down by the lake. Then my mother and I watched as my sister walked up to the window.

At first, she did look out at the lake for Blaze, then she almost fell through the window when she saw that white marigold. She couldn't speak and kept pointing for us to look. We acted confused and unable to understand what she wanted. She hit the floor, panting and crawling toward us speechless, pointing to the window. We both said, *"What? What is it!?"* Then we walked over to the window and acted excited too.

We all went outside and watched her examine the white marigold, which worked until she touched it and got white paint on her fingers. She didn't get mad or upset, but instead was a really good sport, getting the joke right away. That's when we told her our master plan for Roger.

She was to let her marigold team in on the joke and then invite Roger over to show him. We installed a little fence in front of it to keep him from getting too close and trying to examine it. My sister and all her friends gathered around with all the neighborhood kids, and we called Roger over to show him. My sister was so proud as her friends talked on and on, giving long explanations about the combination of fertilizers they'd used to produce a white marigold. The satisfaction my sister got from the look on Roger's face was priceless.

Finally, no one could contain themselves any longer and we all burst out laughing, letting him in on the joke. The white marigold lived for the last few weeks of summer and made my sister the neighborhood celebrity.

4

Mobbed

I had to escort six dignitaries and a European HRH royal for two weeks. When I realized there was a three-day gap in the schedule with no official obligations, I had a quick meeting with the prince about what he'd like to do. I call this "falling off the radar" and normally arrange a discreet party trip to New York City, Las Vegas, Los Angeles, or Florida. I made some suggestions to the prince, and he said he wanted to go to Florida. I told him we'd just missed Spring Break fortunately, since it would have been too crazy to go with his group.

We had our own Gulfstream IV jet, so as a joke, the prince told me to tell everyone except the lead security agent that we were going to Texas. It was funny when the pilots made announcements about the flying time to Texas. After a few cocktails, everybody was oblivious to the fact that we were heading south, not west, from Washington D.C. No one had a clue, and it was really funny when they eventually stepped off the jet expecting to be in Texas, only to be in Florida.

We checked into a five-star hotel on the beach and took over an entire floor, including the presidential suite and rooms for security. I lined up some top restaurants and nightclubs but on the second day the prince asked me to rent a yacht for the day. I rented a 120-foot Benetti yacht and simultaneously discovered that there was a notorious bikini contest at a popular bar on the Intracoastal Waterway where we could hang out that afternoon. HRH approved. In preparation, I dressed in shorts and a white polo shirt and had a limo take me and a security agent over to the yacht ahead of the group. The lead security would bring over the main group an hour later.

When I arrived, I was surprised to find the boat's décor was over-the-top opulent. The whole vessel was done in Versace. Every little detail had the medallion and the vivid blue, red, and gold colors—the designer's distinguished imprint. I had the yacht stocked with everything guests could possibly want for the day.

When the entourage arrived, they also found the décor to be a bit much, but decided it was both funny and entertaining. I told them I'd had to rent the yacht on short notice, which reminded me of a jet I'd had to procure once that was decorated completely in leopard print. The yacht grew on you after a while, and after a few cocktails, it became beautiful inside and out. It was like the old joke *What's the difference between a dog and a fox? Three drinks.*

The weather was great and we cruised along the Intracoastal, looking at other yachts and mansions. Our yacht dwarfed most of the boats we passed. I rode on the top outside bridge with the captain, who pointed out anything of interest. He said he hoped we would be the only yacht at the bikini contest so we could have front row seats. A lot of people were expected. I went down and checked on the group to make sure they were having a good time, which they were. We played some good international music mixes throughout the yacht, and the food and drink kept everyone relaxed and happy.

The crew was very attentive. At one point, the first mate said that the captain needed to see me because there was a problem, so I went up to the bridge and he explained that a yacht was already tied up where we wanted to dock but that they'd given us permission to raft up next to them. He then pointed at the yacht, and I said, "That's a ship, not a yacht."

"That's called a super-yacht," he said. It was massive—almost one and a half times longer and three times higher than ours, making our boat look like the baby to its mother. The captain contacted the other crew by radio and the owner had no problem with us joining them. This meant, however, that we had to walk across or through their ship to watch the bikini contest or reach the beach bar. The captain radioed again so the crews were ready. There were many crew members on board the host yacht wearing crisp white uniforms with epaulets. I asked our captain how much a super-yacht like that would cost and he said in the 40 to 50 million dollar range.

As we approached, I spotted the owner running on a treadmill on the aft deck, completely indifferent to us coming alongside. Two beautiful girls in bikinis hung out on the back of his ship and they smiled and waved as we rafted up. As expected, the ship totally blocked our view and access to the bar, party, and contest. I was anxious to get over to the party to see what the set up might be. Both yachts lined up so we could step onto the other boat easily and then pass on through a door into a very large open lounge and out the other side down a gangplank. The set up actually made it look like we were all on board the other ship.

I couldn't help noticing that the other crew seemed nervous and very serious. Not one of them smiled. Still, I figured I should introduce myself to our host so I asked the first mate of our yacht to go with me since he was a local. My group couldn't have cared less about our arrangement; they were laughing and hanging out all over our own yacht. Our security was dressed casually but as always, kept a vigilant watch. The prince stayed on his cell phone the entire day and never left our yacht at all, so I crossed over to the super yacht when I could see that the owner had finished his treadmill workout. I introduced myself with a fake name and business card, and told him I was entertaining some businessmen from Canada, and we would be respectful of his ship. I always collected other people's business cards and used their names and cards for situations like this. I sincerely complimented his yacht, and he couldn't have been nicer. He said his name was Joey and that he'd done really well in the tech business—which was how he could afford such a magnificent yacht. Joey, in his forties, had a New York accent, wore a jogging suit, and was nice, athletic-looking, with dark thick hair and a tan.

He never took off his gold-rimmed sunglasses but was quite congenial, even saying we could party and watch the bikini contest on his ship if we wanted to. I was relieved that he wasn't a problem and that he was so accommodating. Plus, his ship was really nice! I went down the gangplank which was guarded by two guys and one crew member with the first mate. I didn't think anything about it at the time. The bar was packed and not worth bringing my group to, especially since we could party on our yacht and watch the contest from Joey's. I'd never seen so many tattoos in one place. The contest was over a swimming pool with a runway from one side to the other. I went back to report to the prince and see what he wanted to do. He just wanted to relax, have lunch, nap, and hang out, but said to make sure everyone had a good time.

We stayed barefoot for the rest of the day, going back and forth across Joey's yacht. I could see a few more people had come onboard and he seemed to be holding court on his big round aft deck sofa. The newcomers looked older and rougher but were dressed up in Tommy Bahama type tropical shirts and were accompanied by much younger, beautiful women. So as the day went on, our yacht party, Joey's party of about ten, and the bikini contest were rolling. Loud rock music and a DJ emceed the event. At one point, the DJ referred to Joey's yacht as a condominium at the dock. A few of my group hung out on the top deck of Joey's next to a huge hot tub, watching the contest. The girls took off their tops, only wearing thongs which made the crowd go wild. A typical Florida day, I thought. Nobody ever went into the crowd from my group since Joey's ship was close enough to the action and it was pandemonium if you got off.

I kept going back and forth until the contest was over and I noticed that several of the bikini contestants ended up on Joey's yacht. Near the end of the contest, on my way back to my yacht, I ran into Joey in the huge lounge as he was heading to the master bedroom located at the front of the lounge, under the main bridge. I thanked him again for his hospitality and commented on what a spectacular ship he had. He asked if I'd looked around, and I said no. He then invited me to check it out more thoroughly—to go downstairs to the rooms and up to the bridge, to really look around. He couldn't have been nicer. So I wandered down the stairs which were big blocks of stone; the walls and passageways were some type of exotic, elegant wood with thick carpet under my bare feet. I looked into each of the downstairs bedrooms, which were beautiful and meticulously clean and organized. I did notice, and thought it odd, that each room had a painting or two in them that were well done but of a very urban subject. Back alleys, slum street scenes, back bar rooms. Nothing nautical or having anything to do with boating.

Each room had its own full large bathroom decorated in exotic stone and woods. I headed upstairs through the main lounge past the master bedroom and up more stone steps to the main bridge, which was massive and looked like something out of *Star Trek*. The captain and two crew members were there. They looked serious as I asked them about the different controls and radar screens. The windshield wipers appeared to be 10-feet long. They told me that they'd be heading across the Atlantic to the Med and Italy in a few weeks. I asked how long they'd worked on the yacht and said that Joey seemed really nice. The captain told me that it was their first day. Joey had fired his whole crew of fifteen the day before. Now I knew why they were so serious! It was their first day on the job. I wondered what the previous crew had done for everyone to get fired. I decided to go back to my yacht and went down the stairs.

As I was half way across the huge lounge and almost to the exit door back to my yacht, the master bedroom door burst open, and Joey came storming out towards me. Yikes! What was this about? I was a deer caught in the headlights. He stopped and turned around abruptly—yelling at a blonde girl in the doorway of the master bedroom. Her makeup was smeared and her hair was all messed up. He was furious and used every four-letter word in the book, telling her he

POINT OF CONTACT (POC)

was kicking her off his ship. I was frozen. Joey was volcanic and scary and I had nowhere to go. He was between me and my escape.

He then abruptly turned to me and, like a light switch, without explaining himself, his voice became very calm and he was as nice as could be, saying he wanted to make sure that I was having a good time and happy. I was of course very agreeable because this was so weird and disconcerting that I just wanted to get off his ship. He'd done a complete 180 in the blink of an eye. It was amazing.

I returned to our yacht and got a Heineken and checked on everyone. All were back aboard as the sun was setting. I found our lead security who had stayed with the prince all day and told him what had just happened. He'd worked for the FBI throughout his career on several assignments. He said he'd been watching Joey and his friends throughout the day because something seemed odd about them. He said it had taken him a little while to figure it but he was in fact, pretty sure that we'd probably been rafted to the Florida mob all day.

I grinned. "Okay, got it," I said. "Let's go." We pulled in our lines and disconnected our yachts. I went to the back of our boat and gave Joey a thank you wave and he waved back while the others never looked over. We headed out to sea under a full moon. Everyone stood outside on the top deck enjoying the night ride. I had the steward give me another Heineken in the opulent Versace lounge. Then, by myself, I stood looking out the back of the yacht at the lights on shore as they grew smaller and the full moon rose over the water. I had "Hotel California" blasting in the lounge when I felt a tap on my shoulder. I turned around. It was the prince, all smiles.

He said, "Good job. Good day." He clinked his champagne glass against my Heineken bottle as I thought, Joey couldn't have been nicer....

5

An Electrifying Encounter

I drove a limousine while I was in college and one night I'd just finished driving from the Kennedy Center to the Watergate Hotel. My boss had a tall German bodyguard named Carl. He was German, had graduated from Georgetown University, and his father had been a German embassy diplomat.

When I dropped off my passengers for the night, he was standing in front of the hotel. He was a few years older than me, liked to party, and also the darker side of life. I was surprised to see him since it was pretty late at night. He asked if I wanted to smoke a joint with him. The last time he'd asked me this we'd been outside the Oval Office at the White House. We'd smoked out there on several occasions. I said sure since I was off the clock. So Carl told me to meet him at the back driveway behind the hotel and he'd be there in about fifteen minutes.

I left my limousine in the front circular driveway of the Watergate and wandered through the hotel to the back driveway. This part of the hotel was mainly used for deliveries and not for the hotel guests. It was a small, dimly lit area, the type of place Carl liked. It was a warm night, and I was hanging out waiting for Carl. Suddenly, a silent motorcade flew into the driveway and stopped in front of me. A silent motorcade is usually small—only a few dark vehicles with no lights and sirens, unless needed.

This one was just three vehicles: a car, an armored limousine, and a Sub-

POINT OF CONTACT (POC)

urban. The security people poured out, surrounding the area. They opened the back door. I was staying out of the way, about 20 feet from the limousine, wondering who the VIP was. Out stepped an older Asian man with glasses and maroon monk robes who came right up to me to shake my hand. I immediately felt something like a mild electrical current going up my arm almost to my elbow. The feeling was startling enough that I looked at my arm then his smiling face, then my arm, then his smiling face again, making me smile in response to the weird sensation.

He kind of nodded and half bowed quickly and let go. The sensation stopped. Then he and the whole group disappeared into the hotel. We never said anything to each other, just the smiling and the handshake and then he was gone. The motorcade disappeared down the tunnel that runs under the Watergate complex. Carl came out, casually trying to light up, and said he'd just seen the Dalai Lama enter the hotel. I said, "I just met him," and kept looking at my hand, baffled.

6
On the Lam(b)

I had a VIP trip with a small group from the United Arab Emirates (UAE). I used a Gulfstream IV jet that belonged to Greg Norman the golfer known as "the Shark," to take them from Washington, D.C. to Atlanta, then to Los Angeles. At the last second, one of the group showed up with a whole cooked lamb. He wanted me to put it on the jet and said that his wife cooked it for the group to eat.

This lamb was more the size of a sheep than a lamb, and probably weighed at least fifty pounds. The jet wasn't big enough to accommodate something like this, but we had to make it fit, so we ended up putting it in the cargo hold. While we were loading it, the flight attendant handed me a piece of paper that had come off the bottom of the tray with the name of a restaurant, clearly not the kitchen of the guy who claimed his wife had cooked it!

A security agent stayed with them, and I flew ahead and met them in Los Angeles. We stayed at the Peninsula Hotel, and I had the lamb stored in the hotel refrigerator for a week. I had a really good time while we were in Beverly Hills. Besides having two Ferraris and an unlimited budget, I had a chance to catch up with my good friend Sallie O.

POINT OF CONTACT (POC)

Sallie and I are friends from college days in Washington, D.C. who now lives in LA. She has always had excellent taste, which helped me with suggestions for the very best LA had to offer in the way of restaurants and clubs. When it was finally time to leave and head back to New York City, we needed a larger aircraft because there was still a lamb carcass and more luggage than the Gulfstream IV could handle. So I rented a much bigger brand new 737 that was outfitted as a living room with club chairs and sofas to take us to New York. The lamb rode on the floor in the back of the jet. The main group was in the front first class section that had large plush swivel club seats. I rode in the cockpit for the take off until we reached cruising altitude, then I went to the back of jet to hang out with the flight attendants. When I went to the back, they were on their hands and knees cleaning the carpet because during takeoff, the lamb had slid off the tray and down the aisle.

At this point, I was thinking we needed to throw the thing away. The lamb had been hot and cold a couple of times, and had been cooked more than a week before. It was unappetizing and grisly to look at, especially its face and head.

The weather was crystal clear as we crossed the country. At one point, the crew blasted really cool new age music on the jet's music system as we flew over some spectacular desert scenery. I stayed in the back having a couple of vodka tonics with my nemesis the lamb.

It was Election Day of the Bush/Gore presidential race, and I received regular updates from the pilot to pass along to the passengers. It was a nice smooth flight, and it was evening by the time we reached NYC. I went back into the cockpit with a Heineken for the landing. The view was spectacular as we flew over a stadium, fully lit with a game going on in the Meadowlands. Then across New York City to JFK, since the jet was too big for Teterboro. I spoke to the main VIP about the lamb, and he had me get an extra room for it at the St. Regis. Now my nemesis, the lamb, was getting its own room.

I had the hotel prepare it and put it in the room with plates and drinks. Knives and forks wouldn't be necessary since they'd be using their hands to pull the lamb apart. The room was cleared to only chairs and sofas, and the television turned on so everyone could watch the election results. Slowly, my nemesis, the lamb disappeared and slowly everyone gave up watching the election results since it took days before George W. Bush was declared the winner. No one in my group got sick that night, but I think America woke up a little queasy.

7
One Scared Cop

We were bored one Saturday afternoon, and my trouble-magnet friend Casey had a great idea: sneak my father's shotguns out of my parent's house and go shoot up the woods by his house. He lived in a development called Camotop (Potomac spelled backwards) that was filled with mansions, pools, and tennis courts. There was a huge undeveloped area there, too. We had two shotguns: a 12 gauge and a 16 gauge. We shot at anything—dirt, cans, trees, crows—a completely dangerous and illegal activity.

We were blasting away and at one point even scared a couple in a Jeep Cherokee who looked like they were having a secret rendezvous deep in the woods. They took off the second they saw us, which I would have done in their situation, only faster.

We'd been shooting for more than an hour, making a lot of noise, when we came to a clearing on a hilltop. As we stood there looking for new targets, I heard the proverbial twig snap behind us. I turned slowly to see a Montgomery County policeman, semi-crouched, pointing his gun at us. His gun and hands were shaking badly and I could tell he was really scared. I immediately told Casey not to move and stopped him from swinging around with his shotgun, which surely would have set off the super nervous cop, who would have then shot both of us.

We dropped our guns and put our hands up. It was surreal, something right out of the movies. The cop had us move away from our guns and with his gun pointed at us, he cautiously walked toward us. He couldn't control his shaking hands, and he was right to be scared. As he got up to us, to everyone's relief,

Casey recognized him from the mall where Casey had a part-time job. They were actually friends.

The cop was so relieved. He told us we so outgunned him that he'd been freaking out. We spent the next several minutes calming him down. He told us to get out of there, and he would say he hadn't seen us. That policeman was really brave, and we were really stupid, because it was the second time this had happened.

8

The Last Laugh

I was at the end of a two-and-a-half week dignitary visit, and the only thing left to do was to get the entourage to a private jet the next day, so I decided to have a couple of drinks in a discreet part of the hotel lounge with a couple of my off duty security people. One was a great guy, Chris Caracci an ex-member of Navy Seal Team Six, and two were former members of the Special Forces. It was fairly late so there weren't too many people around.

The guys started talking about hand-to-hand combat techniques, then one thing led to another, and we ended up in the hotel driveway. Caracci, ex-Navy Seal, first demonstrated 180 degree evasive maneuvers in the parking lot with one of our unattended stretch limousines that had me ready to call my insurance company. As I calmed down after watching that I told him that I wasn't expecting a full demonstration. I then asked Caracci what he'd do if he encountered someone and had no weapons. He said, "I'd lock hands," and proceeded to show me. His fingers locked between my fingers and in the blink of an eye, I found myself lying on my side in the driveway in my expensive suit with the wind knocked out of me and a cracked rib. I sobered up quickly when I couldn't breathe. They got me up and Caracci was very apologetic, explaining that he'd simply gone on autopilot. I was pissed, embarrassed, and in pain. I was the boss, which made it even worse, but fortunately no one else had seen what had just happened. I went straight back to my room a bit dazed.

Caracci tried calling a few times but I didn't answer the phone. I just took a shower and went to bed. The next morning, I woke up very sore, determined to figure out my payback. When I came downstairs, the other security guys said that Caracci felt terrible about hurting me, and I assured them that I knew it had been an accident. When I finally met up with him, he started to apologize again, but I told him to forget about it, that things happened, and then with a blank look on my face I went right into the plan for departure. I drew a very confusing diagram and told him that he needed to be the lead agent at the private aviation tarmac where he'd lead the whole motorcade to the dignitary's private jet—and that things had to go without a hitch. He looked concerned as I went through the diagram with him. It had buildings and jets scattered across it and a very circuitous route he'd have to take to get to our jet. I'd drawn a route requiring him to zigzag around the planes, refueling tanks, fences, and buildings. Of course it was all a fabrication, and he'd never even need to leave the hotel but I told him to really study it and not to screw it up. He'd have to leave in fifteen minutes.

    I could tell he felt the pressure of having all of the responsibility of the last play of the visit suddenly focused on him when it wasn't what he normally did, or was comfortable doing, without a dry run. About ten minutes later, I heard a loud burst of laughter. He'd finally seen that the diagram was an optical illusion. Using the buildings, refueling tanks and jets, it spelled out "Fuck You."

9
Let Sleeping Sharks Lie!

I was on one of my usual around-the-world-in-two-weeks trips, which had begun in Washington, D.C., and I was now having dinner with an attractive CIA analyst in Rome. It was a great meal on a cool night at a Piazza Navona restaurant by the Fontana dei Quattro Fiumi, a local eatery frequented by US embassy personnel. I went over the details of my trip with the analyst, returned to my hotel to sleep, and then was off to the Middle East at dawn to meet with some government officials there. It wasn't enough time spent in Rome, but the part of the trip I was really looking forward to was meeting some friends in Thailand in order to go to Phuket. We planned to scuba dive, an adventure that included an organized dive to a place offshore where sharks were known to sleep. My last stop would be California where I'd be mansion shopping in Beverly Hills for a Saudi prince for whom price was no object.

About a week later, I left Muscat Oman, and the only problem I encountered was that the silver dagger I'd gotten as a gift was confiscated at the airport. When the officials discovered who had given it to me, they said the pilots would carry it in the cockpit and return it when I arrived in Bangkok. I rendezvoused with my two friends at the Oriental Hotel then partied around Bangkok for a couple of days. We then flew up to Chiang Rai in the Golden Triangle to try some opium for the first time. Once settled in, we arranged a guide and some elephants to go through the jungle where we ended up in a Akha Hill Tribe village near the Myanmar border. There we were directed to a very sweet Akha woman in a leopard print blouse who never stopped smiling. She supplied her village with just about anything including local opium. We bought more than enough for the rest of the trip from her and were about to leave when she offered to smoke some of it with us. Inviting us into her hut, she laid down on a mat with her long opium pipe and smoking paraphernalia. She lit the pipe with her dark opium-stained fingers showing us how to smoke, smiling the whole time. In between her giving us our demonstration, she would get up and cheerfully put live squealing baby pigs from outside her hut in burlap bags and sell them to waiting village customers. We each smoked a little, but nothing happened, which left us a little bewildered until the opium lady motioned with her hand for us to close our eyes. The velvet slide of euphoria was instantaneous and was so incredibly pleasant you never wanted to open your eyes again.

The next day we flew to Phuket, which for the most part, is a beautiful, exotic paradise, but this time we stayed at a nondescript resort that was still undeveloped. The shark dive rep met us at the hotel and told us to follow him to the port where the boat and tanks were stored. Everyone drove a scooter there, but when we left the hotel, the rep took off like a rocket. We were zigzagging up and down roads, the three of us barely keeping up with him. At a T-intersection where a large tree had stopped many a car, I almost crashed into a huge pile of spirit houses. I found out later that the pile represented everyone killed in that spot in a traffic accident. There had to be a hundred of them, almost a hundred and one that day.

POINT OF CONTACT (POC)

We finally boarded a typical dive boat which was a relief since you never knew what to expect when doing something off the usual grid. Case in point, they didn't check or even ask, but none of us were certified to dive. We had, however, done it enough times to know what we were doing. At least the tanks, regulators, and overall equipment look good.

Our dive master was an ex-pat American who had dropped off the radar. Naturally, I was a little apprehensive about purposely seeking out sharks. I had encountered them before throughout the years, and it was always disconcerting to come upon one suddenly—like being surprised by a snake. There were three other people with us—two guys and a girl from Canada. We headed out to Shark Point, sixteen miles offshore, eventually coming to a pointy rock the size of a small house sticking out of the water in the middle of nowhere. The boat dropped anchor, and we put on our gear. The sun burned hot so we looked forward to jumping into the water. The dive master said to follow the chain down because there was some kind of bioluminescent microbe layer and we would all meet on the bottom. Follow the chain down because we have zero visibility in shark-infested water. Good start, I thought.

I always liked going over the side of the boat backwards because you never feel anything when you hit the water and you start breathing as if you've been thrust into outer space. This time, however, I was shocked to discover I only had a foot of visibility—as if I were in milk. I made my way to the front of the boat where I found the anchor chain and pulled myself down. Twenty feet below the surface visibility burst into full clarity and you could see as far as if you were above the sea—a big relief. We rendezvoused at the bottom, as planned, about 50-feet down.

The dive master checked our entire group for the OK sign indicating that there were no problems. The coral was beautiful, alternating between rocky canyons and white sandy patches. We spread out but stayed in a group following our dive master who swam like a frog, pulling his legs in then kicking and coasting through the water. The colors were deep, clear orange, red, and purple. Many species of fish floated around us, but no sharks. Some of the reef was being destroyed by the Crown of Thorns starfish, which is a large, brilliant purple color. While impressive to see, it was leaving a swath of dead coral in the wake of its feeding, essentially killing the reef.

We swam and floated over the rocky canyons, taking in all the activity and colors of another world. Finally, our dive master pointed down into one of the ravines with a large sandy bottom. I swam over and was startled to see an enormous nurse shark, maybe 14-feet long, just sitting motionless on the bottom. They bite. Our dive master had us head toward a large sandy open area where he indicated we should all lay on our stomachs on the bottom. We were about 60-feet or more down at this point. Once we were all side by side, he had us use our fingers to creep up on the sleeping shark. I had no idea we were going to do this. I just thought we would just look and keep swimming. We got closer and closer to this enormous shark until we were about 2-feet from it. Then the dive master had us stop and take a good look. Both its size and proximity were amazing. In fact, it just didn't look real. Its head looked like it was two feet wide. I was amazed our bubbles didn't wake it up as we lay there. Without realizing it, I was the one on the end at the left side of its head.

I didn't think it mattered until moments later when out of the corner of my eye I saw the Canadian girl reach out to touch the shark. The dive master tried to block her arm but missed. I turned back and looked at this enormous head right in front of me, then leaned back because I realized I might be in danger being near its head and mouth. The girl touched it and it instantly woke up. I stopped breathing and saw its huge eye register our presence in a fraction of a second. I couldn't escape.

In a split second, dozens of razor-sharp teeth and a mouth so wide it could have swallowed my head shot over me, skimming the top of my head and vanishing. The shark could have killed me in a dozen ways besides removing my head, including simply smashing me in the face. The thing about scuba diving is that you have to stay cool no matter what happens so I didn't move for a minute then glanced to my right and everyone was looking at me wide eyed through their masks. The dive master gave the signal that everyone should head back up to the boat. So we followed our bubbles up.

I was one of the last people on board and the girl was in tears by then, the dive master yelling at her, telling her with a lot of "f" bombs, how really stupid it was to have touched a sleeping shark. When I finally got onboard she tearfully apologized. "At least I was underwater," I said, "and no one could hear me scream."

10

Flying High with a Nine Year Old

I was in the middle of a three-week dignitary visit, and it was our last night in Washington, D.C. It wasn't going smoothly this time. There were problems with appointments, hotels, restaurants, security people, even some of the limousine drivers. We'd already been in two cities and the next move was to Miami. The trip was cursed.

The night before had been Halloween, and the group ate at a Thai restaurant in Glover Park just up Wisconsin Avenue from Georgetown. Halloween is insane in Georgetown. The streets are closed and packed with crowds in costumes. So after a big meal, instead of riding back in the safety of the limousines, the dignitary group wanted to walk back to their hotel in Georgetown right through the madness. I tried to talk them out of it, which made them even more determined to do it. There were eight of them, and I only had three security agents to make sure nothing happened to our main VIP, but of course I couldn't let anything happen to anyone. I'd been informed before the trip started that the main VIP was an assassination target by a couple of capable groups. What better place to try something than in a Halloween crowd with everyone in masks?

So off we went down Wisconsin Avenue, two agents walking next to the main VIP, and one at the back of the group. I rode in the front seat of the lead limo parallel to them with three empty limousines following us, creating a wall of cars and also a quick escape if something happened. The big problem would be when we got to Georgetown because the limousines would have to break off. Not even the president of the United States would try to get through such chaos. I talked our way through the first checkpoints to keep the limousines as long as possible until I finally had to abandon them and join the group at Prospect Street. I took the lead, and we dove into the crowds.

It was crazy and funny at the same time. We snaked on and off the sidewalk along M Street. It was a mob scene. We kept up a pretty good pace even though we were squashed at times. The costumes were clever and funny, worn mostly by local college students and, fortunately, everyone seemed good natured. No one even noticed us, and the group wandered, amazed by the wild action. It was a huge, draining chore to finally get them through the melee and safely to the Four Seasons. The dignitaries had a blast; they'd had never seen anything like it.

We got back to the hotel late, and my team was tired. I was leaving early in the morning on a commercial flight to Miami to get a head start fixing some logistical issues involved with their main appointment and to go over final details with the hotel. The group would come down later in the afternoon on the Gulfstream IV.

I barely slept because of the spicy Thai food and some nightmare images from the Halloween walk. At least, I thought, I can get a three-hour break on the flight. I arrived at Reagan Airport later than I wanted to, and they were beginning to board my flight. At least the G IV would have my luggage, and I only had to carry a small briefcase. I could get on and get off the flight and keep moving.

I was on the phone right up until boarding and couldn't wait for my three-hour breather. I had an aisle seat in first class at the bulkhead. I hung up my dark blue suit jacket when I boarded. I was wearing my lucky Charvet tie hoping that would get this dignitary visit back on track. I turned to my seat and was surprised to see that a cute little girl, about nine, was my seatmate. I'd been hoping to ignore whoever was next to me, but I didn't want to hurt her feelings. She introduced herself to me immediately, and I responded. I told her she was very brave flying alone, but she said her mom and stepfather were on the plane too, and that her real dad was in Heaven. I told her that was very sad but that her dad was always with her watching over her, keeping her safe.

When I asked where her parents were sitting she indicated that they were a few rows back on the other side. She said her stepfather was wearing shorts. We were still sitting at the gate, the crew was shutting the door and getting ready for takeoff, but I turned to my left to see if I could see her parents to give them an "all okay" sign about their daughter. Three seats back was a guy with a crew cut, in a t-shirt and shorts, sitting on the aisle. He was so muscularly defined, he looked like he was made of plastic. His eyes were intense, a little bloodshot, and seemed to drill right through me. I gave him a small okay wave. I started to describe the guy to the girl to see if he was her stepfather when suddenly his head appeared between and above us from behind. His face was all American, but he seemed wound really tight. I think the little girl and I were both shocked and scared at his sudden appearance. He asked if everything was okay. I said, "Yes, fine," but the next question was odd.

"Has my stepdaughter said anything? "Anything about what?" I asked.

He said, "Oh no, nothing. Just want to make sure she's behaving." Again, he gave me a long stare with his intense steely eyes.

Then we were saved by the captain announcing that we were leaving the gate to taxi for takeoff; he went back to his seat. I looked at her and she gave me a "yikes" kind of look. She was sweet and innocent, but something inexplicable was going on in her little world. I knew whatever it was was none of my business and I needed to rest. She had dolls and crayons and paper to keep her busy. As we were about to takeoff, I wondered what the stepfather did for a living. The little girl said casually, "He's a Navy Seal." I had a feeling it might be something like that. I asked her was her real father a Navy Seal as well, and she said yes, but that he was killed. I really felt for her, and it took me away from my own issues for the moment.

Once we were in flight, I helped her with the tray table so she could color. The flight attendant came and asked if we would like anything to drink before breakfast. The little girl ordered orange juice, and even though it was only 8:30 a.m., I ordered a screwdriver just to chill after a rough night. I made some small talk about her school and friends. I got up and went to the bathroom for a few minutes. As I went back to my seat, the Seal just stared at me with eyes like bullets. I gave him a small nod. I sat down and reached for my drink. The little girl had already finished her juice.

I never know the policies on airlines about making drinks. Sometimes they give you the little alcohol bottles with your drink and sometimes they mix it in the galley for you. On this morning they mixed it in the galley. Not thinking anything about it, I took a sip of my drink and couldn't taste the vodka. I was about to get the flight attendant when the little girl said that her orange juice had tasted funny. She'd drunk my whole screwdriver! Stay calm, I thought. This was the flight attendant's fault, not mine, but if I said something all hell would break loose on the plane, and the Seal might go berserk.

The girl was sliding around in her seat, loopy. Holy cow. She was drunk!! "I feel funny," she kept saying, with a big smile on her face. I was doing everything to distract her—coloring, looking out the window, anything. I needed to sober her up before we landed. She giggled a lot and drew crazy pictures. I ordered cokes and made her eat her breakfast. She was bleary-eyed for a while but happy and, fortunately, never had to go to the bathroom or throw up.

I tried to eat some of my breakfast, concerned her stepfather would check on her again or the flight attendant that had caused this situation would notice her behavior. Fortunately, neither happened. For me, however, I was flooded with panic for the entire flight instead of chilling out listening to music. By the time we got to Miami, she was almost back to normal. As we pulled up to the gate I told her that life would get better as she grew older and that she was a very special person. I shook her hand. Then I was the first person off that flight.

11
The Misplaced Rolls

The IMF World Bank meetings were starting in Washington D.C., and all the finance ministers and bankers were arriving. I was twenty-three years old and my boss told me to go to The Dolly Madison, a boutique, five-star, all-suite hotel near the Washington Post building. I was to go to the room of a billionaire Saudi Sheikh and drive him and his group to the meetings in their car.

At the hotel, I knocked on the door, and a British butler with a crisp accent answered. I told him that I was there to drive the Sheikh. He was a little hyper and agitated since I'd interrupted him unpacking the Sheikh's luggage, but he ushered me in to meet him.

The Sheikh, I'll call him O, was really nice—a polite, plump, older, balding Arabian man who spoke English with a British accent. Instead of wearing the traditional black or white robe with *gutra* headdress, which I was expecting, he was dressed in a dark blue, Savile Row suit with suspenders, which he had on without his jacket. He asked me a few questions about myself while telling his frustrated butler where to place various items of clothing. I could tell they'd been around each other for a long time, particularly when the butler glanced at me and rolled his eyes. After a while, I asked the butler about the car and he didn't know what I was talking about. I explained that I was supposed to drive Sheikh M in his own car. He gave me a disapproving look and said that I was on the wrong floor and in the wrong room. Sheikh M was one floor up. I was disappointed because in the thirty minutes I'd been there, I'd come to really like this grandfatherly Sheikh. He seemed disappointed as well when I explained I was in the wrong place, but he said Sheikh M was a nice man. What an odd coincidence that there were two Sheikhs in the same hotel and that I'd mixed up their rooms.

Now I was late. I raced to the right room and knocked on the door. A very tall, well dressed and stern looking, middle aged Arab man opened it and said he'd called my office looking for me. Before I could explain, he handed me a valet ticket and told me to park in front of the hotel and that they'd be down in the next half hour. I wasn't anticipating what kind of car it would be because I was distracted by the fact that this guy was not happy with my lateness. Not a good introduction.

I went out front and gave the ticket to the valet and stood there with my little briefcase of maps and miscellaneous pens, pads, and papers, aware that there were a lot of limousines, security people, and activity going on across the street at the Madison, one of the best hotels in D.C. Like all the hotels in town, it was filled with finance ministers and bankers. A few minutes later a big white Rolls Royce Silver Spur pulled up in front of me. I didn't realize, until the valet popped out, that this was the car I'd be driving! Wow, nice!

I got in to get accustomed to the mirrors, seats, foot pedals. The car had New York license plates but must have been transported down because the car itself only had thirty miles on it. This was a brand new Rolls Royce like the two Silver Spirits my boss owned, except this one was white and so much bigger. I felt like I was sitting on a sofa with a windshield. The dash was all electronic with beautiful burled wood and the classic grill with *The Spirit of Ecstasy* hood ornament. I fished around for the owner's manual to help get acquainted with the car. Along with the owner's manual, there was a cassette tape that I unwrapped and planned to listen to when I was alone.

Suddenly, the back door burst open and the tall, stern Arab man got in, ordering me to take him to the Sheraton Convention Center where the main meetings were being held. He introduced himself as Mr. S and said that the Rolls was his. He always bought a new one when traveling to different cities, he explained. He then asked for my home number because he wanted to contact me directly without going through my office. After I dropped him off, I was to go back and pick up the Sheikh and his bodyguard, bring them back to the meetings and wait.

POINT OF CONTACT (POC)

I headed back to get the Sheikh and plugged in the tape from the glove compartment. I thought it would be some type of introduction to the car but instead it was all music about being rich. Too funny. It started with Abba's "It's a Rich Man's World," with the lyrics, *Money, money, money, always sunny in the rich man's world...*

Back at the hotel, I was pleased to see the Sheik wearing the full traditional Saudi black robe with gold trim and headdress. He was a bit elderly with a little mustache and goatee and wore a huge gold watch. He appeared to be right out of Central Casting. The Arab bodyguard was dressed in a suit and helped the Sheikh into the car, then rode up front with me. Neither spoke English and tried to communicate with me without success. The Sheikh seemed to giggle a lot and came across as a benevolent, sweet grandfather with probably several wives and dozens of children. While I waited all day for them, people came by to check out the Rolls Royce because D.C. is such a discreet city, no one sees this kind of car.

My clients came out after six p.m. and had me take them to Le Lion D'Or restaurant the best in D.C.—then back to the hotel after dinner. Mr. S said to wait for him, which was disappointing since I wanted to go home, but when he came back out I took him to Desiree Nightclub at the Four Seasons Hotel for another hour, then finally back to his hotel. He spoke only to give me instructions or ask questions, which made things easier for me because I was tired and liked to mind my own business. He needed me to come back at 9 a.m. the next morning to take them to his private jet at Butler Aviation at National Airport. Mr. S said they were going to New York and would let me know when they were coming back so I knew when to meet them.

The next morning, the bodyguard put some bags in the trunk (or "boot," since it was a Rolls), and I took them to the airport about fifteen minutes away, the Sheikh giggling all the way at whatever he and Mr. S were talking about.

I waited a few days, and no one called. I checked in with my office, and they hadn't heard anything. The World Bank IMF convention ended and still there wasn't any word. I didn't tell my boss or office I had the Rolls and got paid for a full week even though I only drove a day plus one ride to the airport.

Days turned into weeks and weeks into months, and I was having a blast with my friends and the Rolls. We were only twenty-three years old and ended up meeting so many girls with that car. I drove all over the place. Doors opened wherever my friends and I showed up in that car. I used it for everything except driving to work where my boss would have confiscated it. I commuted to school at the University of Maryland, the grocery store, movies, even the McDonald's drive through—to the point where I'd forgotten that I didn't own the car!

The greatest thing I did with the Rolls was for my 85-year-old grandmother. My parents had asked me to stay one night at their house to look after her while they were out of town. She was going back to New York the following day. I arrived at my parents' house in Potomac, Maryland at almost 10:30 p.m. and found my grandmother struggling to put her old pictures into a photo album. She'd had a tough childhood as an orphan in NYC, then married my grandfather who'd been in the New York Police Department his whole career and had passed away. They'd had a long, hardworking life, plus three children.

I told her I wanted to drive her around in a Rolls Royce, and she didn't believe me. I took her outside and she was amazed because she'd never seen one up close before and believed that only Rockefellers rode in them. I helped her into the car. She was delighted and said she felt like a queen. I told her she was "one of the swells now," using one of her terms from the 1920s. She laughed and clapped her hands. Her head barely made it above the window. I found a station playing Glenn Miller, Benny Goodman, and Frank Sinatra music and we leisurely cruised around Potomac's mansions and manicured lawns listening to the music.

She said, "You live the life of Riley," which was a favorite expression she often used with me. After a while, I could tell she was getting tired even though she wouldn't say so, but it was after midnight. I told her we had to do one more thing. I drove into Potomac Village, the local shopping center, and drove around past the closed stores and gas stations. The shopping center was deserted. She asked me what I was up to and I told her she'd find out in a minute. Finally, I drove up to Hunters Inn, the local watering hole and the only business still open, and parked right at their entrance. I could see they were closing up. So we waited for about ten minutes until an older affluent-looking couple came out. They were totally amazed at the huge, brand new, white Rolls Royce and astonished at my little grandmother in the front seat.

"Okay," I said, "now we can go home because somebody had to see you in a Rolls." We both laughed, and she was sweet and humble, as always. I'm sure she was also a little embarrassed, but she did find me and the whole evening funny and entertaining.

About four months later, the call came. A man in an Arab accent told me Mr. S wanted me to take the Rolls the next day to the Madison Hotel and meet a

POINT OF CONTACT (POC)

man who would take the car back to NYC. I cleaned up the Rolls and thought I was so lucky that nothing had ever happened to it. No car accidents or incidents with intoxicated girls. Not even a door ding. I met the man and he handed me an envelope with ten crisp one hundred sequential bills. Within a few moments the Rolls vanished into the morning traffic. My Rolls. I believe that Mr. S had forgotten about it like a toothbrush left in a hotel. He was that wealthy. I never heard anything about keeping the car for so long which was a relief, especially since when I drove Mr. S to his jet, it had had about 100 miles on it and it had over 3,000 miles on it when I gave it back!

12

The Holy Grail

Sam, a good friend from high school loved, deep sea fishing and would often load a rental van with coolers, then drive the five hours from Washington, D.C. to North Carolina where he'd charter a deep sea fishing boat and go after tuna, Mahi Mahi and wahoo. After a day of sea and sun, he'd then haul the catch back to sell to sushi restaurants in D.C. to cover the cost of the fishing trip. On this particular trip, he invited me and two other guys along. We spent the night drinking beer in Georgetown and telling fish stories until around 11 p.m., then headed south. I rode up front, making sure our sleepy driver was sober enough and wasn't going to conk out and kill us.

We arrived at the docks of Oregon Inlet just before dawn, around 4:30 a.m., and climbed aboard the *Seabird*. She was a 50-foot sport fishing vessel with plenty of room for all four of us plus a first mate and captain. The dock was bustling with activity since other boats were also loading passengers and supplies for the same purpose. Ultimately, a fleet of nearly a dozen vessels cast off that morning and, following each other, headed out to sea before the sun crested the horizon.

The trip to the Continental Shelf, where the fish feed, would take two hours, so we drew straws before we went to sleep to see who would fish first and the order to follow. I drew the straw for first up and our order established, we all spread out to sleep wherever we could. In the lounge, near the stern, I was asleep in seconds with a life vest as a pillow. The ocean was calm, the crew quiet, and the boat powered through the night, with only the sound of the engine and the light of the stars punctuating the sky.

POINT OF CONTACT (POC)

It seemed as if I'd barely closed my eyes when I awoke hungover and very nauseous due to the smell of diesel fumes and baitfish, with a hot sun beating down. I was thinking I better get out on deck to put my head over the side when the first mate yelled, "Bait going in the water, bait going in the water!" This meant all six poles were being unreeled and the boat was now going to begin a trolling pattern in sight of the other boats, all of which were doing the same.

The sun was intense, increasingly relentless as it rose, and the sea rolled under us. On a good day, this might have made me a little seasick but hungover, it was more than I could take. From my experience fishing with my father in the Virgin Islands, I knew it could be hours before we got any fish, so I decided now was the time to pay the piper for last night's indulgence—get on deck, be sick over the side, and get in a little more sleep. The more I thought about it, the more pressing the need became, so I hoisted myself up and headed for the deck in search of relief.

Just as my head popped out of the lounge, the first mate shouted, "Fish! Fish! Who's up? Who's up?" I was halfway between the side of the boat, where I desperately needed to be, and the fighting chair. Sam and the other guys were yelling for me to get in the chair along with the captain and first mate. This is one of the most exciting moments on a deep sea fishing trip—one of adrenaline-pumped pandemonium—unless your head is ready to crack open and you just want to throw up.

The first mate busied himself reeling in the lines on the other poles, and the captain stopped the boat. One fishing pole was zinging as the line rushed out of it at what seemed like 10-feet per second. I got in the chair, and the harness was clipped to me, the rod placed in the cup. I only wanted to heave myself over the side but I grasped the rod as the first mate yelled, "Reel! Reel!" I knew what was expected from the days fishing with my father—reel in the slack, sink the hook, reel in the fish—probably a sixty-seventy pound tuna or wahoo. I had never been more motivated, since as soon as I got this fish to the boat I could give in to the nausea consuming all my concentration. So I put the nausea on hold, and with everyone cheering and shouting instructions, I began to feverishly reel in the slack line.

I worked that reel for all I was worth and the slack line slowed, slowed some more, and then felt like cement. I simply couldn't crank the reel over even one more time so in desperation, I pulled back with all my strength, both upper body and legs, and even then, it felt as if I were pulling on a bus driving away from me. The thick rod was bent over, pointing to the port side of the boat.

At that exact moment, I heard a collective, "Whoa, Holy shit!" I turned to look behind me to see what everyone else was looking at—something breaking the surface far to starboard. An enormous blue marlin broke the surface for one shimmering second—magnificent, glittering in the sunlight, an enormous and powerful specimen. As my head spun, I thought, "Wow, that marlin is huge, I wonder what I have?" At that moment, my buddies yelled, "That's your fish!"

My line had arced in a huge half circle and with every pull on it, the marlin leapt from the ocean in defiance. This was the Holy Grail of deep sea fishing—a five-hour fish if ever there was one and it wasn't even 8 a.m. I reeled, my fingers pinched, my arms aching, my stomach roiling, the boat rocking in the waves. Sometimes I'd gain a few inches only to lose them again as the fish leapt repeatedly moving further away in an effort to dislodge the hook. The sun rose higher and hotter.

I didn't want this fish; I wanted a clean bathroom, privacy, maybe some sushi when all was said and done. I told the crew to cut the line—let it go—I was done.

"Are you *crazy*?" the captain snapped. "No way I'm letting that fish go."

I didn't understand at the time that to release the catch, or to switch seats so someone else could reel it in would cost the captain his right to claim a record-breaking fish for his boat. In the charter fishing business, your reputation is your livelihood.

I just wanted to throw in the towel, to throw up. My buddy switched places with me, almost by osmosis, and took the chair after about twenty five more minutes. I made it to the side of the boat, t-shirt stuck to me, in the nick of time. Everything from the night before finally went overboard. I crawled back down to the lounge to lay on the floor, exhausted, while my buddies yelled down a play by play, forcing me to visualize the continuing marathon with that magnificent fish.

Finally, after only fifty minutes from being hooked, that powerful Blue Marlin was pulled through the aft hatch door. We gathered around—it took up all of the back deck. Its eyes were the size of dinner plates and the bill was 4-feet long. The fish itself measured 17-feet, 3-inches and weighed 817 pounds,

And it was beautiful. Unearthly. A privilege to see.

Pulled from its home, wrenched into an atmosphere where it was suffocating only feet from the water it had known all its life, we watched it die. It was a somber moment, and I was sick again, only this time I was sick at what we'd done and my role in it. As I stood there full of regret and remorse, the fish turned its eye and looked directly at me with a consciousness that felt personal, a presence that was unnerving. I wished we'd never crossed paths, that it was still in the ocean. I wanted to tell it I was sorry but then it was gone.

Somehow this wasn't a sport—it was an intrusion, a breaking and entering, a home invasion of the worst kind, and it had victimized the innocent. It hadn't even been a fair fight. I discovered that the double hooks had clamped its mouth so that it ran out of steam hours before it would have—hours before it could have broken free. Since that incident, I've read that marlins can sense when they are caught in such a way that they're not going to be able to break free, and will, in fact, commit suicide, swimming for the depths until the pressure crushes their brains rather than be hauled over the side of a boat to suffocate in the air. I don't know if this is true, but that day I could believe that it was.

The marlin laid on the deck all day as other boats pulled alongside to admire our catch. We also caught three small sailfish that we let go and at the end of the day headed back to the dock where a crowd had gathered to see the marlin since the captain had radioed ahead that we had something special. I had to act like I was happy and even pose for pictures with it until we left the dock at dusk to head back to D.C. I looked back at the fish as we walked down the pier and knew I'd never go fishing again. I could only see her huge black silhouette hanging, alone. The leering, competitive crowds were gone now, driving home, or having dinner, or maybe watching the news. My buddy planned to have the fish mounted and hung in his basement. But for now, there was just this magnificent fish and her silent ocean.

I was transformed by the senselessness and waste of her death since I've always carried the moment with me. It's a fish story best left at the bottom of the sea.

13

Mr. Syriana

At the height of business, the company I'd formed in Washington, D.C. handled motorcades for the White House, embassy delegations, and stealth delegations around the country, providing protocol, security, and private jets as needed. We even provided a point of contact for some of the wealthiest people in the world, keeping everything we did under the radar. At one point, employees at the Four Seasons, in D.C. nicknamed me "Mr. Syriana" after a George Clooney spy movie. We moved people in and out of places around the country so discreetly no one even noticed.

Coincidentally, one very, very rainy night, I went to Cafe Milano in Georgetown in order to have dinner with a top intelligence person and a very high level Middle East envoy. I noticed two men sitting a few tables away not eating or drinking who kept glancing over at us. I mentioned it and I was told nonchalantly that they were Israelis doing surveillance on the envoy and they didn't care if they were obvious. It was all part of the game and by chance George Clooney was having dinner there too.

As the head of the company, I used a fictitious person's name at times to avoid being required to make decisions on the spot. This also allowed me to select what jobs I might want to be involved in first hand, like particularly appealing trips or interesting motorcades. A couple of times a Head of State motorcade would have been assigned to a lead Secret Service agent new to doing them and I'd assist, which was always appreciated.

Which brings me to the fact that I love the St. Regis in NYC. It has the best service, it's discreet, and one of the most elegant hotels in the country. John

POINT OF CONTACT (POC)

Jacob Astor IV, who died on the *Titanic*, built the hotel in 1904. It was home to Marlene Dietrich and Salvador Dali and countless other celebrities over the last century. Parts of the Godfather and Hitchcock movies have been filmed there, too. Over the years, the hotel staff, from the doormen, bellmen, maître d's, security, and gift shop clerks, got to know me and they knew never to ask me questions. I was always generous with all of them in order to keep my visits running smoothly and in order to never hear "no" for anything I might need for a client. I'd learned that even if you're a billionaire or a famous celebrity, if you don't tip well, you might as well go to the back of the line, so I was a walking ATM. I kept hundred dollars bills in my front right pants pocket, fifties in the left, twenties in the right coat pocket and tens in the left, and I wrote an endless list of who I'd doled them out to. When I ran out, I'd just get more.

Normally, I'd take over part of a floor anchored by one of their designer suites done by Dior, Tiffany, Milan, or Bentley. They were big enough to suit my clients with large bedrooms, foyers, living and dining rooms. I had used the presidential suite as well, but had gotten complaints from some guests that it was just too big.

On this occasion, I was back at the St. Regis for three days at the end of an exhausting trip of almost a month around the U.S. Everything was fine, as usual, but there was an older security officer I'd never seen before. He appeared to be retired police—tough and gruff—and very curious to discover what my arrangement was and what we were up to. He asked questions about my group around the hotel, which was disconcerting because my goal was to keep us invisible and only involve people on a need to know basis. He didn't need to know.

I could tell he didn't like me right away, and my people knew never to reveal anything or just to give disinformation to make people like this guy go away. We were there with someone important; in addition to an entire entourage, we were paying a fortune, and never bothered other guests, so my feeling was that he should just back off.

But he wanted to know about our comings and goings, so at first, I just supplied the wrong times. Unfortunately, he caught on quickly and I could tell he wasn't happy with me. Finally, my delegation left on the Concorde (after I'd been allowed to visit the cockpit before they took off). They'd left late enough in the afternoon that the rooms were just going to sit empty until the next day, so I planned to have a small party in the main suite, which was designed by Tiffany. At $8,000 a day, it would have been a waste not to use it. I had the hotel refresh it while we were at JFK, then had my girlfriend, my cousins, and a few friends who worked in NYC come on up to the suite. I had one of the limousine drivers pick up wine, vodka, and sodas and drop it all off at the suite. It was late in the day by this time, my team and the delegation were gone, and everything had gone perfectly for the whole visit. I ordered light food from room service and was relaxing and laughing with everyone. Nice music was playing, we had a great view of Fifth Avenue, and Central Park, and all from this spectacular suite where everything in it said: Tiffany.

Everyone was having a good time when there was an unusually loud knock at the front door. Room Service would have silently put the food in the dining room coming and going through the service door, and everyone I'd invited was already there. And, most importantly, I absolutely knew the Concorde had taken off, so the pounding on the door was unexpected.

Before I could even get up, it happened again, loud and aggressive, like a police raid and I thought, surely the music isn't that loud. I'd had a couple of drinks already and was relaxed and thought WTF is it?! I flung open one of the double doors and there stood the security officer AGAIN, and with him was an attractive blonde woman wearing a pants suit and a security pin. The security officer looked positively triumphant, but I was more startled to see the blonde and she was just as startled to see me.

The security officer began the speech he'd been aching to give me for days. "The president of the United States is coming here today and this is a United States Secret Service agent doing the advance for the president, and I told her that I believe you have weapons in there. We're here to search the suite."

POINT OF CONTACT (POC)

He finished, flushed and pleased with himself, and I looked back at the pretty Secret Service agent. "It figures it's you," she said with a smile.

We'd worked a visit together at the White House a few months earlier, and because it was her first motorcade I'd helped her out. Everything had gone flawlessly. She was very attractive and I knew she'd just come to Washington, D.C. from Georgia. We both cracked up at the absurdity of the situation, and I invited her into the suite. I grinned at the security officer as I closed the door and left him fuming in the hall.

She was still trying to take in that it was me that the security guy was trying to get into trouble, and I was relieved that it was her who'd been assigned to check me out. For the record, she did ask me about weapons and with a smile, I told her my security team was gone and most of the weapons were legal. I introduced her around but she couldn't stay long. The president of the United States (POTUS) was coming.

14

Field of Dreams

I was a new student at Winston Churchill High School in Potomac, MD. It was the first public school I'd ever attended. I'd previously been enrolled in strict private schools in Texas and around the world—wherever my father's job took us—and although I'd already acquired enough credits to go to college, I didn't want to miss out on the experience of being a high school senior. Eventually, since it was just for one year, I talked my parents into letting me go to the local public school. This meant girls and no uniforms.

Most of the kids at Churchill came from wealthy families and displayed an aversion to authority of any kind. Darren Star, who created *Beverly Hills 90210* and *Sex and the City*, attended Churchill, and it was said he based *90210* on his Churchill experience.

One of the first friends I made there, Casey, was also new. Later, I'd discover he was new to Churchill because he'd been kicked out of so many other schools. Charismatic and hugely popular with the girls, Casey was one hundred percent trouble.

Our friendship began conventionally enough: I covered for him in art class every time the teacher turned around Casey threw clay at him. But the fact that he had five beautiful younger sisters and lived in a mansion didn't hurt. Casey was always scheming, especially when it came to girls, money, or marijuana. Though he was a terrible student, he was great entertainment, both in and out of school. The police were routinely at his house but his mother, who knew he was mischievous (to say the least), would automatically deny his involvement in whatever incident was being investigated and always supplied him with an

POINT OF CONTACT (POC)

alibi. She was a beautiful blonde who usually charmed the policemen until they went away.

So one day, Casey informed me that the old caretaker at the stable where his sister kept her horse said that if he could get a ride home to West Virginia, he'd show Casey a place where he could have all the marijuana he could pick. Since Casey had totaled his car, a huge Riviera, right in front of school one afternoon in a spectacular crash, he asked me to drive. I had an older, orange Camaro that I'd inherited when my sister left for college, but it would do.

On the agreed upon day, we drove to the farm on Glen Road in Potomac before sunrise to pick the guy up. I was immediately afraid of him. There isn't much to a back seat of a Camaro, and this guy filled it. He was black as night, wearing an old green plaid shirt and a beat up cowboy hat, and he smelled like a barn. As he got in, I was thinking this was what a serial killer would look like, but I could tell Casey wasn't concerned in the least and that he just wanted to get to the pot fields.

The guy said his name was Lem. He didn't talk much except when he had to give directions. We were going to Moorefield, West Virginia, about two and a half hours west, and I was sure we were going to be murdered once we arrived. Lem's story was that the government had been experimenting with marijuana upstream when a huge flood washed seeds from the plants downriver to Moorefield.

Casey had brought some black trash bags to fill with pot plants but, looking in the rearview mirror at Lem, I thought we would be the only things going in them. Still, the scenery was beautiful as the sun came up, and we listened to the same Aerosmith tape over and over until we finally arrived at our destination, a one-traffic-light town along the south banks of the Potomac River. The only two buildings of note were the police station and a Dairy Queen.

Lem told me to begin driving up a dirt road into the woods and then indicated I should continue toward a bunch of shanties. Again my mind went to the trash bags, and I thought: This is it. Having heard us coming up the hill, entire families started coming outside to investigate. Apparently, cars seldom came up there, and we were particularly suspect since we were a couple of out of place white kids. They couldn't see Lem in the back seat. The poverty around us was startling. People didn't wear any shoes, just dirty clothes, and lived in a kaleidoscope of shacks with smokestacks.

I parked and everyone rushed toward us when Lem emerged from the car. They were so happy to see him; they treated him like a celebrity. A lot of my concern dissipated as their suspicion turned to a warm welcome.

Lem explained we'd given him a ride home in exchange for weed and they all burst out laughing. "It's everywhere!" they said. "You won't have any problem finding it." A kid came up to us with a handful of 1-foot tall pot plants he'd just pulled out of the ground next to one of the shanties and said, "see?"

"Wow!" I said. We walked over and had him show us where the plants had come from—a small patch growing right in the open.

Casey turned to me. "I told you, you had nothing to worry about."

"Don't bother with that little stuff," Lem said. "I'll show you where there's so much weed, you'll think you're in Mexico." We got back into the car with everyone waving and headed down the hill.

When we were back on pavement again, Lem had us make a quick right down a dead end street next to a branch of the Potomac. There was a deserted dog pound a hundred yards away that I wasn't concerned about but the police station at the top of the street was a little disconcerting. Lem said, "This is it," and I parked.

"So just cross the river and start walking around until you see the plants, then fill your bags," he said and thanked us for the ride. "I'm gonna walk back and stretch my legs. Besides, I haven't been here in a long time and I wanna take my time." No one seemed to care that we were in the midst of the mother lode of marijuana.

We pulled out the trash bags and waded across the river. It was about 50-feet across, knee deep, but ice cold, and we tripped and stumbled across the rocky bottom. Still, the water felt good since it was midsummer, and a hot day was well underway.

We climbed up the tree-lined riverbank and came out into to a large open field of chest high grasses and shrubs. The scenery was spectacular; we were in the middle of nowhere. We started to walk around when suddenly Casey took off at full speed. I didn't know what was happening so I took off after him. He'd spotted a grove of pot plants the size of trees. Unbelievable! It was true! They had to be 10-feet high and stretched beyond us as far as we could see.

We started filling our bags then looked around and realized it was everywhere patches of different sizes and colors. So much. Too much. We couldn't believe it. I was only interested in a little free pot and an adventure, but Casey had Pablo Escobar visions that I wanted no part of.

We picked all we could haul home quickly as we each only had one trash bag as well as one small car trunk. We made our way back to where we'd parked expecting a SWAT team to jump us at any moment, but nothing happened. We drove out past the police station and even brazenly stopped at the Dairy Queen for cones—waiting for something to happen.

Still utterly amazed at what we'd found, we drove back to Potomac leisurely, listening to more Aerosmith as Casey calculated how much our cargo would be worth. Finally, I couldn't take it anymore and ejected the Aerosmith tape and threw it out the window. No doubt we'd be able to afford a new tape soon.

We took the bags to Casey's, and he spread out all of the plants on a concrete floor in the basement to dry where no one would bother them. About a week later, with great excitement, we tried to smoke some but nothing happened. We had some other people try it and nothing! Nobody got high. It didn't make sense. It looked good and it smelled good but no high.

A few days later, I went to the library and researched Moorefield. It turned out that there was a government hemp factory nearby which had been used for making rope in WWI. What we'd picked was abandoned industrial hemp that contained zero THC, the chemical component that provides the high.

The joke was on Casey since his Pablo Escobar dreams went up in smoke, but then again, when Casey got lemons, he always made lemonade. Undeterred, he went into a new line of work selling maps at school for $50 apiece to the legendary reefer fields of Moorefield, West Virginia.

15

Oops: Lending a Movie Star a Hand

My college limousine job in Washington, D.C. was great because it gave me lots of time to study and also the opportunity to meet movie stars, billionaires, royalty, and often the chance to go to the White House. On one occasion, I was taking a Hollywood icon, an Academy Award-winning actress to Dulles Airport. Driving people like this always added caché to the ride. Her PR assistant was in the front seat with me and there were two other people with the movie star in the back. I was driving an older black Cadillac limousine. It was a regular Cadillac extended a couple of feet with a back sofa-bench seat where the passengers sat and looked out a little airplane window. This configuration made it difficult for them to get out of the car since it required scooting forward, and I would invariably have to almost pull them out.

When we arrived at the airport, I pushed the trunk button as the Skycap came to help with the bags. I went around the limousine to help the movie star icon get out. I opened her door and reached down to take her hand just as her assistant diverted my attention, telling me when they were coming back.

I looked up just as I was reaching into the limo and completely cupped the movie star's breast. I jerked my hand back but then I had to reach back in and take her hand to help her out. I was shocked and mortified. I had no idea how she would react. I was about to apologize when she looked right at me with a sheepish grin and her beautiful violet eyes and said, "Thank you." I knew I was bright red and couldn't believe her assistant had to talk to me at that very moment. I ended up driving her on several occasions and found her to be very nice and friendly. Once, she even invited me into a small barbecue party she

POINT OF CONTACT (POC)

was having with Johnny Cash's family, Burt Reynolds, and a few other people where I was the only non-celebrity. I even got to hold one of her heavy Oscars, and what happened was always our little secret.

16

Slovakian Humor

I have a good friend, Ben, who lives in New York and who is always on the lookout for new ventures. He was in the Army and went to West Point where he was a linebacker on the football team. In reality, he was a big, colorful guy who was very smart and who now works for some very wealthy and famous people.

So he called me up and asked me if I wanted to meet him in Budapest because he was interested in acquiring some radio stations in Slovakia. It would be a quick, three-day trip. I agreed. A couple of weeks later, we met in Budapest and went to dinner at Gundel, the world famous restaurant. After a few drinks, I felt as if I were in Europe just as World War II was about to roll in. Ben explained the three radio station deal and wanted me to go with him to the meeting the next morning. He had rented an Opel that we drove to the meeting and we would use while we were in Hungary and Slovakia.

The meeting itself was confusing, and Ben wasn't comfortable with the thick accents and fast presentation. He was also being asked for more money than he'd expected. He left a bit discouraged but still wanted to go into Slovakia and have a look around. He was on the Pest side, and I was on the Buda side, so he switched and got a room at my hotel, The Bultschug Kempinski, and we headed across the border into Slovakia.

There was nothing to see other than lots of open farmland and small village towns. At one point, we picked up a Slovakian soldier hitchhiking with a rifle. It was impossible to communicate with him because the language was so different. We eventually dropped him off and stopped for lunch in a small town restaurant. Once again there was no way to read the menu. Nothing was even close to English, so we just winged it and pointed at things on the menu. We did get through that we wanted beer.

The owner seemed to be annoyed by us and turned away a bus full of tourists passing through because he didn't want to deal with them. We figured this resistance to capitalism was a holdover from communism since Slovakia had
been communist for so long. We couldn't really figure out what we'd ordered or were eating when the food came. All I knew was Hungarian and Slovakian food did not agree with Ben because he developed some ferocious silent flatulence that he thought was hilarious. I spent the rest of the trip through Slovakia with my head out the window gasping for air. It was so bad I developed a wind burn on my face that I called a Slovakian tan.

At dusk we finally got back to a border crossing checkpoint into Hungary. I always seem to have a bit of a guilty conscience at those places, leftover from previous sketchy border crossings and airport departures, though we weren't up to anything this time. Ben pulled up to our slot and handed our passports to a very tall, tough Soviet-looking guard in a dark green uniform. He carried a long rifle. There were a few more guards with machine guns milling around behind him not paying attention to us as he examined our papers. In front of us were two wooden barricades about 50-feet apart and then the Danube River in Hungary right in front of us. I was semi-relaxed looking at the Danube and checking out the Slovakian border set up. The guard holding our passports suddenly said, in a thick accent and stern voice, "Ford Opel!" Ben and I looked at each other in confusion. He said it again, "Ford Opel," only a little louder. Now he had our full attention. "What is he saying?" I said, and Ben said, "I don't know. Something Slovakian."

Again, louder, the guard says, "Ford Opel!" and now he seemed to be getting agitated. Earlier, we'd had kind of a minor hit-and-run incident in a town we drove through. At worst, it had caused someone a broken foot. Could this be what this was about?

At this point, the other guards with machine guns started coming over towards us. I had known Ben for a long time and he had a funny little tell—his nostrils flare ever so slightly, when he is going to strike-like a bull about to charge. The guard now yelled, "Ford Opel!" I saw Ben's nostrils flare as his hand slowly slid over the gear shift knob. I thought, Oh shit! We're going to run the border and crash through the barricades. I casually braced myself with my arm against the dashboard. Better to get new passports than be arrested. We were milliseconds from running the border, Ben later told me, but were saved by one of the other guards. He spoke English and explained the guard was making a joke. Ben's last name is Ford and we were driving an Opel. *Ford Opel.* Ha-ha! They all thought it was funny too. WTF!? The guard handed back our passports, and we crossed quietly into Hungary.

17
Ego Alley

Annapolis Maryland on April 22, 2014 was a typical cool spring day with a crystal blue sky. Little did I know what would happen later in the day. Something that could only happen to me: I met the devil.

I'd been living in Annapolis for the past year and it had been just wonderful, the best, most peaceful, sweet year of the last twenty. I'd joked to some of my old associates that I felt like I was in witness protection compared to my old life. It's that different. Each day, I woke up feeling like I was on vacation with my best friend, my beautiful daughter, Lily, who is almost five. I'm an older single parent who put off having a family because of my work and international travel schedule. I give a vague description of what I do to the friends and people I deal with from Lily's school, since it's beyond their realm and would generate endless questions.

In Annapolis everyone is happy, always saying hello, smiling, laughing, plus there are the great bars, boats, music, and most of all the Naval Academy.

That day, I met Lily at her preschool as usual and we walked to Main Street and headed to the Annapolis playground.

At the playground, I sat at a table texting and sending emails while Lily did her usual playing with kids that she'd just met playing her favorite game chasing or being chased. I always have to tell her to slow down and let the kids catch her every now and then because they complain she's too fast, which she is. It was just a relaxing beautiful cool spring day.

Since I'd lived mostly in Maryland for 30 years and had only been in Annapolis for this past year, I continued to watch the D.C. channel 4 news instead of local or Baltimore news. A few weeks earlier, they'd done a report that I watched three different times, then Googled, about Bradford Bishop, a high ranking State Department official on the verge of achieving his career goal of an ambassadorship. Forty years ago, he'd gone to the State Department one day in March, expecting to get his ambassadorship and was told he would not be appointed and not to ever expect it. After being told this, he left work early, went home, and bludgeoned his three kids, wife, and mother to death in their house in Bethesda with a small sledge hammer. He'd actually gone to a hardware store to buy it, picking a horrendous weapon to annihilate his family over the .38 Smith & Wesson he owned. He then drove their bodies to North Carolina, dug a hole, set them on fire, then vanished without a trace for forty years. An absolutely grisly, cold, unsolved murder.

At the time of the murders, my family lived in Potomac about two miles from his house. Growing up, we kids knew everything about him. He was the boogeyman that everyone was afraid would come back.

The last channel 4 news I watched in Annapolis and saw on the web showed an FBI age progressed clay bust of what he'd look like now as well as sketches and old pictures of him. Little did I realize my quirky talent for recognizing faces meant that I recorded these images without realizing it. Over the years, since the murders, there had been many miscellaneous sightings of him all over the world. I suspected he called some of them in himself. He is now just been put on the FBI's 10 most wanted list which makes him one very scary, dangerous, psycho guy.

After about an hour, I asked Lily if she wanted to get some pizza. She did but wanted to throw pebbles into Ego Alley first. Ego Alley is just another of the many great features in Historic Annapolis. It's a small rectangular harbor at City Dock where boats enter to turn around, showing off their boats. Hence the name. All kinds and sizes of power and sailboats are docked regularly on either side of Ego Alley too.

POINT OF CONTACT (POC)

We walked through the driveway next to the Fleet Reserve Club and reached the end of Chandler Dock, which is an eight-foot wide boardwalk. It runs from the Fleet Reserve Club all the way back to Compromise Street. It's usually where the harbor master docks the larger yachts. Lily started collecting her pebbles, and I realize that there were no boats at all docked in Ego Alley. It turned out that they needed it clear for an incoming sailboat show that weekend.

Lily tossed a few of her pebbles into the water, making a silent wish for each one. It was one of the first beautiful cool spring days, and nobody was around. As we turned to start walking up the dock, there was an older, affluent looking couple at the other end about 300 feet in front of us who hesitated for a split second when they saw us, then slowly and cautiously began strolling towards us. I immediately thought that was odd. Lily ran and danced about 25 feet ahead of me, singing "Let it Go" from *Frozen*. She's a happy kid that keeps me happy too. I was relaxed, thinking about our upcoming vacation as we headed toward the couple.

Now, I'd been out of my old life of the alphabet soup world, the secrecy and intrigue of Washington DC, the White House, black-windowed limousines, the private jet set, world travel, kings, queens, palaces, Saudi princes, and Navy Seals—for about two years in order to be Mr. Mom to Lily since I now had full custody.

Right away I picked up that there was something off with this couple. They weren't smiling or talking or holding hands, or looking at Lily or the water and scenery. They seemed to be very focused on me. My radar came on quickly and automatically. My first thought was that the woman, who was around sixty and a bit stocky, looked like she really was in witness protection, with huge black sunglasses that almost covered her face. She had dark, helmet-shaped hair, wearing a dark dress and long coat, on a pretty spring day with a big purse she clutched in front of her. The man was tall, older, and appeared to be in his seventies. He was in very good shape with a small white bushy goatee, which was an odd contrast to his very neat, crisp appearance. He looked like he was really fit and had just walked out of a country club. He didn't have sunglasses on so I could see his face perfectly as we slowly approached each other. He was dressed neat as a pin with a starched white shirt, yellow cardigan sweater, and some serious pleats on the front of his pants. His outfit was in total contrast to the woman. I laughed to myself that he looked like Bradford Bishop. The tall guy had a slow prominent gait of superiority and arrogance, as if he owned the dock.

I glanced away because I didn't want to stare at them as they were staring at me. We kept walking toward each other while I kept an eye on Lily, still dancing around about twenty feet in front of me now. I took another quick glance at the man and thought that he really did look like Bradford Bishop.

They were maybe twenty five feet in front of me and had reached Lily when full power launched in my brain. I've always been able to maintain absolute calm and act cool even in the most dangerous situations and believe the unbelievable because it cuts through doubt, which wastes valuable milliseconds needed to avoid a catastrophe. In this case, I accidentally blurted out "Holy Shit!" as Lily danced near him. It was Bradford Bishop himself!! He reacted as if I'd touched him with a cattle prod. He almost jumped. His arrogance and superiority popped like a balloon. I thought, Uh oh....

He was doing what he'd probably done for the last forty years— hiding in plain sight. His face was spot on identical to the FBI age-progressed clay bust, except he was whiter, not the slight tan of the clay. Still spot on, though, plus he had the goatee the news mentioned he might have to hide his prominent chin.

Suddenly, I was trapped on a dock all alone with a psycho killer who hadn't been seen in forty years and who doesn't want to be seen or caught. I'd outed him with Lily right there. In a millisecond I glance at the woman thinking, "Do you know who you…?" and didn't finish that thought. I saw her startled look of shock even behind those sunglasses, then realized her hand was in her purse. GUN!

I flashed back to him and saw a series of progressively disturbing menacing faces. His first instant reaction was a huge grimace, all his front teeth ground together, then his expression changed quickly to a rabid snarl with his right side lip going up, then to an absolute look of fury as he stared directly at me. He wanted to kill me! The next expression I didn't think was possible on a human. It was like he morphed into what I can only describe as a wolf mixed with a large insect and Satan. All that was missing were the horns. I had just witnessed Bradford Bishop's five faces: calm, surprise, anger, fury and rage in a matter of a few seconds. Immediately, it was game on and Lily and I were in very serious danger.

The State Department used to say that I was always two steps ahead when I worked with the White House and visiting Heads of State and that skill clicked on, my next decisions made in milliseconds, looking for solutions. A Navy Seal Team Six member I worked with once told me that everything is a weapon. I needed one now. I went through the inventory of what I had on me, which was nothing. I realized my only weapon was Ego Alley itself. I was going to grab Bishop, and we were going swimming if he made the slightest move on me. I had to lock eyes with him and continue to walk toward him and not look at Lily, giving away her location behind him now, and if I kept walking it would put more and more distance between them and Lily. I knew that if he grabbed her and put his hand over her mouth, and the woman stuck the gun in my ribs we would have to get in their car. (Later I realized their car was right by the dock where they were headed.) We'd never be heard from again. If I stopped walking forward they'd stop too and it would be on, so I continued walking toward the old psycho and his moll.

It was like a western gunfight as we approached each other, all of us knowing that we all knew I just outed Bishop. He struggled to keep calm, make his face impassive, which he couldn't seem to do. His face went through a series of erratic expressions, as if he were having a stroke. I flexed my fingers, getting ready to grab on to anything I could. We all knew we'd have pass each other eventually. As the distance grew between them and Lily, it lessened between them and me. I saw Lily stop to look back at me for a couple of seconds in my peripheral vision and hoped she wouldn't dart back to me. Instead she just watched; she later told me she sensed something wasn't right because I didn't look at her.

I was completely focused on him never breaking our locked gaze. Fortunately, one of my big games with Lily is a staring contest so I had a lot of practice. I was thinking, tranquillo, tranquillo. Everybody stay calm. My heart rate never changed from beginning to end. I stayed in game mode. I think part of this comes from hanging around Navy Seals for years and growing up in Texas where we'd flip boards or anything laying on the ground to see if there were snakes underneath, like Russian roulette and stay calm and cool when one popped out. This was the same scenario and another snake. If something happened here I'd yell "Run, reindeer! Run, reindeer, run!" "Reindeer" is the code word for "danger" between Lily and me.

I figured that the woman would only shoot me as a last resort because it would draw too much attention. If I grabbed the bag I'd only end up with the bag since she already had the gun in her hand. So that was a secondary issue. If he tried to grab me or push me off of the dock, I'd dig my hands into his sweater and pull both of us into Ego Alley as I yelled, "Run, reindeer run!" That would make a huge commotion. I'd hang on to him so she wouldn't shoot me, long enough for people to come. She probably would flee. If he turned and ran for Lily I'd grab the lady and launch her into Ego Alley, then go after him, all the while yelling, "Run, reindeer, run!"

Those were the plans I made during the milliseconds we closed in on each other. Ten feet, eight feet, six feet, five feet…. A deadly serious countdown. Then, as we were about to meet face to face or side by side, to my sudden surprise he turned robot on me, looking straight ahead and acting like I wasn't even there. As he passed me I tried to absorb the last details of his face. Again, inadvertently, as if I were seeing a rare car or sunset or beautiful woman, I quietly whispered,

"Fuuuuuucccccckkkkk" as he passed, amazed at being so close to this creepy, old, psycho ghost.

We passed and probably to both our relief, no one had made a sudden move. Later, I realized it had been a Mexican standoff. Since we were out in the open, they hadn't wanted to attract attention and were almost to their car. Lily was also there. I also realized we'd both had the same amount of time to react to each other because I didn't fully recognize him until he was twenty five feet in front of me, and he didn't think I would. If we'd been anywhere isolated, I know he'd have tried to kill us both; he couldn't have let Lily go either. The "I want to kill you look" he'd given was so rabid I felt it viscerally, but he knew he couldn't follow through because he was as stuck as I was.

I strolled away from them quickly, breaking free of the bizarre encounter and moving Lily along to get our pizza. I took a quick look over my shoulder to make sure he hadn't changed his mind about letting us go and they had vanished. It was disturbing how quickly they had. If Lily hadn't been there the dynamics would have been so different.

I thought about telling Lily we'd have to wait on the pizza, and to go back to get the make of their car and a license plate number, but that would have been too risky since I lost sight of them.

I walked around the now closed Fawcett's Boat Supply building, thinking I might see them again walking down Compromise Street toward the Marriott but they were gone. We went into a restaurant where I had a great window view of City Dock. I hoped to take a picture but realized they'd gotten out of there at light speed. I'd completely outed him by accident, freaking him out. That must have been one horrible ride home.

I calmly sat and ate pizza with Lily. We watched the late afternoon bustle of Annapolis as I mulled over what had just happened. I thought for a moment about calling the police or FBI but decided not to as he'd vanished. It would be easier to explain that a UFO just landed at City Dock rather than that I'd just spotted Bradford Bishop.

I had one or two quick thoughts about it the rest of the week, but mostly just that life could be bizarre sometimes. That weekend I went to my cousin's daughter's first communion, which his sister (also my cousin) attended too. She's an extremely high ranking law enforcement official. I told her what happened. She knows me so well she only asked me three questions: when did it happen?, where did it happen?, and what was I going to do about it? She didn't even question the plausibility of me running into a man on the run for forty years, an FBI most wanted. She completely gets me and knows I wouldn't even remotely want to deal with something like this.

POINT OF CONTACT (POC)

    I told her I wasn't going to report it and she said I had to. She said to call it in and then forget about it. It wasn't as if I'd seen him in a car or a restaurant. It had been a long, bad, scary encounter that could have had a horrible outcome. I knew it would be an almost pointless huge, aggravating Mount Everest kind of uphill battle convincing the FBI anyway.

    Of course everyone would ask why Annapolis? Which is an easy answer that all Marylanders know and that is "Marylanders love Maryland." We don't even like crossing into Virginia or Washington DC and Bishop is a Marylander and he came back.

18

Richie Rich

I had a small VIP group in NYC with a free day so I arranged for a yacht to spend the afternoon touring the Hudson and the East River. The yacht was made for 200 people, and my group was only eight people, plus they'd hired a band. Since I had food catered from the main VIP's favorite restaurant, I had the yacht's food donated to a homeless shelter. The funny thing about the yacht was that it had a large, open top deck with another large lounge and a nonfunctioning helicopter welded to the top of lounge.

We boarded the yacht down in the financial district almost under the shadow of the World Trade Center twin towers. It was a beautiful day to be out on the water. I kept the band and the singer at the back of the yacht and told them not to interact with the group or security. The singer and band were really good and performed music and songs from the VIP's native country. I checked on the VIP group a few times in the massive main lounge and saw that they were fine and happy, talking to each other and listening to the band all day. The only time they went outside was for five minutes to look at the Statue of Liberty.

POINT OF CONTACT (POC)

I was happily camped out in the upstairs lounge with my cell phone and papers. I had the stewards bring me food there throughout the day. When we pulled in alongside the *USS Intrepid* aircraft carrier at Pier 86, I went outside on the top open deck under the helicopter. I was dressed casually that day, wearing a blue blazer, open shirt and Ray Bans. I couldn't believe the massive size of the aircraft carrier. I called my girlfriend, told her what I was doing, and I was describing the *Intrepid* to her when I started seeing camera flashes and realized tourists were taking pictures of the yacht with the helicopter. I then realized they couldn't see anyone except me on the top deck in my blue blazer. I told my girlfriend that they must think I'm Richie Rich, talking on my cell phone on my yacht. Just as I said that, a uniformed steward came out on deck and handed me a flute of champagne.

19

Skipping School

Two weeks after I'd gotten my driver's license, I talked a friend into skipping school for a few hours. I was going to Jesuit Prep in Dallas, Texas, and my sister, who had a brand new, bright orange Camaro was going to Hockaday, a short walk away. I had borrowed an extra set of keys to her car, and we were going to go joy riding and eat lunch at Las Colinas in Irving. We'd return the car and no one would find out. I was surprised school security didn't spot us walking to Hockaday. My friend, Bill, and I were both sixteen and were incredibly conspicuous in our gray pants, blue blazers with the school crest, white shirts, and blue and gold ties, plus Bill was 6' 7". Yet no one noticed us.

It was easy to spot my sister's orange car, and we got right into it. My huge friend barely fit as he wedged himself in using every inch of space possible, with his head pressed against the car ceiling. I had no business driving yet, and really didn't know how, except in the classroom. This would be my first time on the street with my new license. On top of that, the Camaro was a really fast, two-door racecar with too much muscle for an amateur driver. We slinked out of the parking lot, passing Jesuit Prep and headed to LBJ freeway, neither of us wearing our seatbelts.

It would only take thirty minutes to get to Las Colinas once I got on the LBJ freeway, and I started playing around with the car. I would speed up then slow down, change lanes, then speed up again. The response and power of the car was amazing. I cranked up ZZ Top's "La Grange," the Texas theme song, and decided to see how fast I could go. I stomped on the gas pedal, and we took off like a rocket. The last time I looked at the speedometer, we were doing 115 mph. That's when I saw our exit two lanes over.

I turned the wheel in the direction of the exit ramp, and that's when the back of the car started fishtailing badly. Somehow, without hitting any other cars, I got the Camaro into the funnel of the exit ramp. I was probably still going around 100 mph as it continued to fishtail wildly, and we shot down the ramp.

What I did next probably saved our lives. At close to 100 mph, with an out-of-control car, no seatbelts, no experience driving, I let go of the steering wheel and put my hands in my lap. It seemed like a dream or a nightmare as I sat there thinking this couldn't really be happening. Everything went into slow motion. The Camaro shot down the ramp, fishtailing like crazy, and shot across a couple of curbs, across a road, into a rain ditch, out of the ditch, through a tall cyclone fence, then spun out in a huge dust cloud over the pitcher's mound of a little league field that wasn't being used, finally coming to a stop over third base.

We were both fine and just looked at each other. *Did that just happen?* We were so lucky that we didn't hit another car, or person, or go airborne, and flip over. The only thing I saw was a small crack in the side of the windshield and I thought, Oh no, my parents are going to find out that I had the car. I attempted to start it.

Meanwhile, I'd ripped the entire bottom out of the Camaro, bent the front end down, flattened the tires, destroyed the transmission, and left a trail of car parts behind us. That was a tough phone call to make to my parents, and I think I was grounded for five years after that. The only good thing about finally coming to a stop on a baseball diamond and third base was that I was SAFE!!

20

Celebrity Sightings

When I was in college, I talked a friend of mine into driving a limousine, too. He got hooked right away because it was such an easy, fun way to make money, and we got to study in the back of the limousines while waiting for our clients. One night, we were both out on jobs driving people to dinner so we planned to go into Georgetown for drinks and dinner ourselves while we waited instead of studying.

The plan was for me to leave my limousine at my passenger's restaurant so he could pick me up in his stretch limousine. That night, D.C. was all crazy and pumped up that Michael Jackson was going to be in town. There was so much hype before the King of Pop arrived that the city was now in a frenzy about his concert. On our way into Georgetown, I knew we'd pass the Regent Hotel on M Street where he was staying. We slowed down as we drove by the hotel. There was a mob of about thirty groupies across the street, each wearing a sequined glove. Suddenly, I got a great idea and told my friend to pull over.

I got out and went over to the groupies and found a beautiful girl with caramel skin and a sequined glove. I was young and those were simpler days, so when I explained my plan, she was totally game. We got into the back of the stretch limousine, which had dark tinted windows and had my friend drive around the block. The groupies were all facing the hotel and when we got close, I had my friend toot the horn. The whole crowd swung around to look at the limousine. I partially rolled the window down and the girl reached out so they could only see her thin, caramel arm and sequined glove. She waved. The crowd instantly went nuts and stampeded toward the limo. We took off before they could reach us.

POINT OF CONTACT (POC)

I couldn't believe it had worked so much better than I'd expected. So we had to do it again. We went around the block, tooted the horn, she waved, and they stampeded at us. We took off again and headed into Georgetown. We stopped at an outdoor café, out came the sequined arm, and people were practically turning over tables to get to the car. We did it all over Georgetown, even waving to people just walking down the street, which gave them a thrill.

It was so much fun that we never got around to having dinner. We finally shut it down when several cars started following us. I never got the girl's name, but I know she'll never forget that night. We took her back and dropped her near the Regent where we'd picked her up and all the groupies were still there. We then quietly went back and waited for our clients to finish dinner.

21
Gigi Saves the Day

My parents were upper middle class people who came from humble beginnings. My father was the son of a New York City policeman, and my mother was the daughter of a Chase Manhattan bank teller. My father was a WWII retired Navy Lt. Commander Seabee who served in the Pacific and who would always refer to those as the best years of his life. After the war, he worked very hard building his international engineering company. We moved almost every other year as his projects took him around the world.

Near the end of his career, the family finally settled in Potomac, Maryland. The children were all grown and had moved out, so my parents bought a modest but very nice house in a park-like setting and invited my grandmother, who was almost ninety by then, to live with them. My father was close to retiring, and his health was failing rapidly. He was spending more time at doctors' offices than at work.

One afternoon, the doorbell rang and my mother opened the inner front door. A tall, very dark, African man with a knapsack was clearly visible through the Plexiglas window of the outer security storm door. He explained through the door that he was from Nigeria and had to deliver a package to my father. My mother said my father was at his office and to please deliver the package there. But the gentleman now protested that he'd already tried the office. Again, the guy said he really needed to deliver the package and asked if he could simply leave it with my mother.

But something about this guy just gave my mother an uneasy feeling. So she said that she was sorry but she couldn't accept it, and that he would, unfortunately, have to go back to D.C. in order to deliver it to my father's office.

Disappointed, the man asked to use the phone, but again, my mother said no. He asked to use the bathroom, and she said no, feeling worse and worse, but still uneasy. Finally, the man asked if he could just have a glass of water. At this point, my mother felt so bad she was ready to give in, but just at that moment Gigi, my mother's geriatric, incontinent, deaf, almost blind poodle, started limping into the foyer. My mother turned and sharply ordered the dog to "Stay," but the man, who could not see the dog himself, but now knew that my mother had one, looked terrified and took off.

My mother saw him walk quickly away and abruptly realized he didn't even have a car. He must have walked from the bus stop at Potomac Village, the local shopping center, which was more than a mile away, after riding the bus all the way from downtown D.C.

When my grandmother woke from her nap and heard what had happened, she felt my mother should have taken the package and said they needed to find the guy. It had to be important if he'd come all the way to Potomac to deliver it. She raised enough doubt in my mother's mind that they both got into her car and drove to the Potomac Village bus stop looking for him without success. When my father got back to his office, he confirmed that the guy had been there but didn't know what the package was or who it was from, and told my mother not to worry about it. That seemed to be the end of things.

The next afternoon, I stopped by to visit and to have dinner with everyone when my father got home. By now, I already knew the story of the package delivery guy and we were just sitting around visiting when the doorbell rang. My mother said, "Oh no, not again" and I went to the door. This time there were two Montgomery County detectives standing there.

We all sat down in the living room, and they showed my mother a series of mug shots to see if she could pick anyone out. It was tough but she eventually identified the delivery guy. The detectives said that shortly after leaving my mother's house, he went to Potomac Village, frustrated, where he then carjacked and kidnapped a doctor's wife who had been grocery shopping. He was trying to get a ransom from the doctor, and the police had traced the call to a place near the Jefferson Memorial. There, they ambushed and captured him and the doctor's wife was unharmed. She was so flustered in the moment however, that when the police swarmed the kidnapper, she just drove home!

The police interviewed her later that night by which time they'd found a gun, large knife, and a long ransom note to our family in the kidnapper's backpack! Inexplicably, the guy had targeted my father and had been stalking him for a while, but his big plan fell apart when my father wasn't there to be kidnapped. In the end though, everyone decided it was little deaf, blind, limping Gigi who had saved the day.

22

Contagious

I'd stayed up too late drinking port wine, a gift from the president of Portugal, with my friend Clair who was taking care of me since I had a bad cold. Unfortunately, I had to get up at 7 a.m. to take a scion of an iconic American family to the White House to see President Bush #41. I felt really bad and almost called someone else to do it but then decided to muscle through since it would be quick.

It was early Saturday and a spectacular late spring morning as I drove up to the South Portico after clearing the USSS checkpoint. The entrance is the more private one to go to since it's reserved for visiting heads of state, ceremonial and personal arrivals to the White House. Most people come in through the Northwest Gate or the Old Executive Office Building. After dropping him off I, parked near the awning next to the Rose Garden and got out of the car and took a couple of deep breaths. My cold was getting worse, and I felt a little hungover.

I walked around sneezing a little, occasionally looking over at the Oval

Office, then out over the great lawn where the president's white top helicopter lands. There was hardly anyone around and no Secret Service or park service groundskeepers. Everything was very quiet and all mine for a moment until a Secret Service agent came out of the South Portico, looked around,  visually locked onto me, and told me to get back into my car, turn off the engine, and stay there because POTUS (the president of the United States) was coming out.

I was excited since it's always fun to see the president up close inside the White House. I had another quick sneezing session which confirmed my need to get back to bed. Some USSS agents started to make a perimeter outside the South Portico and along the driveway. The agent who ordered me into my car stood over near the South Portico doorway whispering into his sleeve. Suddenly, there was a burst of activity, and U.S. Secret Service agents came streaming out. All right, I thought, I have a front row seat. The president emerged, dressed casually in a tweed jacket, open shirt, no tie, and with him was Mr. Scion. They reached the end of the awning at the driveway and stopped. Mr. Scion looked around for a second, then at me in the car, and they both came straight toward me. Instinctively, I jumped out of the car. Mr. Scion was diverting the president of the United States to meet me!

He introduced me to the president, and we shook hands. I didn't have much to say since Mr. Scion had just made such a glowing introduction. I just added that it was really nice to meet him. The president said a few nice things as well, but I can't recall anything specific because I was so stunned by the exchange. Then they explained that they were going to the Oval Office, but I was only thinking about what an exciting moment I'd just had. The USSS agent who first ordered me into the car gave me an annoyed look as he followed the two men to the Oval Office. I gave him a friendly, Cheshire cat grin.

About two days later I was watching president Bush speak at a news conference on TV, and I suddenly had a flash of guilt. He had a really bad cold. My cold.

23

Chicken Little

While I was in college, friends and I would sometimes go exploring by air, usually in Cessna 172s. On one particular trip, we'd formed a group of three planes, flying around the Bahamas, landing on small islands off of the radar to almost everyone except perhaps drug dealers. The wreckage of other planes were visible everywhere—mostly wings and tails with black burn spots in the middle.

Most crash sites were near roads, beaches, or at the end of runways, although there were a few intact planes underwater near the beach, including a DC 3, which is pretty big. It was obvious that most of these planes had gone down trying to land at night or had been overloaded for drug runners. So we decided to check out the island of San Salvador because we understood that there were monuments around the island marking the exact location where Christopher Columbus landed.

We never planned places to stay, and sometimes we'd end up camping out next to the plane. It usually worked out fine but could be unexpectedly exciting. For instance, one of our planes went off to scout out another island we could explore and found one with an abandoned mansion near a landing strip. My friends buzzed the house a couple of times, and when they started to land, a bunch of guys with guns came pouring out of the not-abandoned-after-all-mansion and our pilot aborted the landing and got everyone out of there. This was the scary, tricky thing about flying around the Bahamas back then.

So we ended up on San Salvador. We were unloading our plane when an open flatbed truck came by with some sketchy Americans on their way to their plane. They were probably traffickers. We asked if they knew of a place to stay, and they said yes. There was a guy with a shanty house that was nice enough and only cost $5 a night, including dinner. We were happy to hear that because we were all hungry and tired. We arranged for the truck to come back for us and we all climbed into the back and rode up a hilly tropical road to the house.

Upon our arrival, the owner came out in a tattered shirt and dirty work pants—an older black man who introduced himself as George. He confirmed that it would be $5 bucks each to have dinner and spend the night. He took us into the house where we could smell the delicious aroma of chicken cooking in the oven and showed us to a couple of rooms with mismatched couches and paperback books stacked floor to ceiling left by previous guests.

The house had indoor plumbing, although the rooms were little more than a bunch of different large wooden boxes slapped together. We crashed on the sofas for a couple of hours, chatting, looking at the books, all the while smelling that delicious chicken cooking and getting hungrier by the minute. George was kind of grumpy and never smiled. He just sort of barked at us, although the plan was that we would have dinner with his family at a large picnic table.

When dinner was finally ready, we all sat down with his wife and teenage daughters who were quite friendly and asked a lot of questions about the United States. George brought over a beautifully cooked chicken and some roasted potatoes. As we were admiring the meal, he brought out four plates with two slices of green tomatoes and a slice of day-old birthday cake on each and placed them in front of us. I said, "what's this?"

"Your dinner," George replied. "The chicken is for my family."

24

Partying with the First President

I had a VIP group of eight from Dubai, including a Sheikh, that I was escorting around the U.S. We were in Washington for three days staying at the Four Seasons hotel. They had nothing official scheduled for the next night so the head of the group wanted to have a party where no one would see them cut loose. He wanted Indian food, a tape deck for their music, and drinks. He emphasized that he wanted total discretion because of their identities and purpose in the U.S.

I spoke to a few of my Washington contacts and came up with Woodlawn Plantation which used to be part of George Washington's Mount Vernon estate. Woodlawn was given to Washington's stepdaughter and Martha's granddaughter as a wedding present. It was perfect, an elegant Georgian mansion on 126 isolated acres close to D.C. I called the curator, and she was game so I arranged to meet her for a tour and to firm up the details. The next day while my group was in meetings at the hotel, I went to Woodlawn with one of my security agents in a sheriff's car. The entrance was just past Mount Vernon; it was discreet and formal. The long driveway wound through a forest to the main house. It was perfect, I thought. I met with the curator, and she gave us a tour of the house. The house was beautifully decorated; each room was a different color of traditional blue, yellow, and red with many breakable antiques, including a large harp. There were also all kinds of George Washington related memorabilia, including valuable paintings and marble busts.

As I was looking around, I told her she should put away as much as she could so nothing would get broken. I warned her that the group was small but I wasn't sure whether they would get wild. I also assured her that I'd have two security people there, as well as myself, to keep things in check. I asked that only she be present without other staff to minimize witnesses. I felt a little bad because the staff of this house would normally not accommodate my group or my requests. I had a feeling they needed money for the expensive upkeep.

I went back to the hotel and set everything in motion. I had one of the town car drivers pick up all the food, drinks, and other requested items and drop them off at Woodlawn. I then spoke to the lead security agent with the VIPs and told him to call me when he saw Mount Vernon so we would be ready and waiting at the door for their arrival. I returned to Woodlawn with a security agent in a sheriff's car at dusk. I picked the largest room with the least amount of antiques to set everything up. It was really dark there in the middle of the woods when I got the call that they were passing Mount Vernon so I went to the front door. I asked the curator to stay out of sight so they would feel like they were alone.

As I stood there, four black town cars pulled up in front of me. I was only expecting three. Everyone started getting out of their cars, checking out the house and grounds. From the fourth car, three beautiful belly dancers emerged. I smiled and shook my head. I quietly told the lead driver to leave with the other cars and to wait at the circle at Mount Vernon until I called them. I escorted the Sheikh and VIPs inside and showed them around, ultimately depositing them in their party room.

I then took the belly dancers upstairs where they could have a bathroom and place to change into their costumes for the night. Before I reached the second floor, I heard the music already blasting and lots of loud laughter. The party had started.

I hung out in the foyer area the whole night with the two security agents and the curator. We directed the occasional stray to the bathroom or around the antiques that were roped off.

We watched the belly dancers come and go, which was a nice diversion throughout the long night. We never saw the Sheikh or a few other members of the group until they left. There was only one stray that kept coming out and wandering around the house. He'd flirt with the belly dancers, then careen past the antiques, making us hold our breath. He was the only one who seemed to have had too much to drink. I finally put a security agent on him to look after him any time he appeared. He was funny and friendly but looked like he was walking on a boat, especially, it seemed, when he was near the antiques. At one point, he had to be pulled out of the ancient boxwoods in front of the house when he went to light a cigarette and fell backwards.

They were really loud but sounded like they were having a great time, and I was happy nothing was getting broken. I got the signal that the party was end-

POINT OF CONTACT (POC)

ing from one of them, and I called the town cars back to the house. It was late, and they were really happy to have been off the radar for one night. All of the George Washington memorabilia, marble busts, and antiques had made them think they were actually at Mount Vernon not Woodlawn Plantation. They were particularly impressed that I'd arranged to have their stealth party in the home of the first president of the United States! I thought it was funny and didn't correct them. They finally left, and I met with the tired curator to settle up. We were both very relieved that the house and priceless antiques had survived the party. We'd agreed on four thousand dollars for the night. The curator was astonished that I ended up giving her much more than we agreed upon.

25
Airborne

My parents had lived in Bangkok, Thailand for three years early in my father's career. I was born there during that time and had never been back. Now, twenty five years later, my parents asked if I wanted to return to the land of my birth. What made the invitation even more appealing was that they meant a trip without my siblings, just me. I was thrilled, of course. My father's health  was getting worse, and we all knew this would be their last big trip to Asia. His company was taking care of the expenses, to the consternation of his partners, but my father had worked hard his entire life, and now in these last years he was going to live it up.

The plan was that I'd meet them at Narita airport in Tokyo then continue on to Bangkok with them after a one hour stop in Taiwan. I didn't realize I was facing twenty six hours of nonstop traveling to get there when I left. I flew up to New York's JFK and caught a Pan Am fourteen hour flight to Japan. I thought I was in the twilight zone sitting on a plane that never landed. Cycling through movies, food, and more hot towels than I could count, and still we just kept flying....

I'd finagled business class tickets through the company I was working for at the time so the trip was as nice as it could be, but when I finally landed at Narita, I felt like pulp. My parents had said to just keep following the disembarking passengers off of the plane and at least one of them would be waiting. We did the usual twists and turns in corridors then ended up on what seemed to be a mile long moving walkway. There was at least a 100-foot gap between myself and the people in front of me on the walkway.

To this day, I've imagined that was what it must be like to go to heaven. There, at the end of the moving walkway, waiting for me, was my beautiful, beaming mom, dressed in all white. She honestly looked like a waiting angel. I knew instantly I was safe and had connected with my parents halfway around the world. We were both so happy to see one another.

My parents had been in Hawaii and Japan the previous month and had another month to go before returning to the States. They still had Thailand, China, and Singapore ahead of them. They were consummate world travelers yet I was still always impressed at the ease with which they acclimated to any culture. They wanted me to make the rest of the trip with them but I would have lost my job if I had. Looking back, I regret not taking the risk. My father wasn't feeling well again, and my mom took me to the Pan Am lounge where he was waiting. We weren't there very long before we had to board the jet to Taiwan, and then it would be back to the land of my birth, exotic Thailand.

We were seated on a Pan Am 747—my parents were in first class and I was in business class. Unlike the packed flight from the U.S., this one seemed only half full, and luckily no one was sitting next to me. I dozed off as soon as we took off and woke up to see my father coming back to sit with me. I wished it was the other way around that I could join him in First Class. I always had a great time traveling with my parents, especially without my siblings, who always brought along their personal issues or drama. By contrast, I was easygoing, laid back, and genuinely enjoyed my parents' company.

My father sat with me for a while. He knew his health was failing and we talked a little about that, but then switched to the adventures we were going to have once we got to Thailand. Of course, at the time, I had no way of knowing that he'd be gone forever in only four years.

Growing up, the entire family had globe-trotted the world and always on Pan Am. Even as infants, we'd flown over the Pacific a couple of times on Pan Am, and that was when the planes had propellers and bunk beds for passengers. Ironically and sadly, my father's company had designed the iconic Pan Am flagship world port terminal at JFK. He told me this was the very last Pan Am flight to Thailand and possibly to Asia as well, because United was taking over all their flight routes.

Eventually, he went back up front, and after a while, we landed for a one hour layover in Taiwan. It was nice to get out and walk around the airport which looked a lot like Dulles. When we got back onboard, there was a crew of new flight attendants seemed to be made up entirely of inexperienced, pretty Asian girls. I'd been traveling at this point for twenty four hours straight, and at last, I was only two hours away from Thailand with the world's best guides, my parents. My father had arranged for a huge suite at the five-star Oriental Hotel in Bangkok. It had a giant balcony overlooking all the action of the Chao Phraya River and my room was next door. I was full of happy anticipation as we taxied out to the end of the runway and turned for takeoff.

That's when I realized something was wrong. I could see a bluish smoke as the 747 began to roll. The pilot hit the throttle and we rocketed down the runway as the smoke began visibly pouring into the cabin, burning my throat and eyes. It started to get thick fast and I thought, Abort takeoff! Abort!

Suddenly a fire alarm sounded in the back of the jet, then another, and another, and we still rocketed down the runway with me thinking, Don't take off! Don't take off! My eyes burned and I started to have trouble breathing. Now all the fire alarms from front to back were going off. And we lifted into the air! We are doomed, I thought. It was some consolation to at least know I was with my parents, but damn, I'd almost made it back to Thailand!

Higher and higher we ascended as the flight attendants ran up and down the aisle as the 747 climbed, taking the batteries out of the smoke alarms to shut them off. I thought, this is definitely the last Pan Am flight since we are clearly going to crash.

Within a second, the pilot hit a switch that sucked all the blue smoke out of the cabin in the blink of an eye. He apologized and said that the ground crew had spilled a lot of oil on one of the engines.

We weren't going to crash! And I would finally get to see Thailand.

Upon our evening arrival, we were met by Lek, my father's company driver. Lek and my parents acted like long lost friends, and perhaps, in a way, they were. Lek got us through Customs quickly, seemed to know absolutely everyone, and was completely solicitous to my parents, taking care of their every need. It was actually very entertaining to watch him in action.

Lek was a stocky Thai in his late fifties with a crew cut. He drove a white, four door car of some kind that he easily weaved through Bangkok traffic on our long ride to the Oriental Hotel. There, we were greeted by Ankana, the doyenne of the establishment. Ankana had married someone from my father's company who had passed away, so she and my parents really were old friends. She may have been the person who saw to it that my parents' suite was filled with orchids.

The hotel had a twenty minute newsreel running continuously any time the TV was first turned on, depicting every newsworthy item that had occurred the week before. I must have seen the Challenger blow up at least thirty times that first week as I came and went from my room. It was sad and strange.

During the day, I toured the city with my parents and Lek. We went to temples, the king's palace, Jim Thompson's house, took boat trips—including very fast, long-tail boats—saw a crocodile farm, and had a scary ride in a Tuk Tuk, during which we almost crashed into a baby elephant. My father would come and go since he had some meetings he had to attend.

One day, I accompanied my mother to lunch with one of the queen's ladies-in-waiting, a member of her inner circle, and some other people. Afterward, we visited the hospital where I was born, the church where I was baptized and then, our old home.

The house, with its unique architecture, looked the same as in the pictures my parents had shown me over the years, but now it was surrounded by high fences and major security. As we stood looking at it, the person living there drove up and allowed us in to look around. He was an American from the US embassy, head of the DEA in Southeast Asia, which explained the need for security. The house was still beautiful with a large yard, marble steps and dark exotic woods—just as I'd seen in family pictures. A photo of me at three years old, sitting on the marble steps, hung in my parents living room, so I sat on the same spot and my mother took a couple of pictures.

On another day, I accompanied my father to a meeting with the Minister of Commerce. It took place in the biggest, emptiest office I've ever been in. The room was the size of a huge gymnasium that could have accommodated an entire hockey or basketball team comfortably. All that was in it was an official desk, the king's picture, and a Thai flag on one end, a spirit house on one side, and a living room where we gathered on the other end.

The nights were as interesting as the days. We had dinner one night across from the Oriental and sat on the floor, watching an elegant performance of Thai dancers in native costumes. On another night, we went to the home of a Thai prince and princess. The prince was my father's Thai business partner—a requirement in order to have a corporate presence in the country. This couple, older than my parents, were very gracious. We went through large gates to get into their estate, which was spectacular, located right in the middle of Bangkok. It was much like discovering an entire opulent estate in the middle of New York City. The residence was comprised of several buildings, lit up, yet seemingly dark and mysterious at the same time. Everything was surrounded by lush gardens and orchids. We sat by their large, flowing pool and had cocktails as Thai music drifted in the background and the staff floated around us like butterflies.

It was surreal—right out of the movies. When we finally went to dinner, we followed the couple in their two Jaguars. The second one was for their security team.

At the restaurant, we sat in a private room while the prince commanded waiters to bring specific foods he wanted us to try. At one point, he ordered a dish of fried sparrows, including beaks and legs. I'd never seen anything like it and felt the prince was testing me to see what I would do. Fortified by a couple of vodka tonics, I smiled, picked one up and ate it. This thrilled everyone so I asked for another which kept us all laughing.

On another night, we had dinner at Nick's Number 1, a very authentic place which seemed to be housed in a bombed-out building but had the best Kobe steak in Bangkok. On other nights, my father, with a wink, had me go with Lek to see the darker side of Bangkok, which included Lek getting me some really strong Thai stick to smoke. One

POINT OF CONTACT (POC)

night, we went to a Thai boxing match that was ferocious. On a couple of other nights, we went to Patpong, where he showed me the night market, girls with numbers, darts, and of course, the infamous ping pong balls.

Two weeks flew by, and one of the best things that came out of the trip, one of the things I'll remember and treasure the most, was a quiet dinner I shared with my parents alone at the Oriental, where together, we planned out the rest of my life.

26

Get Around, Get Around, I Get Around

A friend and his brother owned houseboats. On the Fourth of July, they'd raft them together on the Potomac River to party on all day, then watch the national fireworks from them at night. My friend had canoes to take people back and forth from the shore. The plan was to party for a while on the houseboats, then head to shore and watch the Beach Boys concert on the Mall, then return to the houseboats for the fireworks. There were lots of boats anchored all around us with the Park Police patrolling in their boats. We were near the Memorial Bridge and the jets landing at National were deafening as they flew low over us.

My friend had a water cannon that he was really good at using. It was basically a slingshot that attached to your feet and you launched water balloons from it from between your legs. It was unreal how far they could go and hilarious when they landed. He'd pick out snooty people on their yachts, or kids, or the Park Police in their boats. He did it so intermittently, no one could ever pin down where the balloon assaults were coming from. He'd launch and we'd watch the water balloon sail through the air, then explode on unsuspecting people, soaking them. On impact, we'd all look the other way and pretend it wasn't us and we didn't see anything. It was great, harmless, Fourth of July entertainment, and the nearby boats were in on it, too.

Because it was a hot, sunny day we decided to go ashore and had the canoes drop us off. I knew my friend Carl was driving one of the limousines for the Beach Boys so we went around to the back of the stage to see if I could find him. There were masses of people everywhere. There was a huge cyclone fence around the whole backstage area with a bouncer and some Park Police at the entrance checking for backstage passes. There were limousines parked all over the place outside the fence. I told my friends to wait away from the entrance so the bouncer wouldn't see us together until I found Carl. It wasn't hard to spot him since he was so tall. He was chatting with one of the Hawaiian Tropic girls that were all over the backstage area in their bikinis.

I asked someone walking by on the inside of the fence if they could get Carl to come over to me, which he did. I asked him if he could get us in backstage, and he said he only had one extra pass, which was a colored plastic band. I said I could work with that, and he passed it through the fence to me. I had my friends move away from the entrance but stay next to the fence.

I went in first, loosely putting on the pass, then met my friends and passed it through to them one at a time, and did that routine until all of us were in. Backstage at the Beach Boys on the Fourth of July! It doesn't get any better than that.

There were picnic tables and plenty of free food and drinks. There was a really tall staircase up to the stage as the Beach Boys played above us. We got some food and sat at one of the picnic tables. Michael Jackson's parents were at another, and at one point, Ringo, La Toya Jackson and Julio Iglesias were walking around us. But we were all mesmerized by the tan Hawaiian Tropic girls milling around in their bikinis. There was lots of activity and people so we just hung out and enjoyed the music and action. Carl checked on us briefly, but was up to his own shenanigans with some of the backstage crew. The Beach Boys took a break and came down the stairs passing right by us as they headed to their hospitality trailers to chill out.

I don't know what we were thinking but we were feeling pretty bold by this time and decided to walk up the stairs to check out the stage. We didn't care if we got caught at this point since we'd had our fun getting in and eating. It was amazing to get to the top and look out at a sea of people that extended all the way past the Washington Monument.

The stage crew were moving instruments around and getting the stage ready again, completely indifferent to us. We wandered across the wires and past the instruments and went to the left side of the stage in front of the speakers. There was a tall wooden fence keeping the crowd back about 10-feet from the stage. People were jammed together as far as we could see and we had all the room in the world. We were about to head back when the Beach Boys came back on stage and the crowd went wild! We were trapped, and the only thing we could do was sit down on the stage in front of the speakers.

It was really loud, but we thought it was really funny and cool. My one friend, who could be a jerk, got a girl on a guy's shoulders to lift up her shirt, then pointed to another girl and made a gesture indicating she should come over the fence and join us. She immediately got nailed by Security. We told him to cut it out before we all got caught. It was just amazing sitting there on the side of the stage listening to the music and looking out at a sea of so many people. The music finally ended, to the relief of my ears, and the band finally left the stage. We got up and casually meandered across the stage, down the stairs, and out the way we'd come in. The canoes picked us back up. We'd had the best seats in the house for the concert and for watching the incredible fireworks that night. A week or two later, I saw a picture in a national magazine of the Beach Boys concert taken from far away. You could see some black dots on the side of the stage. That was us.

27

Blowing Bridges

A friend of mine who's in the intelligence defense security business wanted me to have dinner with Nathan Perry and Jose Romero at J. Gilbert's restaurant in McLean, Virginia. This had always been the watering hole for the CIA since the restaurant was close by and the food was good. They were already there when I arrived and had a table near the back with a good view of the whole restaurant. These guys were the real deal; they even had their own listing on Wikipedia. Both had very colorful histories working for the CIA, mostly in Central America, Europe, and the Middle East. Nathan had written a fascinating book about his CIA career.

We had an interesting evening and conversation. At one point, Nathan asked me about myself and I shared a brief history. When I mentioned that my family had lived in El Salvador for about five years when I was a kid, he asked why we were there. I told him that my father's company had been building all the bridges through Central America for the Pan American Highway. Nathan smiled at me and said, "I blew up two of those bridges." These were bridges I remembered my father talking about.

"That was you!" I said.

He replied, "Yeah, I hope your father wasn't mad."

I wished my father was still alive so that I could have told him this story.

"No, he wasn't mad," I told Nathan. "He got paid to rebuild them! He probably would have been happy if you'd blown up a few more."

28

Heaven Sent

My father died on October 27th, and my family decided to have his funeral November 1st instead of October 31st so the service wouldn't be on Halloween. I decided to spend the night before the funeral at my parents' house with my family. It was surreal sleeping and waking up in my old room after so many years. It was so hard to take in that my father, my best friend, was gone, and that today we'd be attending his funeral. He was everything a father could be and now was gone forever.

It had been a mostly sleepless night, so as soon as the sun rose, I got up while everyone else still slept and decided to go for a run to clear my head before the day's events. I didn't have anything with me, so I dug through my old closet and dresser for running clothes. Everything I came across now had new meaning and some connection to my father. I finally found a sweat shirt from Maine, shorts, and old sneakers. I wanted to listen to music and could only find an old broken Walkman in my childhood desk. The radio was the only part that worked, but that would be good enough.

Since no one else was awake, I wrote a note and quietly went outside, tuning into a local rock station for my run. I was relieved that at least it was a beautiful fall day. As I started running, I listened to some classic rock music, which brought back memories of growing up, and the tears streamed down my face. I ran through the old neighborhood, reflecting on how fast life seemed to be flying by, especially now at such a profound watershed moment. An hour later, near the end of the run, I had to cut through a path in the woods that came out at the back of my parents' house. I walked through the woods looking up at the bare trees against the blue sky, then walked out onto the street along the split rail fence that runs along the side of my parents' property. I'd passed this spot thousands of times while my father was alive, going about his usual routine inside the house, and now he was gone.

Something caught my eye. I couldn't believe it, but a tiny red rose was blooming along the fence. I'd planted the bush with my Dad years earlier. It had been forgotten, overtaken by brush and tangled vines that had all but smothered it. Yet there, on this morning, one bright red rose flowered on a bush that hadn't bloomed in years. A momentary sense of peace came over me. Hot and sweaty, I walked back to the house, bracing myself for the day ahead. I was about to take off my headphones when the DJ announced, "Today is November 1st, All Saints Day. If you are going to heaven, today is the day."

29

A Coppola Birthday Party

During my college limousine job, my boss's assistant, Ali, asked me if I wanted to go to a party with him in NYC. He was from a wealthy Persian family exiled in the US after the fall of the Shah, and who had movie star looks, in addition to being suave, sophisticated, and charming. Basically, he was a babe magnet, so it was always fun and easy meeting girls when I was with him. He always wore black or purple silk shirts open to his chest, and gold chains, which was both funny and cliché.

Ali rarely did any driving, so since he'd driven some people from New York, my boss must have had a personal connection to these people if Ali was driving them around. So that's how it happened that Ali got invited to the big NYC birthday bash, and I went along.

We drove up to NYC and got a couple of rooms at the Hilton, which were hard to get since the Democratic Presidential Convention was in town. The next day we drove over and picked up his friends on the West Side. I recognized one of them from a science fiction TV program. We drove over to house on Staten Island, and I was surprised it was a normal house in a normal neighborhood. I'd been expecting a big mansion. We were met at the front door and went through the house to the party in the backyard next to a pool. Ali introduced me to the host whose birthday was being celebrated. He was a very jovial Italian who wanted us to have a good time and feel at home.

The theme of the party was a Hawaiian Luau with all the decorations, the food, music, and flowered leis. They had a band by the pool that played all kinds of music in between the Hawaiian stuff throughout the day and into the night.

POINT OF CONTACT (POC)

I looked around at maybe forty or fifty people I assumed were members of his big Italian family and personal friends. I recognized a few other people from TV there as well, which I liked. I tried talking to a few of the girls and some of the people, but they didn't want anything to do with me, almost to the point of ignoring me and giving me suspicious glances. So I pretty much just hung out with Ali and the people we came with. Ali picked up on the unfriendly vibe too. As the day turned into night, we just drank and ate. In between, I wandered around the party. As I passed a table at one point in the day, I heard a guy say, "So I broke his finger and he still wouldn't tell me."

I thought that was kind of weird and then didn't think anything about it again. I was ready to go, but had to stay longer since the people we brought weren't ready to leave yet. I went back for more food after a while, and then overheard someone in another group say, "Okay," I said to him, "don't carry the gun. I'm going to put it in the glove compartment so at least you know it's there." That's when I understood, which made me more uncomfortable as the band started up again. It was definitely time to go when, of all things, the band began to play, "Speak Softly, Love," the theme from *The Godfather*. When it was over the host called out, "Again!" and when that ended he said, "Again!"

30

A Close Call with the Soviet Military

I was in charge of supplying the limousines for the motorcade of the first USA visit of a general, whom the Pentagon referred to as the most dangerous man in the world: the Chief of the Soviet general's staff, the man with his finger on the nuclear button. He'd arrived the night before at Andrews AFB and we'd taken him to Maryland House, the VIP Officers Quarters at Bolling AFB. I showed up alone at dawn, before my people or even the security detail for General Moiseyev, in order to set up the motorcade. I got out of my car and could tell it was going to be a nice Washington day. It was the first Monday in October and would also be the day the Supreme Court would reconvene. This was a major event, attended at the invitation of Colin Powell, Chairman of the Joint Chiefs of Staff.

I was thinking about how to position the motorcade for departure when I noticed someone emerging from the OQ. It was the general coming out for a smoke, completely unattended. He was wearing his military pants, boots, and a white tank top tee shirt. He walked right up to me and offered me a cigarette. I declined since I didn't smoke, but he stood near my car smoking and hanging out with me.

He couldn't speak English, and I didn't understand Russian, but we seemed to communicate. He didn't seem scary; he smiled and laughed trying to make himself understood. He finally shook my hand, said something in Russian, and went back in. An hour later, we were all in position for the departure to the Pentagon and an arrival ceremony. The general, now in full uniform with the accompanying medals, regalia and an imposing hat, came out with his Russian military entourage. *Now* he looked impressive but scary.

POINT OF CONTACT (POC)

We loaded the general and his entourage into a few limousines for the ride to the Pentagon to meet with General Colin Powell. The general naturally sat in the power seat of the limousine, which is the right rear seat of the car. We had military CID and D.C. police providing security as our silent motorcade left Bolling AFB. I rode in the limousine that followed the general's with police cars both in front and in the rear of the motorcade.

We weren't five minutes out of Bolling AFB when a car suddenly appeared, rocketing out from an underpass right at the door where the general was sitting. The car must have been doing at least 50 mph, having blown through a red light. It was about to T-bone our motorcade, killing the head of the Soviet military! I shouted and our driver slammed on the brakes, launching a few Russians to the front. The renegade white car practically skimmed both the back of the general's limousine and the front of the limousine I was in, narrowly missing us as it zoomed in between, never even hitting its brakes. If we'd been one second earlier, it would have been a major international incident. That thought kept me up a few nights wondering, as I do to this day, whether or not it had been an attempt on the general's life that had simply failed.

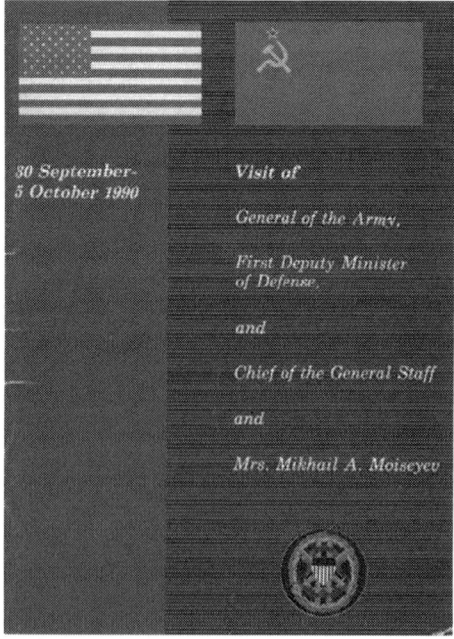

93

31

Speeding to Las Vegas in a Purple Haze

My friend and I were eighteen, doing our first cross country road trip, and had ended up in Moscow, Idaho to see his old girlfriend. We'd run out of weed days earlier, and we were hoping she might have some. A road trip without being stoned would be boring and uncool. Our plan was to fill up our little Honda Civic in the morning and drive straight to Las Vegas. In the meantime, Idaho was a beautiful place, full of spectacular mountains, pine forests, emerald fields, and lakes. It happened to be the Potato Capital of the U.S. I spent the day walking around in the fresh air and watching TV, waiting for my friend to come back from visiting his former girlfriend. As I thought, he'd gotten lucky one way and unlucky another when he showed up the next morning.

"Did you get more weed?" I asked.

"No, the whole area was dry, but I did get laid," he said proudly. "And I do have something else," he added sheepishly.

He opened a napkin to reveal two BB-sized purple balls. I'd never seen anything like them before and ask what they were. He said, "You know that Jimi Hendrix song, 'purple haze all through my brain?

"Are you serious!? That's LSD?"

"Yes," he said.

Neither of us had ever tried it before. "What's it going to do?" I asked.

"She said it would creep up on you until you peaked and that you would know what that was when it happened. The rest is a Disney movie."

"Can you drive on it?" I asked.

"I guess we'll find out."

POINT OF CONTACT (POC)

"Okay, let's think about it," I said, "and get on the road." We were looking at almost a seventeen hour, 900 mile drive south through Boise to Vegas. We figured maybe we'd take the LSD when we got to Vegas. That plan lasted a couple hours until we stopped for lunch at a roadside stand and the curiosity was too great. We decided to take them and joked that at least it was a straight line and all downhill the rest of the way to Vegas. What could go wrong?

My friend took his and then, to his horror, I told him I'd changed my mind. It was really funny for a couple of minutes then I took mine and we headed down the highway. The radio was on and I was about to push another Steely Dan tape in when the news confirmed that Elvis Presley was dead—possibly from a heart attack.

Wow, the King was dead. Not that we listened to his music but he was Elvis, the King. It was an odd feeling to realize that an icon you'd thought had the ultimate life and a kind of immortality, was suddenly gone forever. I'd had a similar feeling recently when I'd noticed the Playboy Centerfold was my age, when previously they'd always been older.

For the next hour we kept asking each other whether we felt anything yet, as the fields began to look like green paint, the lakes like giant mirrors and the mountains like they were covered in ice cream. We were laughing so hard we had tears in our eyes and couldn't breathe. I saw alphabets and geometric shapes everywhere. My arms looked really long then really short. I thought I was the first person on this highway, then I was a dinosaur, then we were traveling underwater, everything was melting. So many wacky thoughts. We finally had to pull over at a scenic overlook and get out of the car. The overlook was located above a massive valley with cows that looked like cardboard cutouts miles away and trees that walked around as the mountains winked and laughed with us. The huge, white puffy clouds against the blue sky appeared as an entire spectrum of happy creatures. This must be peaking, we thought.

We sat on the wall and laughter started deep, tickling our stomachs, then bubbled up like an erupting volcano. Everything was funny, and everything was alive. We tossed a couple of rocks down the hill and it looked like we were bowling for cows. We were there for a while, maybe minutes, maybe hours, until we got a handle on what was happening and got back on the road. I asked my friend how long it was supposed to last, and he said he'd forgotten to ask.

"I hope it's not forever," I said, which made us laugh even more.

We weren't out of it—it was more that we were hyper aware with a splash of Disney, and driving wasn't a problem. Laughing was the problem because it became exhausting. Everything was vivid and alive. My thoughts were crystal clear, and we had deep abstract and ridiculous conversations as we drove, young and free and completely bonkers. We drove and drove. My friend never got tired and kept hitting "repeat" over and over to listen to "Pretzel Logic," trying to sing along, changing the words. I felt like I was in a chair at a window and everything outside was just a movie. As the sun set and it got dark, our hallucinations changed frequency and we finally began to mellow but were still intense. We just kept driving through the Disney night, but I was ready for it to end and be normal again.

We passed a bunch of gas stations that were closed and we needed gas badly. It was almost 4 a.m., and we were on fumes. The last thing we needed was to run out of gas on the side of the road while we were tripping. So as we came through a small, dusty Nevada town, we just pulled into a closed, dark gas station and parked at the pumps to wait for the station to open. We sat listening to Elvis music which was on every station and to updates on Elvis. We rode the light fantastic and waited.

After a while, we got out and stretched but stayed close to the car, as if it was our spaceship and we were in deep space. The intense laughing had finally subsided, but things were still funny and we were more lucid but still tripping away. Suddenly, another car pulled into the gas station out of nowhere in this totally dead, sleeping town. He pulled up on the opposite side of the pumps from us, and our eyes and hallucinations had to adjust to the blast of headlights. It was a cop!!

Not only was it a cop, it was a cop with a cowboy hat! Somehow we both stayed calm and relaxed when he got out of his car, probably because it felt as if it couldn't really be happening. We weren't doing anything wrong, and the circus was only in our heads, so we had to keep it together. He asked why we were there, and we told him we were on fumes and just waiting to get gas in the morning. He was taller than us, almost 12-feet tall, at times, his face and hat morphing into all kinds of freakish shapes as we spoke.

My friend and I knew not to look at each other, maybe by instinct, or we'd burst out laughing. Like laughing in church, except it would be jail. To this day, I don't know how we pulled it off. He then said, "You boys are in luck." I thought, You are not going to arrest us? But he only meant that he had a key to the pumps and he let us fill up and pay him. He was there to fill up his car before his shift.

We filled up and let him do all the talking so we wouldn't say something insane. He was an Elvis fan and maybe hearing his music on our radio gave us a pass. He never asked for IDs or any of the usual "you're in trouble" questions. His face, his car, which looked like another, cooler spaceship, the station and everything around him, kept morphing and changing colors. I couldn't tell if he was thirty, fifty or eighty years old; he kept morphing. We thanked him and couldn't get out of there fast enough. I almost said, "Viva Las Vegas!" when we were leaving but stopped in case it came out like "moon marshmallows" instead.

We waited until we were far away to burst out laughing; it had been amazing! About an hour later, dawn slowly appeared in the desert with more colors. It was incredible to see two such dramatically different landscapes separated by the night. We pulled into Vegas as the sun came up. The purple haze was finally diminishing but the colors and lights of the strip were still incredibly vivid and alive. I was worn out, my sides were sore from laughing, and I was exhausted from being up all night. It was still early in the morning as I changed from my shorts and t-shirt into a pair of jeans and shirt in the casino parking lot. It was like wrestling an anaconda to get it done. As we walked toward Caesar's Palace, and even though we were coming down, we were still zinging along until we passed an Elvis impersonator. We looked at each other and smiled. Boy did the news get that story wrong! He's still here walking around!

Amazed and mesmerized by the bells, lights, and so many people, we strolled around to adjust to civilization. We got something to drink and attempted to eat. We'd put our brains and bodies through a triathlon and the race, to our relief, was ending.

Two hot girls came up to us as we sat on a sofa and asked us if we wanted to party. I was about to say, "We've been partying all night," when one of them gave me this look, and I realized that she meant the for hire kind of party.

Elvis had left the building.

32

Going to the Prom in Style

After I had gotten into big trouble for introducing my limousine to a tree one night when I fell asleep, I had to redeem myself with my boss. His method of extracting punishment for this lapse in judgment was to have me do the worst, lowest limo jobs the company had: pickups in the middle of the night, bachelor parties, weddings, and proms. I hated them all and wanted to get back to motorcades, private jets, and Arabs.

On this one occasion I drove three couples to their prom located at a place made for parties and events. Driving rich prom kids around was easy providing they weren't crazy, drinking, or doing drugs. I'd drop them off, wait four hours, during which I could study in the back of the limousine, then bring them home. So I found a good spot in the parking lot after I dropped them at the entrance. I was parked a good distance from the front door but close enough that I could still watch it.

The school had a photographer taking pictures of the kids arriving by limos in their tuxedos and gowns. Limo after limo arrived, and pictures were taken. Most of the limo drivers would take off to get something to eat since the kids would be in there so long, but I had to study so I stayed. I was getting ready to get in the back with my books when I saw a pretty loud, old beat up, white pickup truck drive past me and park. I watched and two kids got out dressed for the prom. I could tell by their clothes that they weren't going to really fit in with all the gowns and tuxes, but no doubt they'd done the best they could with the only outfits they could afford. Before they passed my limo, I got out and asked them if I could drop them at the front door, since they were taking pictures. The couple was beyond thrilled. Neither one had ever been in a limousine before. I said, "Just sit back, enjoy the ride, and let me open the door to let you out. Don't tell anyone where you got the limo."

I circled around, took them to the grand entrance, and dropped them off at the red carpet, in front of popping flashbulbs and their friends. It was obvious that the people who knew them couldn't believe that they'd arrived in a limo.

They got out, and the boy gave me a healthy handshake and the girl gave me a dainty peck on the cheek. They were all smiles, and I think we made each other's night. I went back to my parking spot and got back to studying.

33

And You Thought This Was a Safe Neighborhood

My trouble magnet friend and I were skipping a day from Winston Churchill HS in Potomac, MD, as usual, driving around smoking pot, when suddenly a police car shot up behind us with lights and sirens. Oh shit! I thought, and pulled over just as the police car rocketed away from us. I was about to get back on the road when two more cops flew by us, lights and sirens blazing, then more and more. Something was going on, so we followed them, continuing to get out of the way as more police cars came up behind us.

They were heading to Montgomery Mall and had swarmed an undeveloped field and wooded area behind the mall. We parked and walked up as close as we could, which turned out to be pretty close. The police were all over the woods with shotguns and pistols drawn. An ambulance was leaving as we arrived at the scene. We wondered what in the world could be going on. My friend, who is very gregarious, knew several of the Montgomery County police from his own encounters. He finally spotted a detective he'd interacted with before and asked him what was happening. The detective told us that the bank in Potomac Village had been robbed, but something odd had happened. The bank robber waited around for the police to get there then drew them into a big police chase that had ended in the woods where we were. Then the bank robber had lured the two police officers into the woods as if to surrender, but he was apparently an expert marksman and had caught them off guard, shooting them both in the head, killing them instantly and escaping.

POINT OF CONTACT (POC)

This was extreme for any area, but for sleepy affluent Potomac, it was unthinkable. I felt so bad for all the policemen searching the woods who looked frantic and distraught. The bank robber/cop killer had left his shotgun in the woods and had run across I-270, which was really dangerous, and disappeared. We left for a few hours then decided to drive back by to see what was going on behind the mall.

When we got there I thought there would be lots of police, crime scene technicians, and crime tape but there wasn't anything. So we decided to park and walked into the woods to look around just in case we could see anything. We found the crime scene pretty quickly, and it was horrific. We saw blood-stained gauze and worse left behind on the ground and all the fresh BB scars on the branches around the spot from the shotgun blasts. We tried to figure out where the bank robber/cop killer had stood when he fired. It was starting to get dark and we quietly left the tragic scene that was now burned into our memories.

About a week later they caught the bank robber/cop killer and it turned out to be Robbie Angell who had been in our high school class but dropped out to join the Army. That's where he'd learned to be an expert shot. He'd been AWOL when he committed his crimes. I didn't know him, but I was told we were around him at Great Falls Park the day before he'd robbed the bank and killed the policemen when a big group of us were partying there. Later, I also heard he'd been at the same big party we'd attended after shooting the policemen. The police later also linked him to a random murder of someone just walking down Seven Locks Road in Potomac.

The weird part, too, was that one of his neighbors, Bradford Bishop, who was in the State Department and supposedly the CIA, had murdered his whole family—his mother, wife, and kids with a sledge hammer—then completely vanished and was never heard from again. Both tragedies happened within a month of each other. We always said that there must be something in the water in that neighborhood.

34

Dropped by a Drink

I was in NYC briefly and planned to meet my cousin for a late dinner at Isabella's on the West Side. In the meantime, I called a good friend of mine, Ben, who worked at Rockefeller Center to see if he wanted to meet for a drink before I met my cousin. He did, and we decided to meet at a five-star hotel bar off of 5th Avenue. The bar was thinning out when I got there. Ben is a big guy who played football for West Point who could easily have several martinis and never show it.

He'd already had one when I got there and ordered himself a second one and one for me. We laughed and caught up on things when I started to notice there seemed to be almost as many working girls as real patrons in the bar. Ben had noticed too and thought it seemed odd that the hotel would allow them in since it was five-stars. He asked if I wanted to go with him when we finished our drinks to meet another friend of his nearby who wanted to introduce Ben to someone. As we spoke, there was plenty of activity around us, but we didn't notice anything odd except the working girls.

I finished my martini, ordered a second one, and went to the bathroom. Ben was still on his second martini when I left the bar. As I walked to the bathroom, I started to feel funny, as if I was walking on a slow motion, rocking boat. Something wasn't right, and when I got back to my bar stool a working girl stood next to it. I told my friend that I felt drugged as my second martini was placed in front of me. To my surprise, Ben, who could drink ten martinis without being affected, said he felt the same way. We were both woozy, and there was no way I was going to have a second drink.

POINT OF CONTACT (POC)

I've never been roofied but doubted that's what it was since we were still lucid, just loopy and woozy. The working girl tried to talk to me, but I politely declined a conversation. I wondered if it was she who'd drugged me but how would she have gotten to Ben's drink? It was a really weird feeling, not like we were out of it, more like we'd taken something that would make us let our guard down and be easily handled. I said we had to get out of there.

Ben took care of the check, and as we were leaving I knocked over my second martini. Before I was out the door I heard the working girl cry out as my spilled martini splashed her. We didn't stop and kept moving to get outside the hotel. Ben was laughing because he saw it happening. We were both in suits but were really high on whatever we'd been slipped. I decided to go with him to meet his friend and hoped the drug would wear off if I walked around.

We had to go to the Sheraton Hotel on 7th Avenue just a few blocks away. We were trying to walk down the sidewalk and did a pretty good job but banged into each other about four or five times. We weren't staggering or anything, just walking under some kind of unbalanced drug buzz. We kept it together really well and doubted that anyone could tell there was anything wrong. We got to the Sheraton and met Ben's friend in what seemed to be a second floor lobby. He was speaking in a thick Irish accent which was funny since he hadn't had one the last time I'd met him.

I thought we were going into the hotel bar to meet his friend, but instead he opened a door to a huge banquet room. There must have been 500–600 people seated at round tables having dinner. We were both woozy from being drugged, and we followed him around all the people to the center of the room. Everyone must have been watching us since we were the only ones walking around. I was worried I was going to lose my balance and fall down so I grabbed the back of a few chairs as I moved through the crowd. We finally got to the main table, and Ben's friend introduced us. The man stood up, and I didn't know who it was until he turned around to shake my hand. It was Gerry Adams, the head of Sinn Féin.

It was an interesting surprise and I'm sure all of my contacts at the British Embassy wouldn't have been too happy about me being there. My friend did all the talking which impressed me since he felt the same way I did. I wanted out of there fast and was glad when we headed to the door a few minutes later. We got outside the hotel, and I said that it had been another interesting night. I got into a taxi to meet my cousin at Isabella's and he sauntered back to Rockefeller Center.

35

The Curious Guest Saves the King

I had to redeem myself with the boss of the limousine company I worked for in college because I wrapped a limousine around a tree then took off for California while he was out of the country. I wrote a contrite letter to him from San Clemente, California, asking for my job back. My boss knew Richard Nixon, who lived there, so I told him, jokingly, in my letter that he said hello. When I returned, my boss took me back but not before giving me the worst limousine jobs they had.

Finally, he saw that I'd soldiered through everything without complaint. He wanted to take a few of us up to the Waldorf Astoria in New York City for his childhood friend, King Hussein's, speech to the UN. He asked if I knew my way around NYC, and I said absolutely. I just wanted to go. I really had no clue and only vaguely remembered going to Rockefeller Center when I was six or seven.

My cousins lived there and told me it was fairly easy using street numbers and avenues. The good part turned out to be that most of the time, I was in a motorcade in one of two Rolls Royce cars my boss owned. We went to JFK for the arrival and I could actually see the king in the pilot's seat taxiing his royal 727 jet up to us. The rest of the time we waited and waited on the Wal-

POINT OF CONTACT (POC)

dorf towers side. Finally, there was some action when the Secret Service was setting up a motorcade to go somewhere. At the last second, my boss told me to get into the motorcade with a couple of Jordanians, and off we went through NYC: nonstop, lights and sirens. I had no clue where we were going, we just seemed to be zigzagging, playing follow the leader, flying through NYC.

We kept going until the city turned to country, and we arrived at an enormous brick-gated entrance that looked like it was from another time and shot right through past the guardhouse. We followed the driveway through the manicured lawn, past elaborate turn of the century outbuildings until we arrived at a giant rectangular stone mansion at the top of a hill. My passengers couldn't speak English so I couldn't ask them where we were. The fifteen people we transported there disappeared into the building. The Secret Service directed the cars to a staging area to park. I got out and went up to the lead agent to ask him where we were and he said, "the Rockefeller Estate. It's called Kykuit."

Wow, how cool. I couldn't believe it. It was a spectacular place. He told me there was a room inside with food and drinks where I could wait and we'd leave after the king had dinner with David Rockefeller. It was around five so it was going to be a long wait. I went in and found the room. It was big and windowless so I didn't want to sit there while it was a nice fall day outside. There were sandwiches and sodas on a table. There was a mix of people going in and out of the room. I got bored after an hour and decided to explore. I was in a suit and I had a security pin on my lapel so I figured I could wander around until someone stopped me.

I got up and eased out of the room of embassy people, Secret Service, and house staff. I went down a long white cinderblock hallway with some of Nelson Rockefeller's modern art on the walls. I thought, I have to get some type of souvenir to prove I was here. I wandered around under the main house until I found the perfect proof. There was a stack of magazines with the mailing labels on them addressed to Nelson Rockefeller at Kykuit. So I tore off two of them and put them in my wallet. I continued my wandering, occasionally passing someone who nodded or said hello but no one stopped me.

I made my way upstairs to the main floor, my confidence bolstered, and wandered around looking at John D. Rockefeller's home. It was beautiful, yet a time capsule of statues, furnishings, and art work. I was standing where he'd once stood—such rarefied air. The household staff scurried around as if I were invisible.

I came across the dining room just as the staff had just finished setting the table where dinner would be served. There were portraits of John D. Rockefeller on one wall and John D. Rockefeller Jr. over the fireplace. The table, set for about ten, already had the place setting cards for the guests. I went around the table reading each name including David Rockefeller's and King Hussein. I touched the king's plate just to do it. I continued looking at each beautiful room, including one that had an oval opening to the second floor. I strolled the checkerboard foyer until I found myself at the front door. I walked out onto the portico which had a high step for people arriving by carriage. There was a huge statue and fountain directly in front of me at the far end of the driveway overlooking the golf course that surrounded the house.

It was still a beautiful day, and it was almost sunset, so I walked out to the big fountain and watched the water. I was surprised that there weren't any security people or guests around. I couldn't get over the fact that I was really walking around the Rockefeller estate. As I leaned over the wall looking out over the golf course, I saw another fountain below me that was between two large concrete staircases. I could see the glow of NYC above the forest at the edge of the golf course in front of me. I thought I'd better look at the lower fountain before it grew too dark, then go hang out in the bunker room before King Hussein's motorcade arrived. I casually walked down the giant staircase to the golf course.

At the end of the railing on each staircase, there were huge concrete planters. The fountain was surrounded with beautiful detailed astrological symbols and another large white statue embedded in the wall. I stood on my Scorpio symbol for a moment, and when I turned toward the stairs something caught my eye. Far away, there were two bright, white lights skimming the treetops. It looked like a car driving on top of the forest, growing brighter. As they reached the golf course, both bright lights dropped down what looked like only 10-feet above the golf course and rushed directly at me. Oh no, helicopters!

POINT OF CONTACT (POC)

I had nowhere to run, and it wouldn't look right if I took off in a mad dash up the stairs. I was stuck frozen as they both came right up to me at the fountain and landed. I was caught and in big trouble now; my boss was going to kill me when he found out. They were two identical slick looking, small hot rod helicopters that only had four or five people in each. The front was a huge, clear bubble of a window, which made it very easy to see that the king was flying the one on the left. I was only about 30-feet away from both of them.

The passengers started getting out of the helicopter on the right and I looked over at the king getting out of his helicopter. Since they were small hot rods they only had about a ten inch plate to put your foot on to get in and get out. I figured I'd just stand there and pretend I was security and let them go past me.

The people on the right started coming up to me when I saw the king catch his foot and trip on the small foot plate getting out. He started doing one of those running falls, trying to catch himself, but he was going down. Without hesitation, I ran forward and caught him, stopping his momentum before he fell completely, even startling myself. The king was all smiles and shook my hand, pleased that I'd saved him.

The only thing I could think of saying was, "welcome" like it was my house, and I waved my hand towards the stairs. The others had seen what I did and paraded by me, each one shaking my hand. I watched them all go up the stairs then looked at the helicopters up close for a little while, giving the guests enough time to get into the house.

I then kind of did a Bill Murray-golf course-Caddy Shack move, the part after the priest got hit by lightning, and got out of there fast. Twenty years later, through several twists of fate, I stood on the same spot when I was David Rockefeller's golf partner at Kykuit. I also proposed to my fiancé on the back terrace of the main house overlooking the Hudson River a few years later.

36

Crete, Armed and Dangerous

I had one year where I was traveling all over the world almost nonstop. I liked using Amsterdam as the jumping off point in Europe because of the beds at the Marriott, the food, and, of course, the infamous coffee shops. It was a good place to acclimate to jetlag before intrigue or shenanigans. This year, I'd gone in and out of Amsterdam seven times. On this one trip I went with a friend from Washington who was going to Moscow while I was going on to Crete.

We were both meeting girlfriends first, and then planned that we'd meet back in Amsterdam in about five or six days. The Marriott was perfect for several reasons besides the beds. We used the third floor credenza, outside of the elevators, as a drop spot for messages for friends crisscrossing Europe or the Middle East. Anyone who knew about it could check even if they weren't staying there.

I'd never been to Crete before and wasn't interested in going back to Moscow again before Crete. We hung out for a couple of days, wandering around Amsterdam, looking at the window girls, and camping out in different coffee shops. There were awesome Indonesian restaurants and pastry carts all around the canals, perfectly situated when you had perpetual munchies.

We split up, and my friend went to Moscow and I headed to Athens, then on to Heraklion, Crete. My girlfriend, Caitlin, was staying with a very wealthy girl, Ivy, at her family's villa there. There were some other friends from the States staying at the villa, too. I was going to stay at St. Nicolas Bay, a resort in the town of Agios Nikoloas overlooking Mirabello Bay and the Sea of Crete. Caitlin gave me directions to the villa that seemed really circuitous. The plan was that I would pop by, visit, and we'd explore Crete for a few hours each day. Then I'd return her to the villa.

I'd never met Ivy before. She was Greek but lived in Washington, D.C. most of the year. Caitlin said that our plan for visiting shouldn't be a problem, and it would be good for me to meet Ivy. I rented a jeep and left the very picturesque Greek town my hotel was in, heading off into the mountains of Crete. It was hot and dusty as I zigzagged through mountains carpeted in olive trees. Every time I stopped to check my directions whatever kind of insect lived in the olive trees were absolutely deafening.

I started on the east coast and my destination was somewhere on the southern coast, on the Sea of Libya. I thought it would take about an hour but it was more than two hours before I reached the vicinity of the villa. I finally came to the last town before the villa and thought how strange it was that I had to go through a very narrow alley then out the back of the town and back up into the mountains towards the coast. I knew I was getting close when I came around a bend and suddenly was stopped by two guys with rifles.

I had nowhere to go except off the side of the mountain. One guy pointed his rifle at me while the other one came up to my window. I thought I was about to get robbed. The guy who came up to the window was holding an old long antenna walkie-talkie and a rifle. He didn't speak any English and what he was saying was literally Greek to me. I started saying Ivy's name, and he nodded okay, then immediately called someone on his walkie-talkie. They said something back and forth, then waved me through. I thought, What is this all about. What's with the *guards*!?

I thought I was close, but it was almost two more miles until I arrived at the villa. The funny thing was that it wasn't a villa, but a 4 or 5-story former hotel on the ocean that had been turned into a house. I parked and saw someone walk into a large open garage on the right side of the tower hotel villa. I also got out two pairs of wooden shoes from Holland that I'd brought for Ivy and Caitlin. I went into the garage where I'd seen the person walking and found three guys sitting around, sleeves rolled up, playing cards in between several different old and new cars. Two of the men had pistols in shoulder holsters. They casually looked at me and I just said Ivy's name, and they pointed to steps at the end of the garage that would take me up to the back of the hotel.

I started up the stairs that curved around, and I could see as I got to the top that it came out on a grand lawn. There were tall hedges on either side at the top step so when I stepped out on the lawn and looked up at the hotel, I was caught off guard by someone who slugged me in the chest knocking the wind out of me. I had surprised a big burly guard holding a rifle when I'd stepped out onto the lawn. He grabbed me by my shirt and hung on. I kept saying Ivy's name. The guy said something to someone on my right and when I turned and looked, it was like something out of a movie.

At the end of the lawn overlooking the ocean was a big desk, which seemed totally out of place sitting there outside, and an older, thin Greek man was behind it who remained expressionless as he spoke back and forth with the guard. On either side of this man stood two guys holding rifles, and behind him there was a big palm tree with burlap wrapped around it and what looked like a Thompson machine gun tucked into the burlap. Immediately, I thought Greek Godfather. He said something to the guard and he pretty much dragged me into the hotel, never letting go of me.

There were some young kids and women playing in the open atrium and all of a sudden the whole place was yelling Ivy's name. I stood there for a little while in the grasp of the guard, looking around at the bizarre sight of the big desk on the lawn and the Godfather. Finally, a small chubby, pissed off looking girl in a sundress came up to me. "Who are you? Why are you here? How did you find this place?" she demanded.

I said, "Are you Ivy?" and she said, "Yes." The guard's grip got tighter as I explained I was a friend of Caitlin, I was in Crete, and she thought it would be okay if I stopped by. I told Ivy I was from D.C. too, and had brought her wooden shoes from Holland, which she took, but put down right away. She calmed down a little, but still seemed very angry at my presence. She said something to the guard who finally, reluctantly, released me. Ivy said Caitlin was down on the beach with everyone, and I could go down and see her. She pointed to a big stone staircase off of the lawn that descended down to a half moon beach where I could see about eight people. There were terraces as I went down where there were more guys looking around with rifles watching over the group on the beach. I was wondering if they were expecting something to happen. There must be a pretty good reason for all the guards and guns.

I met Caitlin and some of the other people from D.C. and some people who had gone to school with Ivy. There were two of Ivy's relatives there also. The Americans all seemed nervous and uneasy. I started to say something to Caitlin about my arrival and got a look from her to be quiet. We all made small talk until the two Greek ladies decided to go back up to the villa hotel. As soon as they were gone, everyone said that I had to help them get out of there. They were prisoners and couldn't leave even to go sightseeing!

They called the man at the desk Dr. Scaremonger from James Bond and said they were constantly watched by the guards. I told them I'd realized pretty quickly that something wasn't right. They said they couldn't even go in the wa-

POINT OF CONTACT (POC)

ter because you could actually see big sharks swim by 20-feet out. I said I really didn't know what I could do because they were pretty isolated; there were lots of guns and I only had a small jeep. Caitlin, my friend, and I left them and walked back up to the villa hotel past the guards.

I thought I needed to get myself out of there first. Caitlin didn't seem as concerned as the people on the beach but did want to take a break from the place. I asked whether she could go to Agios Nikoloas and hang out at the pool at my hotel. She left a note for Ivy since it was her nap time and said she'd call her once we got to my hotel. I told Caitlin to grab her passport for ID just in case. I gave a small wave to Dr. Scaremonger who turned out to be Ivy's uncle, but he remained expressionless as we crossed the lawn to the stairs down to the garage.

The guard who'd slugged me just gave us a look of disgust as we passed him. We jumped in the jeep and got out of there. When we got to the guards on the road they actually made me stop again and looked us over then waved us on. At first I thought they were going to turn us around and make us go back to the villa hotel. We made it back to my hotel a lot faster since I knew the way. The resort was all done in beautiful Greek architecture and we had lunch and swam in the enormous pool overlooking Mirabella Bay. The weather was hot and spectacular the whole time we were there.

Caitlin called Ivy to let her know what she was doing. Caitlin turned white as she listened on the phone. Ivy was ferociously nasty and couldn't believe that Caitlin had left the villa hotel without her permission even if it was only for a few hours. She wanted to know who I was and her uncle wanted to see me and know where I was staying. Caitlin played dumb, knowing that that would be trouble for me. Ivy said she was keeping Caitlin's luggage and plane tickets and hung up. I told her to just relax. She had her passport and Ivy would eventually calm down. Talk about a buzz kill. Caitlin was very upset, but I said she wasn't stranded since she was staying with me at a five-star resort and we could get new plane tickets. I assured her that after Ivy calmed down Caitlin, would get her suitcase back and that's what happened two days later.

When these people asked about me, and asked how I'd found their place and where I was staying, I had Caitlin tell them I'd already left and that she was staying by the airport where she would meet one of the guards in Heraklion, a very public place, to get her suitcase and tickets back.

We got there earlier than the rendezvous time so I could get a good spot to watch the drop. To our relief, two big guys met Caitlin outside of the terminal and gave her the suitcase and plane tickets back. I waited until they drove away before I picked her up. She checked that she had everything except the wooden shoes I'd given her. We spent that afternoon exploring the ruins of the palace of Knossos and finally had a nice, relaxing last day in Crete. She was relieved and happy to be going home the next day. I was staying one more day then heading back to Amsterdam.

After I took Caitlin to the airport, I found a nice restaurant on the water for lunch. I was ready to leave too, since I'd thought this would be a relaxing trip instead of cat and mouse with Don Corleone. I was enjoying my lunch, looking forward to going for a swim later, and relaxing before leaving in the morning, when suddenly a big earthquake hit the island. I was picturing the runway opening up and getting trapped on Crete. Fortunately the airport was fine—only a few cracks—and I got out of there on time.

It was such a good feeling zipping down the runway and leaving Crete. Later that night in Amsterdam, I looked forward to seeing my friend and his Russian girlfriend who was coming back with him. They weren't registered at the hotel when I got there so I dropped my stuff in my room and went to third floor credenza. Under it was a note to meet them at a hotel in London with a small stone pipe and some hashish.

37

Clandestine Candelabra

I had an unusual request come to me while working at a company I helped set up right after college, partnering with an eccentric woman. We normally dealt only with the White House, the State Department, royalty, billionaires, and Hollywood celebrities. The request came from a regular contact to meet a VIP who normally traveled by private jet but who would be arriving by a commercial jet at National Airport. They wanted a security limousine and chauffeur, as well as an armed bodyguard.

My boss, with a smirk on her face, said she wanted me to meet them personally. I was supposed to meet them, introduce them to their bodyguard, and escort them to the limousine—a job which I did on occasion. I lined up one of our toughest security guys, Bennett, and told him the job was very sensitive, that it was of major importance to national security. I said it was super top secret and no one could know. Our mission was to get this VIP through the airport quietly and discreetly so no one even noticed us. He could have an assistant with him, I added. I told Bennett the visitor was staying briefly in Washington, D.C. and that he should stay with him and keep the limousine available until this VIP left DC. Bennett said, "No problem, standard operating procedure. I will take good care of him."

I told Bennett I knew what the client looked like and that we'd meet him coming off of the plane. Having set everything up, I went to National Airport to meet Bennett and wait for the commercial flight. The plane finally arrived, and we waited for our secret passenger. Normally, I never asked anyone's name or what they did; I just did what I was asked to do, and most of the time, the clients were average people of no interest to the public. Although this time I knew who we were expecting, but I'd kept Bennett in the dark. I told him one more time that we had to be completely invisible going through the airport and Bennett agreed. I said, "don't forget that national security is riding on this one."

The mystery passenger appeared with his assistant, and they were the first people off of the plane. I gave him a small wave to indicate that we were the ones he was meeting, and he came right up to us. Bennett was confused for a second then realized that I was having some fun with him. It was Liberace and his boyfriend, both in full regalia. They glittered, they dazzled, they sparkled, and they shined. They were both wearing enormous fur-trimmed capes and diamond rings on every finger. Liberace came up to me, a little bigger a man than I was expecting, and I introduced myself and Bennett. He shook my hand and it felt like my hand had just been engulfed by a baseball mitt made of plastic with plastic sausage fingers. He said it was soooo nice to meet me in his low, nasal voice. His boyfriend seemed disinterested and wouldn't even look at us. It seemed like they were both kind of upset, as if they'd just had a fight. I led them through the airport, which was about as low key as leading a fire engine with lights and sirens blaring. People actually froze in shock as we passed. I put them in their limousine and Liberace was very nice as I said goodbye. Bennett, the bodyguard, got into the front seat. As the limousine pulled away Bennett turned to the window and slowly mouthed the words, "Help Me!"

38

Quality, not Quantity

I'd been escorting a European prince around the U.S. for ten days when he arrived for the final meeting of the trip with about forty people. There was a big commotion upon his arrival and, as usual, when working with royalty or a VIP, I stayed in the background but within eyesight, until I saw him look for me. I made my way through the throng of people streaming into the meeting room to see what he needed. He leaned over, and he said, "I want Cristal Champagne," then continued on into the room. Since this was the last meeting, I assumed he wanted to make a toast, which in itself, was a normal request; when price is no object anything is possible.

Cristal Champagne is normally around $200 a bottle but at the Four Seasons, no doubt, it would be at least twice that, and we'd need about twenty bottles. I spoke to my hotel contact, and she said she'd get back to me but that it wouldn't be a problem. As she walked away, it suddenly struck me that something was odd about the way the prince had asked for this.

The meeting had started and the lights were lowered for a slide presentation. Fortunately, the prince was seated in the back of the room near the door. The security agents gave me permission to enter the room so I slipped in, leaned over, and quietly asked the prince if he wanted the Cristal for the meeting room or on his private jet? He turned, looked at me, and he got it right away, letting out a small laugh that made some people look over at us. Then smiled at me and said, "One. On the jet."

39

Welcome to the Rockies

It was a moonless night as we began our journey through the wild west of America, August 1977, and rumors of Elvis's death crackled through the radio as my best friend, Jack, and I finished loading the last of our supplies into his new Honda Civic. I pushed Pink Floyd's *Dark Side of the Moon* into the tape deck and steadily increased the volume as we flew into the darkness on our Maryland to California journey.

We spent thirty hours driving straight through the night to reach Colorado. We were eighteen, fresh out of our first year of college with what was left of the summer in front of us, experiencing a sacred rite of passage for the American young and free—the epic cross country drive—high and fast.

We'd underestimated our supply and demand and nearly ran out of weed. We'd made a pact not to smoke again until we saw the Rockies. We flew through the night, driven by the wild inertia of the newly carefree, with a heightened eagerness to see the peaks of the mountains rise over the endless horizon. Late the next afternoon, we could tell from the road signs that we were nearing the Colorado state line. We decided we'd held out long enough even though we couldn't see the Rockies. We decided to light up. The rapidly approaching state line was close enough to break our non-toking pact.

Jack had the wheel while I readied the simple pipe we used for smoking on the road, an ingenious design with a bowl suction-cupped to the windshield, and two long hoses coiling out to the driver and front seat passenger. I packed the wooden bowl full of the last of the herb and twirled a pack of matches between my fingers with anticipation as I lit it. The flat countryside sped by as the reefer slowly crept over us, and we became pleasantly stoned. We shot through Goodland, the last town in Kansas on Interstate 70 before Colorado.

Looking in the rear view mirror, a now very stoned Jack said, "Fuck!"

"What? What's wrong?" I said.

"We're being pulled over!"

Mildly puzzled, thinking he might be joking, I rolled my head around to look out the back window thinking, if anything, that we'd have ten or twenty seconds to compose ourselves and air out our crime scene.

"We're being pulled over." Those words will do strange things to the stoner's mind—blinding fear and paranoid confusion, particularly when you still have a lung-full of reefer smoke.

I looked behind us thinking the cop was racing up after us but instead, he was right on our bumper. As I focused, I realize a Kansas State Trooper was staring right at me through the rear window, so close that he was practically in our backseat. I could almost read his badge number. We were fucked.

Not today, I thought. This can't be real; we were so good, so smooth. We can't go to jail now.

We went into stoner battle stations trying not to move around panic stricken in the car. Smoke had to have billowed from the windows as Jack and I quickly and coolly rolled them down. I discretely yanked the smoldering bowl off the windshield into my lap and shoved it between my legs, wrestling with its tentacles and putting out the smoldering ashes as we eased over to the side of the road. The Trooper got out of his car in all his glory: mirrored sunglasses, 9 mm pistol, broad shoulders, broader hat, and approached Jack's window. Dead-pan, with the unreadable face of the law, he moved his thin lips in slow motion. The voice came from somewhere else, distant. "You blew through a right turn lane back there without signaling. License and registration."

We sat frozen, my mouth suddenly dry; my heart beat in awkward random thumps and my vision swirled. Jack turned to me to get the registration out of the glove compartment. "I wish we'd waited for the Rockies," Jack said gloomily. I saw doom in his bloodshot eyes. The officer had to be able to smell the lingering reefer smoke.

"Step out of the car, son," the officer said then, and reached his giant gloved hand toward the door handle. At that very second, suddenly and miraculously, his radio squawked to life, loud, unintelligible, but full of urgency, and as quickly and surprisingly as he'd appeared, without saying a word, he was gone. Spinning his car around with a squeal and a cloud of dust, his tail lights disappeared behind us as we sat stunned and confused.

"Did that just happen? Did that really just fucking happen?"

"Let's get out of here!" said Jack.

Moments later, we saw a sign that said, "Welcome to Colorful Colorado." We'd made it! About an hour later, like a distant explosion, as stunning and as perfect as we could have ever imagined, the Rockies rose straight out of the nothingness of the flat farmland and towered into the sky. We beamed, enthralled and victorious, smiling from ear to ear. Steely Dan's "King of the World" blared through the small car's speakers. It was a magical moment; we were at peace with the road and at peace with the world, with nowhere to be but right there.

40

Babysitting the Family Jewels

While working as a limousine driver as a college student, I ended up driving for a truly royal American family for a couple of days. They came in on their own jet with a bodyguard for a private event at the National Gallery. They were staying at the Madison Hotel, which was the best hotel in Washington at the time. The bodyguard with them carried a soft, dark leather bag about the size used for a bowling ball.

The passengers went to the National Gallery Gala on their first night but when it was over, the bodyguard couldn't find them in the departing crowd. He came back to tell me, then left again to search for them. I quickly dove into the sea of black ties, gowns, and famous faces and found them, escorting them back to the limousine.

They were a very friendly couple in their late seventies with a good sense of humor. I told them I had to go back to the gallery to find their bodyguard, and they thought that was funny. When I found him after several minutes, he seemed distraught that he hadn't been able to find them. I told him that they were already in the limousine.

The next day, they visited several places, planning to leave that evening after a dinner event during which they wouldn't need me or the bodyguard for three or four hours. So when I dropped them off, the bodyguard pulled the mysterious leather bag from the trunk, sitting in the front seat, clutching it to him. He said he felt like having a good steak dinner, and price was not a problem since his boss was paying. I decided we'd go to Morton's Steakhouse on Connecticut Avenue since it was the closest to the event. This was one of the best perks that came from driving wealthy people while being in college—a great steak dinner in a restaurant. It was like Christmas.

The bodyguard patted the leather bag and said he had to bring his football in with us. I asked him what was in the bag, and he said, "Let me show you." He unzipped it and reached in, pulling up something to the opening as I looked away for a second to click on the light. When I looked down, I couldn't fathom what I was seeing. It was a dazzling mountain of jewelry made of sparkling, massive diamonds and all kinds of other jewels. He said, literally, "These are the family jewels, and I'm in charge of keeping them safe." I asked how much he thought they were worth, and he said, "Who knows? Maybe thirty, forty, or fifty million dollars, but they're really priceless since they go back generations."

We walked into Morton's and, jokingly, I asked for a table for three, the third chair for the jewels. When the waitress came over I even got a third menu and put it in front of the bag of jewels. I figured this was the meal of the week so I ordered a big appetizer and a huge filet mignon. The bodyguard ordered all kinds of things, as well as a massive steak. He said it was okay for me to have a beer and then he proceeded to get absolutely trashed. He drank everything imaginable, topping it all off with after-dinner drinks, which to me, was like drinking gasoline. Twice he got up and went to the bathroom and both times I put the bag in my lap, just in case. Just in case I wanted to leave with it!

I was thinking how cool it was having dinner while next to me on a chair was something so incredibly priceless and yet nobody in the restaurant had a clue. At the end of dinner I carried the jewels back to the limousine because the bodyguard had almost forgotten both them and his credit card. Then I had to carefully pour him into the front seat, eventually rolling down the windows because the limousine reeked of his after dinner drinks. I went back to wait for my passengers.

When they finally appeared in the doorway of the restaurant where the bodyguard should have been waiting for them, I had to wake him up. I got them to their jet and even though they were in their late seventies, I doubt they missed the fact that the bodyguard watching the family jewels was blitzed. That almost became the most expensive steak dinner in history.

41

College and the Caribbean Cartel

Around 1980, while in college and on one of my many small airplane trips exploring islands in the Bahamas, my friends and I decided to check out one called Norman's Cay. We had flown over Norman's Cay a couple of times; it was a big whale-shaped island dotted with houses. It had a really big, wide, long runway, which was unusual for the Bahamas, and there were numerous planes of all kinds parked on both sides of it.

There were four of us, two girls and two guys, and we camped out next to the plane by the runway. As we locked up the plane and set up the tent, a few planes took off and a couple of private jets landed. Then I realized that was why the runway was so big to handle jets. If private jets were landing, this must be a jet-set island hangout, I thought. From the air we'd seen that there was a rancho bar at the highest point on the island not far from the airport. A rancho is a building with a big triangular cone roof made of thatched coconut or palm leaves. We zipped up the tent and walked to the place on the hill.

The weather wasn't so great, unfortunately. The sky was gray, it was windy, and a little cool, not the sunshine we were hoping for. We got up there and it was a good-sized rancho from which you could see for miles in every direction. They played Jimmy Buffett, Calypso, and reggae music. The other people at the tables seemed to be laid back Americans or South American-looking guys and a few Bahamians who barely took notice of us. We decided this would be our hangout while on Norman's Cay. The chair I sat in had a photograph of William F. Buckley in the rancho thumbtacked to the wall behind it. It looked like he'd been there while he was sailing around. We met some Canadian college girls who were there with their parents. They had a car and to our relief, gave us a ride back to our tent. They told us about a few large half-built mansions on the island that we should check out—mansions where it seemed that the owners had just vanished.

The next day was cloudy and a little rainy so the Canadian girls gave us a tour around the island, and we ended up at an abandoned mansion. We thought about staying in it but it turned out to be too spooky. It was big and long, overlooking the main bay and some sailboats. We chased some scraggly, wild dogs out of it that had startled us as we started to look around. It looked like it was almost finished except that it had no windows and the bathrooms had been vandalized.

The house was dark, and there was an eerie feeling about it, especially since we knew the owner had vanished. Most likely he'd been in the cocaine business and was now feeding the fish. We went back and hung out with the girls at the rancho a few more times. We'd made some casual acquaintances, some of the people we kept seeing when we walked back and forth to the airport and who we also saw at the rancho.

There was one Latin guy around thirty, who kind of stood out and always showed up in a group. He seemed to hold court whenever he was at the rancho. It seemed everyone on Norman's Cay knew him. He bought us drinks and was friendly but, while we were polite, we kept our distance. Finally, the Canadian girls left with their family on a sailboat, and we flew on to Nassau almost crashing trying to land.

Decades later, I read about Norman's Cay and found out it was controlled by a drug lord named Carlos Lehder. Now I wonder if he was the friendly Latin guy at the rancho. He was co-founder of the Medallion Cartel with Pablo Escobar and Norman's Cay was their huge cocaine distribution center to the United States. The jets would bring it in from Colombia and the planes would take it into the United States from there. Except for the young Canadian college girls, I think everyone we saw and hung around with were probably cocaine traffickers and almost every plane at the airport belonged to the operation.

I don't know if they thought we were part of it or if they just didn't care since we were only college students. Ironically, we were always on guard on every trip, trying to avoid drug smugglers and yet we ended up hanging out at the Medallion Cartel's Caribbean operation center!

POINT OF CONTACT (POC)

Years later, I saw the movie *Blow* with Johnny Depp. Norman's Cay and Carlos Lehder were both featured in the movie, which further confirmed how naive and how close to the flame we'd really been.

42

Everyone Remembers their First Time

The first time I drank alcohol was by accident when I was fourteen. My family was on vacation in Hawaii, staying at the Royal Hawaiian on Oahu. My father took us to a luau at the hotel one night. I'd never been to one before. The drums, the hula dancers in grass skirts, and a huge roast pig were so much fun. We all sat at long tables with other hotel guests. We had on our Hawaiian shirts and flower leis. They had plastic pitchers of Hawaiian punch up and down the table. Some contained rum, some didn't, but there was no way to tell which was which. The one pitcher in front of me was the wrong one for a kid my age but my parents and I didn't realize this.

The show was getting better and better as I started feeling funny. I realized that this was what it felt like to get drunk, and I really liked it. By the time the poi was taken away, I had a good buzz going, and I didn't want it to end. At that age, I always traveled with a fishing pole, and after dinner I told my parents I was going fishing on Waikiki beach. I got back to the room in a hurry, changed into shorts and a t-shirt, and grabbed a towel and my fishing pole.

My plan was to get back to the luau before the tables were cleared, grab a leftover pitcher, and head out to the beach. I felt great. I got to the tables, clutching my towel and fishing pole. The staff was already cleaning up and didn't care that I was sampling different pitchers. Bingo! I found one that had rum and that was almost full.

I casually walked away with it like it belonged to me, took off my flip flops, and headed out to the shoreline to drink and fish. I set up my camp, spreading out my towel, casting my fishing line into the ocean, then sitting down to drink my punch straight out of the pitcher. Life was great! It was a clear Hawaiian night, and as I looked down the beach at all the lights and at Diamond Head, the last thing I remember was seeing all the lights become blurry and seeming to bounce up in waves.

I don't know how long I lay there until I heard some people around me talking, wondering if I was dead. They poked me. I had completely passed out. I came to splayed out on the towel. I never said anything; I felt so bad and weird. I just drunkenly reeled in my line and to my surprise, I'd caught a crab that let go as soon as he came out of the surf. I abandoned my towel and flip flops and staggered back to the hotel with my fishing pole.

My parents didn't know what had happened when they woke me up the next morning to tell me that they were going to the pool. I told them I didn't feel well and would meet them later. I felt awful, like I had the flu and had been hit by a car at the same time. I swore I'd never touch alcohol again, the downside was worse than the upside. Of course this pledge only lasted until high school.

After I woke up in the early afternoon, I ordered room service and emptied the minibar of every soda. As I headed to the pool to check in with my parents, I realized I had a hangover. I sat with my parents for a while as my siblings swam in the pool. I wanted to get back inside to the air conditioning and out of the bright sun. I went back in the hotel and idly wandered around looking at people and poking around, just watching the hotel run.

Eventually, I noticed some activity in a building next door. I walked over, cautiously watching people come and go. I noticed there were big, fat black electrical cords all over the ground. I eased closer and closer, waiting for someone to stop me but no one did. I made it to a large room and discovered I was on a location set of *Hawaii Five-O*. It was so cool, and nobody cared that I was there.

Eventually, I went over and started looking at a script on a big production table where a couple of the actors were hanging out in between scenes. I finally was comfortable and bold enough to sit down at the table with them. They were filming an episode about a family of killers who only robbed people after they killed them because then it was okay. The two big stars at the table were Slim Pickens and Jerry Reed. There were also some other minor actors. They completely accepted me for the whole afternoon. The director and whole crew came and went from the table all afternoon without asking who I was. Slim Pickens rambled on, telling funny stories in his very distinct voice, and Jerry Reed laughed and egged him on. All day I hoped I'd get to meet James MacArthur, the star of all the Disney movies I watched growing up, who played Danno in *Hawaii Five-O* but it never happened.

Robert H. Remmert

More than thirty years later, I was staying at the Four Seasons Washington, D.C. with a delegation I was in charge of. They'd just arrived, and I was going up and down the elevators getting everything settled. The hotel is not very tall and I was on the fourth floor waiting for an elevator when the doors opened and there stood a slightly stocky man, with curly, bushy white hair, maybe seventy years old, with big clear glasses, dressed to the nines in black tie. I nodded hello as I got in the elevator with him and said, "You look sharp." When he thanked me and I heard his voice, a big smile crossed my face. It was James MacArthur! Book 'em, Danno!

43

Hotel Oasis

I'd become friends with a high ranking HRH prince through my work with the embassy. His uncle was the king and he was traveling around the U.S. with his father, his father's wives, and a dozen children in their own 747. The prince called me up out of the blue to say he needed a break and wanted to get out of the hotel. No one likes traveling with their parents as an adult, no matter who they are. I had no idea the prince was even in D.C. so it was a nice surprise. I'd just gotten back from vacation and always had a good time with him. He told me his family had the top three floors of a hotel in Tyson's Corner, Virginia and said I was to go to the top floor and let their security know I was there to see him.

The prince was very low key and about eight years older than me. Unlike the stereotype, he never wanted to attract attention to himself. On several unofficial occasions over the years, he'd worn shorts, a t-shirt and a baseball cap. At other times he'd dressed in the finest custom-tailored clothes ever made. He was urbane and witty, spoke perfect English, French, German, Spanish, and Arabic, of course. Occasionally, a sentence would contain three different languages but it seemed to be the perfect way to describe whatever he was talking about.

The prince was unbelievably oil rich, had several children, and a wife who is a princess and lives in several palaces around the world. That night, he said he couldn't be away too long, he just wanted to sit in a casual restaurant away from his entourage. I decided Clyde's was perfect. It had an upscale atmosphere and no one from the embassy would be there who might recognize him.

I got to the hotel, which was teaming with limousines and security people, parked my Porsche on the side of the hotel for a quick, discreet exit to the restaurant, which was only five minutes away. I'd been to the hotel at least a hundred times running my own dignitary visits. Even though I was dressed casually in jeans and a polo shirt instead of a suit, security didn't question me as I made my way past them through the lobby to the elevators where another security agent waited. I identified myself and explained who I'd come to see. The agent had been expecting me and radioed their command post that I was there, then he keyed the right floor in the elevator, unlocking the access button.

When the doors opened on the prince's floor, there was a long desk with more security people, camera monitors, clipboards, and visible weapons but they knew I was coming and told me to wait in the lounge. The lounge, which I'd been in too many times to count, was normally full of food, drinks, and Chippendale-style furniture. Now it was empty. I paused, then slowly approached. It had been transformed with white silky drapery at the entrances, and over the walls. The big windows lined one wall and framed the distant glow of the D.C. skyline. The floor was covered with several giant, brand-new, beautiful Persian rugs that shimmered in the light. Along all the walls were beautiful bright silk pillows to sit or lean on. That was it, no western furniture.

I slowly realized I was inside a tent, in the top of a building, and it was amazing. The prince came in dressed in jeans and a sport jacket and greeted me in his usual manner. "How are you doing young man?" he said in a very British accent. As usual, our plans had changed. Who we met, where we went, and what happened is classified.

44

Timing is Everything

Blair House, the president's guest house, located across the street from the White House, was being renovated. The State Department designated the Madison Hotel on 15th Street across from the Washington Post as the temporary Blair House until the renovations were completed. I was waiting for the prime minister of Australia one day, standing outside the Madison waiting for his arrival. I could hear the sirens of his motorcade getting closer on L Street and in a few moments I saw the first Harleys of the motorcade come around the corner. The sirens were pretty loud when I heard a louder *pop* somewhere near the middle of the block.

A small, deep purple cloud rose from where I heard the popping sound. Within seconds, the cloud had grown huge, spreading across 15th Street, and I could no longer see the motorcycles, police cars, or the rest of the motorcade. Suddenly, the Harleys, police cars, and armored limousine with the Australian prime minister, and Secret Service popped out of the purple cloud and drove right up to me at the hotel's front entrance.

The deep purple cloud had now floated across the street. The motorcycle cops, without missing a beat, didn't even stop at the hotel. They swung around and sped back to the alley from which the purple smoke had originated. The prime minister got out of his limousine in front of me and gave me a quick nod of hello as the entourage scrambled to surround him and disappeared into the hotel. Seconds later the motorcycle cops caught the bank robber who had set off the dye pack. Talk about bad luck! You go to rob a bank, step outside, and discover dozens of law enforcement officers coming around the corner. Timing, once again, is everything.

45
Sushi

I was in my mid-twenties and had a crush on a beautiful Swedish girl who worked in my office building. I flirted with her whenever we ran into each other and tried to get her to go out with me but she played hard to get. Finally, she agreed and said she wanted to go to Sushiko, a sushi restaurant in Glover Park that the Japanese embassy staff frequent, so I knew it had to be good.

I'd never eaten sushi before, but I love all food so I wasn't concerned about eating raw fish for the first time. We went to the restaurant and I wanted to be suave and debonair but realized quickly that I better just let the waitress bring us a sushi assortment. I knew how to use chopsticks so that wouldn't get in the way of impressing my Swedish beauty. The sushi came in an elaborate presentation and since I had no idea what I was looking at, I ate the whole mound of green wasabi first.

46

Spring Break 1976

It was 1976 and I was in my senior year at Winston Churchill High School in Potomac, MD. I'd moved into my trouble-magnet friend Casey's parents' mansion since my nightmare older brother had reappeared unexpectedly at my parents' home. Something had happened in Colorado where he had been going to college but now he was back. So I left because I could not be in the same house with him.

We barely went to school and life was good living at Casey's huge home. Their refrigerator and pantry were like a grocery store and his five sisters doted on me night and day. I almost became like a family pet. They kept me hidden from their parents, which wasn't hard because they were hardly ever there. After a few months, their mother finally realized I was living there but didn't care. Casey's father never did find out. We had near-nightly parties in their huge basement pool room with all kinds of stuffed big game fish looming over us on every wall.

Casey was madly in love with Ashley who had moved to Potomac from Texas about the same time I had. She was new too, and came to Churchill at the same time we did. Spring break was coming up, and Ashley was going back to Texas and Padre Island to party with the friends she'd grown up with. Casey decided since he couldn't go with Ashley that we should drive to California. The trip would be our first cross country trip and would keep his mind off of Ashley. Casey somehow finagled a Jeep Wagoneer from a company in D.C. that needed it dropped off at their office in Los Angeles. All we had to do was pay for gas. This would not be a problem Casey assured me, since we had $22 between the two of us.

We threw some clothes into a bag, his sisters filled a Styrofoam cooler with food and sodas and Ashley dropped us off in downtown D.C. where we picked up the Jeep Wagoneer. I couldn't believe they were actually giving such a nice Jeep to Casey, the wild child. He could really pour on the charm in an Eddie Haskell kind of a way when he had to and people ate it up. It was amazing to watch. The Wagoneer was cream colored with fake wood sides and perfect for a cross country. Not only was it big, it had four-wheel drive and the front and backseat were the perfect size to use as beds. We had a full tank of gas, a map book, a cooler full of food and sodas, some pot, and $22 as we headed west out of Washington, D.C.

We drove all day and part of the night drinking sodas, smoking pot, and eating the sandwiches his sisters had made. It was getting late and we were both tired when we realized we were running out of gas. I said, "We better find a gas station," and Casey gave me a Cheshire Cat grin and said, "No, we need to find an abandoned car on the side of the highway." I didn't know what he was up to until we found a broken down car. He slowed down and pulled up behind it. What was he up to? I wondered as Casey jumped out to examine the parked car. Cars and trucks whizzed by us. He got back in and put the Jeep into four-wheel drive and pulled off the highway and alongside the car. Out of the back he pulled a long syphon hose with a hand pump to get things flowing. It went into the broken-down car, he gave the pump a couple of squeezes and the gas began flowing into our Jeep. So criminal, yet so clever. This scheme got us all the way to California. I don't know how many cars we did this to but it sure worked perfectly the whole way. We slept in the Jeep at rest stops and made our way to Texas where I thought we'd spend some time and could stop in on friends of my parents.

After a couple of days, we made it to Dallas and stayed with a friend of mine from Jesuit Prep who I always thought had the coolest first name: Sterling. After we recharged in Dallas, we drove to Irving to visit the McKennas. They were wealthy and lived off of a fairway at Las Colinas country club. Our families used to vacation together in the Virgin Islands and Wyoming when I was growing up. Their house was built with two large steel I-beams they'd gotten from a building that was being demolished in Kansas City. They'd gone dancing there regularly during their courtship. The I-beams made the house cantilever out so it looked over the golf course. Mr. McKenna's fleet of white cars, including a Cadillac El Dorado and a Rolls Royce, were parked underneath.

We showed up unannounced at their door like two stray dogs looking for a meal. They were naturally surprised and shocked to see me appear out of the blue. They invited us in. There were several of their grandchildren running around. We sat down in their huge living room taking in the spectacular view of the golf course as we caught up. Mrs. McKenna seemed like herself, but Mr. McKenna did not. He'd always been happy, talkative, and welcoming, but something was off, and he seemed depressed. We chatted for a little while, and Mrs. McKenna encouraged him to take us out to lunch so he could get out of the house and hang out with us. I was thinking about asking them if we could stay one night but after seeing all the kids and Mr. McKenna not himself, I decided it wouldn't be appropriate, and we would move on after lunch. I hoped we'd go in one of his cars but instead he jumped into our Jeep, which was a mess on the inside. He took us to a nice Mexican restaurant and treated us to a feast. He said he was envious of us being young and free, going to California, that every young man should do it. He told us that when he'd been our age he'd had no money or commitments and he'd done the same thing with his best friend. Instead of driving, they'd bummed around the country jumping on railroad cars. He and his buddy did it for a summer until his friend fell off of a train and got really hurt, ending their travels. It really made me feel good hearing that story since he'd become extremely successful, which meant there was hope for me. We took him back home and he slipped me $40 as we said goodbye, without having ever asked why he seemed depressed.

I'd always admired Mr. McKenna and looked up to him as a great person and role model but it was the last time I ever saw him. I found out a few years later why he'd been depressed. A couple of months before we showed up, his son had bought a new twin engine plane in California and when he was flying it home for the first time over the Rockies, he'd flown higher than the plane had been made to withstand and a wing snapped off.

That afternoon we continued to head west and spent the night in the Jeep again outside Amarillo, Texas. The next morning when we woke up, stretching after another night of sleeping in the Jeep, Casey decided he wanted to look for snakes, especially a rattlesnake. There were some big broken pieces of plywood on the side of Highway 40, and we took turns flipping over one piece of plywood at a time. It kind of felt like we were playing Russian roulette, and I wondered who would get the bullet. Sure enough, I finally flipped one over and slowly stepped backward because there was about a foot and a half long, fat, tan snake. It didn't really react or move, and before I could figure out if it was poisonous, Casey had picked it up behind its head. Casey explained that from the shape of its head and tail he knew it wasn't poisonous. I still wasn't sure and just wanted to let it go but he wanted to take it with us so we dumped out the last of the contents of the Styrofoam cooler, put it in there, and hit the road.

We were now only two states away from California and heading into the desert. On the way, Casey played with the snake when he wasn't driving. He'd collect bugs and things to feed it, and the snake got so used to him that it would wrap itself around his forearm and stay there for a long time.

We'd run out of food and drinks so we started eating at busy diners along the way, parking out of sight at each one. We would have a really good breakfast, lunch, or dinner ask for the check and leave a nice tip. It was dine and dash time since we had so little money. The tip for the waitress wouldn't alert her or anyone as we slipped out while the cashier was busy with customers. We were long gone before they probably realized it but it was survival. Although, knowing Casey, he probably would have done it for the thrill even if he had $500 in his pocket.

Another idiosyncrasy about Casey was that he was notorious for falling asleep at the wheel so this added to my uneasiness when he was driving, especially at night. A couple hours after a rather big dine and dash dinner in Arizona, he was driving and I'd dozed off. Casey was really trying to make it to the California border before we stopped for the night. I don't know how long I was asleep but I felt the Jeep shake right to left a little bit, which woke me up. I opened my eyes a little then closed them again to go back sleep, but the Jeep did it again. I could tell we were going pretty fast. So I slowly opened my eyes again and saw something white in front of us. I was so tired, however, that I almost went back to sleep. Luckily I focused quickly, suddenly realizing that the white thing in front of us was our headlights reflecting off of something. I screamed Casey's name and he reacted instantly, swerving back onto the highway. Sparks exploded off the right side mirror as it skimmed the concrete bridge abutment we'd been about to slam head-on into at 70 mph. Not only had Casey fallen asleep with the cruise control on, but his legs were crossed Indian style on the seat.

The next afternoon, glad to be alive, we were well inside California and past the Mojave Desert when it was Casey's turn to drive again. He put his snake back in the cooler and took over. He wasn't driving for more than an hour before he got us pulled over for speeding by the California highway patrol. That's when he told me his driver's license was suspended for having too many points. Shit! He needed mine or he was going to jail and I'd be stuck with about $36 in my pocket.

For some reason, at the time, a Maryland driver's license was just a typed paper card and no picture. So when the CHIP came to the driver's window and Casey couldn't talk his way out of it, he gave the cop my driver's license and the Jeep's registration. I got three points on my license and an $80 speeding ticket. Once again, Teflon Casey, which was one of his nicknames, got out of trouble at my expense. I shook my head. I should have figured he would drive completely across the country without a driver's license.

POINT OF CONTACT (POC)

We made it to the drop off in downtown Los Angeles and cleaned out the Jeep. We threw away the cooler, the syphon hose, and a bunch of trash, then dropped off the Jeep. It had made it with only a broken side mirror. Casey then put the snake in his gym bag with his clothes. "Now what?" I said as we walked out of the building. "We made it to California, Now what are we going to do? We have hardly any money, we've lost our ride, and we have no plan." We went back into the office building, and Casey asked to use the phone for a couple of local calls. He called Ashley in Austin, Texas, then his mother in Potomac who had no idea he was in California. She'd thought he was somewhere in the house.

He hung up the phone, smiled, and said we needed to get a taxi and get to LAX in a hurry. We had just enough money left between us to pay for the taxi. When we got to LAX we found two tickets to Austin that Casey had gotten his mother to buy for us. We were going to stay with Ashley and her friend at Padre Island. When we walked into the LAX terminal, Casey quickly went into the bathroom and changed into a long sleeve shirt. I didn't think much about it at the time as we rushed to our plane. We finally reached our seats on the jet, and I asked why security hadn't seen the snake in the bag during the X-ray screening. That's when he lifted his arm where I could see the snake's head peeking out of his sleeve. It was wrapped around his forearm once again with its tongue licking the air. I almost jumped out of my seat because I still wasn't convinced it wasn't poisonous. "No wonder you changed your shirt," I said, and he just smiled.

We had something to eat and both fell asleep. About two thirds through the flight I woke up to see the snake completely out of Casey's sleeve, resting on his lap and leg. I slowly nudged Casey to wake up so as not to startle the snake to either bite me or take off in the plane. We were lucky no one was sitting next to us and that no flight attendant had seen it because it was pretty menacing looking. Casey calmly stuffed it back up into his sleeve. When we landed in Austin, he put it back into his bag.

We were met by Ashley and her friend Shannon, for the drive to the beach. Ashley was very attractive but Shannon was beautiful and completely out of my league, a prom queen or head cheerleader type or both. Two classic Texas beauties. Shannon still lived in Austin where they'd both grown up. She even drove the same car Ashley had in Potomac, a light-colored, two-door Impala. I couldn't believe that we were back in Texas after driving all the way to California and literally only spending a couple of hours there once we got rid of the Jeep. And those hours had been mostly in LAX. Plus the snake had come with us on half the trip and now it was back in Texas too.

It was a four or five hour drive to Padre Island, and it was nice to sit back and watch the scenery go by. We got to their rented beach condo, and it was full on Texas spring break pandemonium. There were shrieking girls in bikinis and muscled guys guzzling beer, chasing after them as we cut through the throngs to get to their place. It was a large two-bedroom apartment with a kitchen, a big living room, and a balcony looking out at the beach and ocean. Shannon took over when we walked through the door. She said, "Ashley and Casey, you're in there," pointing to one room, "and I'm in here." With a sheepish smile, she told me, "You're on the couch."

The girls had already spent a few days in Austin and were only there for three days before Ashley had to go home. We also had only three days to figure out how to get home ourselves.

The next couple of days we partied, eating and drinking off of Ashley's parents credit card in the funny chaos of a Texas spring break. Shannon was definitely her school's royalty with everyone coming by to say hi and to see what parties she was going to attend. Finally, we loaded up the car and left Padre Island. Casey was in the backseat with me, and when I looked over at him, he lifted up his arm. The snake, which I'd totally forgotten about, was back wrapped around his arm again. The girls never knew he'd had it in the condo.

The music was loud enough in the car that he whispered he planned to let it go at the airport. Ashley was buying us our plane tickets home and we'd figure out how to repay her once we got back to Potomac. Ashley's parents naturally hated Casey, knowing he was nothing but trouble, so she'd have some explaining to do when that bill arrived. After all the partying and late nights, Casey and I both fell asleep on the long ride back to Austin. The girls woke us up when we arrived at the airport and sleepily I looked around as Shannon parked the car. I glanced over at Casey who had a funny look on his face. He kind of grimaced then held out his arm. I looked and the snake was gone! It was hiding somewhere in the car. We both tried to look for it casually without alerting the girls. When we got out of the car we both quickly looked under both seats. No snake.

I asked Casey what he thought we should do and in his typical fashion, he shrugged and said, "Let's go home." We said goodbye to Shannon and walked into the terminal. Casey gave me a sly smile knowing he'd just left a snake in her car. When we went to check in at the ticket counter, to my dismay there was only one seat available on the jet back to Washington, D.C. that day. With a sinking feeling I knew at that moment that I was going to be left behind. Ashley had her reserved seat and bought Casey the last seat but assured me that when she got back she would book me a seat as soon as she could. Casey gave me a nod of agreement but I knew he just wanted to get on that jet and go home. The guy had just left a snake in a girl's car. So that was it as I walked with them to their gate. I'd have to wait in the airport. As we approached the gate, the loudspeaker exploded, calling Ashley's name over and over like it was an emergency. Casey and I both looked at each other thinking the same thing. The snake!

Ashley went to answer the page and was gone for about ten minutes. She came back looking very angry. Casey tried to fake not knowing what was wrong but she knew him too well. "You left a fucking snake in Shannon's car!" she yelled and went on like that, screaming at him. I just stepped aside out of the line of fire. Apparently, Shannon had left the airport and gone to a 7-11, and when she came out, the snake was curled up on her seat. When it saw her, it slithered back under the seat. Shannon was furious and cursing up a storm at Ashley. She said she never wanted to get back in that car ever again. Casey kind of gave her an "oh well" look, a smile, and put his arm around her to calm her down as we all walked to their gate.

I reminded Ashley to please not forget that I was in Austin and to get me home as soon as possible, which she assured me again that she would. I trusted her. I thought Casey would have forgotten about me as soon as the jet door shut. It was a very lonely feeling watching their jet take off and disappear, leaving me there. I only had about $6 in my pocket and a big blank of time in front of me not knowing when I could go home. I asked the ticket agent when their jet would get to D.C. and if there was anything available yet, which there wasn't. I bummed around the airport watching people come and go and jets land and take off. I rationed my money, only eating peanut butter crackers and sodas.

By that night I'd heard nothing from them and the airport seemed to be closing down. I had figured at this point that I'd just have to camp out overnight inside the terminal until the next day. That's when a policeman came up to me and asked what I was doing since I was the only person in there. I told him I'd missed my flight and had to wait until the next day for another one. He told me I had to leave the terminal because they were locking it up. My heart sank. I had nowhere to go and hardly any money. I went outside as the doors were locked behind me and wandered around trying to find a place to spend the night. There were some huge bushes along a decorative cinder block wall where I could look out at the runway and still stay hidden, I thought. I used my bag as a pillow and went to sleep. A couple of hours later I was awoken by a flashlight in my face and two cops. Fortunately, one of them was the one I'd spoken to earlier so he knew my story. They got me out of there and told me I had to leave airport property. I felt awful as I walked away. I was alone, homeless, broke, in a place I didn't know and so far from home. I thought it couldn't get any worse and then it started to rain.

I looked around, and there was no shelter. I couldn't go back to the terminal. I stood there as the rain started to pick up when I saw a jacked up pickup truck at the far end of the parking lot. I had no choice but to climb under it to get out of the rain. I put my bag under my head and went back to uneasy sleep worrying that if the owner of the truck drove away, he might accidentally run me over. At least I was out of the rain for the moment but under a truck.

When they reopened the terminal the next day, I was at the door and the first one in. It felt like a small victory that I'd survived the night. I sat there all day waiting and waiting, not knowing if anybody was even trying to get me home. I was losing hope by the hour as I watched people and jets come and go all day long again. I made sure I kept a quarter as a final bullet to make a kamikaze collect phone call to my parents for a rescue if this went on for a couple of days. I hadn't spoken to them in three months, not since I'd left home.

It was now almost five o'clock, and I hadn't heard anything. My dread started to build about spending another night outside under a truck again. I was really hungry and had eaten the last of my peanut butter crackers that morning. I was really thinking about using my quarter since my spirit was about as low as it could go when suddenly, in what seemed like a call from out of heaven, I was paged to go the ticket counter. My spirit soared when I found out I was leaving in two hours and it was a dinner flight. I couldn't believe my crazy trip was finally over as my jet shot down the runway that evening. I was going home. I always did wonder what happened to the snake and hoped he had somehow gotten away.

47

Paying in Cash

I had to pick up $120,000 in cash as payment for the president of Argentina's visit. I always called this "meeting the rooster" when I had to collect cash so I wouldn't have to reference money. I went to the Hotel Washington on 15th Street and up to a room on the fourth floor. I had an undercover cop along to shadow me and escort me out of the hotel and into the waiting car when it was over.

I knocked on the door, and a very large Argentinian man without his suit coat on let me in. A soccer game blared from the TV and a smaller, skinny man shrugged a hello from where he was sitting at the edge of the bed watching it. The room was tiny and had barely enough space to move around in. The big guy, in thick Spanish, said, "$120,000. Right?" I confirmed the amount. He then went to the closet, picked up a big brown box, and put it on the bed. When he opened it, I was stunned to realize that there had to be at least two million dollars in cash in the box. He casually counted out twelve packets of $10,000, each in a sealed plastic bag with a bank band around the bills. He said, "You need to count it," which I was, of course, planning to do. He put the box back in the closet and sat down next to his associate to watch the soccer game.

I tore open all the plastic bank bags and used the bed to count each pack. The two Spanish guys were smoking up a storm in this tiny room, completely ignoring me, laughing and talking in Spanish about the soccer game. It felt like I was part of some Colombian drug deal—a big box with a couple million in cash and me counting stacks of hundred dollar bills!

It took me almost twenty minutes to count it all and the process was exhausting. When I was finally finished, I pulled out a shopping bag and dumped all of the money into it. The men got up, shook my hand, and I left. Mike, the undercover cop, took me down the stairs, out the side door, and into the open door of a waiting sedan. I didn't mention to him or anyone that there were millions of dollars in cash upstairs in an unguarded hotel room.

Best to keep that to myself.

48

Defensive Moves for the Federal Government

Some of the best people to drive during my college limousine job were people with private jets. They were an ultra-rich breed that always somehow surprised you. On this day, I had to go out to the private aviation center at Dulles airport and meet a jet. Private jets are identified by their tail numbers like N244RH. You give the tail number to the control desk for the in-bound plane and they track it for you. Then you wait on the tarmac until it lands.

When the plane touches down and stops, you follow an escort vehicle out to the jet to pick up your passengers. The last thing anyone wants is a limousine banging into a jet and causing millions of dollars in damage. The passenger on this day was a bit mysterious because I was only given the pilot's name. Whoever I was driving was to be taken to an office building in Bethesda, Maryland, where I was to wait until he finished his business and then return him to his jet. A super easy job.

I waited on the tarmac when my jet came in for a landing. The jets we normally met, besides the big ones used by royalty or that land at Andrews Air Force Base, were routinely small executive jets like Gulfstreams, Falcons, Challengers, or Lears. I got word that my jet was now taxiing to park, and that's when I saw it. Not only was it a 737, which is big and unusual for a private jet, more like a commercial jet, but the whole thing was bright lime green. I was thinking, What is this about? The ramp stairs were pulled up to it. I was waved over to the giant lime, and the pilot came down and met me.

First, he had me go back and forth to get me exactly in the right spot at the bottom of the jet ramp stairs. Then the crew perfectly aligned a red carpet between the stairs and my car door so the passenger would not touch the tarmac. Then the pilot got in the limousine, looked it over and put up the electric divider window between the front and the backseat. People don't realize the chauffeur can hear everything even if that window is up because the sides are just cloth. I was then handed an instruction sheet and saw they were using a Mr. X type euphemism for his name.

The sheet had a numbered list of rules on it: Don't talk to him, don't look at him, don't look in the rearview mirror, open the doors when X gets in and out, lock the doors when X is in the car, don't drive fast, don't drive slow, know where you are going, if he asks you a question answer it then be quiet, don't try to shake his hand.... I'd never been handed a sheet like this, and suddenly my passenger became a bit intimidating. I wondered what he was going to look like.

He slowly came down the stairs, and the whole crew stood lined up along the red carpet outside the limousine. The pilot opened the door. I saw him for a few seconds before he got in. He was in his late sixties, very distinguished, wealthy looking, and reminded me of a wise owl. He was well dressed in a tweed jacket, shirt, tie, tan slacks with expensive looking shoes. I quickly became comfortable because I didn't have to interact with him, and it was an easy drive to his destination.

I gave him a smooth, good-paced ride. When we arrived, I jumped out and opened his door. When he got out, to my surprise, he said, "thank you." I was taken aback since usually people like this never acknowledged your presence. There was no one around as he walked to the building alone. About two hours later he came back out of the building by himself. I popped out of the front passenger seat and opened his door. This time he didn't look at me or say anything.

We were about halfway back to the airport when my heart skipped a beat. The electric divider window was going down. He asked me my name and then began a discussion which I found very interesting. He wanted to convince the U.S. government to move its whole operation to the center of the United States, then make Washington, D.C. a ceremonial city just for parades or inaugurations and events like that. He was concerned that the United States was completely vulnerable to a nuclear weapon attack that could wipe out our leadership in one fell swoop. By being in the center of the country, our governmental buildings and officials would be harder to attack. the White House, Congress, Pentagon, and Supreme Court wouldn't be clustered together and instead, could be miles apart.

I realized he was right as he described the possibility of a future event like the attack on Pearl Harbor. I found his idea fascinating and insightful, whoever he was. When we got back to his jet, to the horror of the pilot, I got out of the

POINT OF CONTACT (POC)

car, shook the man's hand, looked at him and told him I'd really enjoyed our conversation. He gave me a smile and a pat on my shoulder and walked up the stairs. The pilot just shook his head and followed him up. To this day, I wonder who the man was with the smart idea to move all branches of the federal government to secure it from a single devastating nuclear attack, and why his big jet was lime green.

49

Waiting for War in the Alps

It was 1991, and the U.S. was on the brink of the Persian Gulf War and getting Saddam Hussein out of Kuwait. Washington, D.C. was completely shut down, bracing for the war and business was dead. Saddam Hussein only had five days left before the UN deadline for him to leave Kuwait expired, and he wasn't budging. So since there was nothing to do, I decided to go skiing in the Alps with two of my friends and wait for the war to start. Just before I left for Dulles airport, I watched CNN give an advisory warning of terrorist threats against all Americans traveling around the world especially to Europe, our destination.

We flew into Amsterdam to pick up "supplies," then took a 400-mile, all-day train trip to Munich for a one day breather there before skiing. We relaxed all day in our comfortable train cabin drinking German beer and smoking different things we'd picked up in Amsterdam. The scenery changed continually as we flew along the Rhine River, passing many medieval villages with their big castles looming over them. Around dusk, and in the middle of a huge blizzard, we finally arrived in Munich.

My friend had the address of a hotel that was supposed to be close to the train station but when we stepped outside we could barely see 50-feet in front of us; the snow was coming down so fast. There were no taxis, no cars, no people to ask for directions, and almost a foot of snow already on the ground. There was no option but to begin walking and hope we found our hotel.

We put our suitcases over our heads and started trudging through the drifts. We zigzagged up and down streets searching for more than an hour in the relentless blizzard. It was now night and we were cold, wet, and starting to feel like we might just freeze to death. Finally a car came down the street and we flagged the driver down. He barely spoke English but clearly said we were crazy to be out in the blizzard. He directed us to the hotel which fortunately, was close by. Freezing and drenched, we felt as if we'd just conquered Mount Everest as we finally entered the lobby.

We spent most of the next day at the legendary Hofbrauhaus talking to girls, drinking huge steins of beer, and eating awesome German food. After a day of partying, we were ready to get back on the train and head to Austria. We planned to hang out and ski at a small resort called Igls just above Innsbruck.

The day we left the hotel turned out to be beautiful, with a bright blue sky. Totally opposite to the killer blizzard in which we'd arrived. We asked the doorman for a taxi to the train station, and he looked at us funny, then pointed across the street. We'd almost frozen to death the night we arrived, searching for our hotel, when all we'd had to do was cross the street! We hadn't even noticed the austere station entrance when we went to the Hofbrauhaus because it was so typically German.

The three of us sheepishly walked across the street and down the stairs to the train platform.

When we made it to Innsbruck, we had to switch trains for the trip up to Igls. While we were waiting for our last train, the platform speaker announced, "Stand back from the tracks because there is an express train coming through the station." At least that's what we assumed the announcer was saying, since it was in Austrian, when we saw the other people waiting back away from the tracks.

The train came blasting through the station and it was so loud, so big, and so fast. We decided to slowly creep up right next to it, within inches, to see who could get the closest. The incredible, deafening clackity-clack sound and the wind blasting in our faces was absolutely exhilarating. If there had been one thing sticking out of the train we would have been cut in half.

Our train showed up and we got to Innsbruck easily, laughing about being lost in the blizzard.

The scenery in the Alps is always breathtaking and Igls, which was new to all of us, wasn't a disappointment. We found our hotel without a problem this time, a classic Austrian lodge. We were all anxious to begin skiing so we quickly changed and rented our skis. The best thing about skiing in the Alps, besides the spectacular scenery, was that the ski runs were really long. We took two separate cable cars to the top, passing through clouds, which I love, then burst out into a crystal blue sky.

We put on our skis and skied over to the top of a short but steep hill to start our first run down the mountain. As we stood there, we watched a big jet fly by below us in the valley, we were up that high. I said that we should all take it easy until we warmed up, as it had been a while since any of us had skied. The most athletic of us went first for the milk run, getting to the bottom of the hill easily. Then it was either my turn or our cocky friend in the group, so he decided he would go next. Just before he went I said, "Take it easy. Get your ski legs, don't show off." My friend who had skied down already watched from the bottom and I watched from the top as he dangerously schussed the hill, meaning he went straight down. At the bottom he disappeared in a huge cloud of exploding snow.

I skied down to find him lying on the ground in pain. He'd broken his leg on the first run of the day, on the first day of a week of skiing. We were at the very top of the mountain above the clouds and didn't know how to reach the snow patrol, when to our great good fortune, a Snowcat came by. We got them to stop but could see they didn't speak any English as we tried to explain our friend had broken his leg and asked if they could take him down the mountain.

They seemed to understand and agreed to help get our friend down. He said it was okay for us to leave him and that he would get it taken care of and see us back at the lodge. So we took off and left him with the Snowcat guys. We skied through the clouds several times throughout the day, making countless runs. We had lunch and wheat beers at the restaurant halfway up the mountain and enjoyed a great day of fun and skiing.

POINT OF CONTACT (POC)

When we got back to the lodge, exhausted, we found our friend in front of the TV next to the fireplace with a cast on his leg. It was kind of funny. He told us that as soon as we'd left, the guys in the Snowcat just drove off leaving him there in the snow. He said he'd had to crawl all the way down the mountain until he got to a road and forced some guy in a Mercedes to drive him to the hospital. We'd never gone back on that run again that day since there were so many to choose from, so we hadn't come across him struggling to get to the hospital. Then pointing his new cane at the TV he said, "Look, the Persian Gulf War has started."

50

The Midas Touch

As the guest of a high ranking HRH prince, I was touring all over Saudi Arabia with an assigned military escort. I toured Riyadh, the capital, then flew to Daharan, where I saw the well-guarded oil fields. I also saw, unauthorized, the abandoned Khobar towers which had been blown up by Osama bin Laden and where nineteen U.S. servicemen died and 372 were injured. I couldn't get closer than the security fence, but I could see the devastation. We then flew to Jeddah, which is the beach and vacation area for the Kingdom.

Jeddah was a large, clean city with several rotaries and many royal palaces built along the Red Sea. The king had an oceanfront vacation palace there too, right in the heart of Jeddah, and I'd heard it was so large that it had its own traffic signals on the grounds. On the way to the hotel, I was amazed by the size of one palace, completely visible in the downtown area. The main palace seemed to be the size of the U.S. Capitol, yet there were two more guest, or children's, palaces as well, built in its front yard, each the size of the National Gallery of Art.

The architecture was beautiful, more European than Middle Eastern, and not only was the enormous scale amazing, but the entire place was covered by a stadium-sized roof with movable panels to block the sun. It was a bizarre sight when you put it all together. My military escort said that it was nothing compared to the palaces along the Jeddah coastline. Now I had to see them as well.

We checked into the Meridian Hotel, exhausted from a long day of traveling and touring. I was just about to lie down when the hotel manager called to invite me down for a fruit drink and a tour of the hotel. I politely declined, but he then claimed that he had arranged a tour of Jeddah for me that was leaving in fifteen minutes. Again, I explained that I was exhausted and that I was doing that the next day and politely declined. Every time I declined, he came back with something else for me to do in the next ten or fifteen minutes, and I kept declining, trying to politely get him off the phone. I just wanted to close my eyes. I think he finally could tell I was getting exasperated because he burst out laughing. It was the prince, using a phony Indian accent, checking up on me to make sure I was having a good time.

The next day, the military escort drove me around, pointing out the sights. At one point we walked through a *souk*, which is a large marketplace. There were all kinds of people there, and my attention was especially drawn to the women, who were completely covered in their black *abayas*. As we walked through the marketplace, I did get a lot of suspicious glances as I admired swords, genie lamps, perfume bottles, rugs, and all kinds of silver Saudi objects. My escort explained that it was not that busy in the daytime because of the heat, but that the whole city came alive at night.

I then asked to see all of the palaces. He'd rented a sporty Cadillac and we headed along the coast. We made a quick stop to get something to eat at a nice Tiki-like restaurant built out into the crystal clear water of the Red Sea. I looked down into the water to see it teaming with beautiful bright yellow sea snakes, which are more poisonous

than cobras. It was hot and sunny but comfortable under ceiling fans and with an ocean breeze. Fortunately, my companion could speak perfect English and was explaining everything to me about Saudi culture and customs.

After lunch, we drove along the road, admiring all the royal palaces, but I couldn't really see anything but beautiful entrances and guard houses engulfed by date and palm trees and tropical flowers. The palaces themselves were all hidden behind high walls and elaborate ornate gates.

We drove for miles and miles past what seemed like a limitless row of palaces without even a glimpse of anything but entrances. Then I had a great idea. I'd seen a Sea-Doo rental place near the restaurant, located in a large inlet from the Red Sea. I asked my escort if he wanted to rent some, and he said he didn't know how to swim which, of course, made sense since he'd grown up in a desert. He also seemed nervous about letting me do what I planned to do and told me not to get too close as it was very easy to get into trouble. Of course, he wasn't concerned about my drowning, but about my possible arrest.

I rented a Sea-Doo and took off. The great thing about a Sea-Doo is that it's big and fast like a water motorcycle. I took a few minutes to get used to it because I'd be alone on the Red Sea, which had lots of dangerous things in it. My plan worked! The palaces were completely exposed from the  sea for the water views. They were absolutely spectacular, one right after the other, each one different from the one before and none like anything I'd ever imagined. I thought they would be huge, gaudy, wedding-cake castles but they were beautiful. They looked like Four Seasons resorts designed by Disney and Citizen Kane, but on an even more massive scale, surrounded by incredible tropical gardens and trees as far as I could see up the coast. Edens of oil wealth. I went up and down the coast admiring them, stopping at times to take in what was visually incredible. I did this for more than an hour until I finally became bored. I never saw one person the whole time, not even a groundskeeper.

The Sea-Doo could go really fast, up to 70 mph, so I decided I'd shoot out into the Red Sea. As soon as I got out of the inlet, the sea became quite rough. I realized I'd gone out too far when I almost capsized. I carefully rode the waves back in, zigzagging back into the safety of calm water where I could open up the Sea-Doo again. I flew up and down the inlet thinking about calling it quits for the day when I spotted a bunch of fish jumping out of the water. I thought, I'd zoom over to them since there was nothing left to look at.

I throttled up and went straight toward the jumping fish. About fifty feet from them, an enormous Hammerhead shark, also chasing the fish, and more than twice the size of my Sea-Doo, breached right in front of me! I immediately cut the throttle and glided right across its wake. Yikes! I'd almost collided with this sea monster and could have ended up in the water with a hungry, pissed-off shark! Of course, I realized, a bit after the fact, the fish were jumping for a reason.

POINT OF CONTACT (POC)

Time to head back to the dock. My escort was as relieved to see me as I was to see him. We left Jeddah for Riyadh and my flight back to the U.S. Before I left the hotel, I was presented with everything I'd picked up, or looked at, in all the *souks* throughout Saudi Arabia. The prince, who was extremely gracious and generous, had instructed the different military escorts to buy anything I seemed to like or looked at. It was great surprise.

51

On a Wing and a Voodoo Prayer

There were four of us on a trip: my friend Charlie, his girlfriend, his sister, and myself. We'd just spent the night in a tent next to our airplane at a small airport in South Florida. We had an older Cessna 172 that was pretty much a Volkswagen with wings. The 172s had high wings, which meant that they were above the cabin and you could see straight down. Also, the plane was only a single engine, so if the engine stopped, we'd have to land whether we wanted to or not. The joke was to never fly higher than you're willing to fall. I rode copilot.

We were on our way to Haiti to see if we could find a real voodoo ceremony and to check out the island in general. We took off after breakfast and corkscrewed up into the sky to get up to our 12,000-foot flying altitude. We had the coordinates of a city called Cap Haitian along the coast, but we had to be careful not to accidentally fly into Cuban airspace because they would have shot us down without hesitation.

We headed out over the Caribbean with life jackets but no raft if we had to ditch. At 120 mph, it got a little boring puttering along seeing nothing but water. If we'd had more planes with us, we would have had mock dog fights, buzzing each other, clicking the radio like a machine gun for fun, although this required a strong stomach, but we were solo on this expedition. Instead, Charlie decided to cut the engine, and all the noise stopped as our propeller came to a standstill. The nose of the plane immediately pitched down at a steep angle and began to rapidly descend. There was absolute silence, only the sound of the wind whistling, slowly getting louder, then alarmingly louder. Charlie restarted the engine easily, and the power of the engine pulled us back up into the sky.

After a while dark, clouds started to appear, then more clouds, until we were starting to lose sight of the ocean. We hoped there weren't any other small planes or drug runners lost in the same clouds. I had a sinking feeling that our plans had seriously changed. Our plane did not have radar or GPS, only a compass for navigation. Within an hour, we found ourselves deep inside a tropical storm, completely alone.

We were bumping up and down, bobbing and weaving, our plane engulfed in the clouds right up to the windows. This got to be very claustrophobic since you could only see up to the propeller, windshield, and inside the plane. Charlie, the pilot, was my age and looked pretty concerned as he wrestled with the plane. He had me focus on the compass to point us in the right direction using my hand every time we went off course. We were both worried about missing Haiti completely and ditching in the ocean or being shot down by Cubans. He said we had to go lower and get out of the clouds to see something, anything, so we started doing 500-foot drops at a time, still with zero visibility. When I asked him how low we'd go, he said, "I guess we'll know when we hit the ocean."

We couldn't see anything, just a white, 1-foot wall around us, and still barely even the propeller at the front of the plane. We dropped another 500 feet, then another 500, until suddenly at about 1,000 feet, we popped down out of the storm clouds. It was a huge relief to be able to see again and more than a couple of miles in every direction. We had a gray flat ceiling of clouds above us and a raging violent ocean below with massive white cap waves, sandwiching us between two things you don't want to be in between while in a small plane.

Now we needed to see land before we ran out of gas. We weren't seeing Haiti even though we were coming up to the coordinates. I think I knew exactly how Amelia Earhart must have felt. We were silent, scanning the rainy horizon for any sign of land, our little engine droning away. Finally, after about fifteen minutes, Charlie yelled, "Land!!"

It was just a big, fuzzy, dark mass rising up from the ocean miles in front of us. We heard some faint, unintelligible, scratchy voices on our radio that meant that we were getting close to civilization, but were still too far away to respond. So we figured we'd wait to contact the tower once we saw the airport or had to do a mayday call. We weren't exactly sure as we approached the Haitian coastline whether our Cap Haitian landing strip was to the right or left of us. Charlie said he had a map of the island and reached into his top pocket and handed me a used shiny red matchbook from a bar. There was an outline of Haiti with Cap Haitian and Port au Prince marked with a star. Charlie said, "See if you can match it up when we get closer. Unless it's the Cuban coastline."

I wasn't sure whether he was serious or not, since he'd never pulled out any other map. If this didn't work we could at least follow the coastline until we ran out of gas. The compass said to go left and we banked left. It was better than nothing since now our fuel was starting to get low. The storm had been so unexpected. We tried the tower for a little while but got no response; not a good sign. At least the storm started clearing as we flew along the coast. The island was enormous and the scenery was amazing —lush green jungles on craggy mountainsides that shot straight out of the ocean. The sun was going in and out of the fleeting tropical storm making the steamy lush flora shine, and there were huge 20 acre-sized patches of land where parts of the jungle had washed out into the ocean in massive landslides from the storm. I couldn't believe it, but within a few minutes I could actually coordinate the outline in the matchbook with what I was seeing out the window. We were going in the right direction and only a few bays away. We tried radioing the tower again, and again received no response. The first signs of civilization were little rusty metal roof shanties dotting the mountainsides. Then there were hundreds of rusty metal roofs jammed together on a ridge, and we knew we'd found it.

We flew pretty low over the ridge and shanty roofs, and it appeared to be a good-sized city inside a bowl-shaped valley. The runway was right in front of us, running perpendicular to the beach. We started radioing the tower several times and still got no answer. We circled the airport—still no answer—and so we buzzed it. Someone came out of the small control tower and waved to us to come in for a landing without any clearance. It was just a landing strip with a small tower, a couple of hangers, and no activity. We landed and taxied up to where the Haitian man wanted us to park. We were happy to see him, but he looked mad. He started yelling in Creole, then English. We tried to tell him we thought no one was in the control tower and the airport seemed abandoned.

POINT OF CONTACT (POC)

It turned out our microphone had broken somehow. We could hear if someone called us, but no one could hear us, so it would have been pointless if we'd tried to call out. Like a mayday call that we were ditching in the ocean!

We were so lucky. We'd just flown over the Caribbean in a big storm. We finally found our authentic voodoo ceremony in the back of a nearby village one night. We were the only whites and stood behind the small crowd gathered facing a large campfire. There was an altar, singing, chanting, drums, chicken heads, blood, fire, and a zombie woman. Let the voodoo spookiness begin.

52

Soybeans

I had a fun summer job after high school: pumping gas at Mitch and Bill's Exxon in Potomac Village, a shopping center in the heart of Potomac, Maryland. Potomac is the Beverly Hills of Washington, D.C. and it's where I graduated from Winston Churchill High School. I met so many new friends and interesting people who came in for gas, especially girls to whom virtually everyone gave free gas. Customers told me about parties and rich people gave me advice for my future. I don't think the books ever balanced at Mitch and Bill's, but it was rare that anyone got fired. Friends from high school, even strangers, came in with joints burning and gave me a couple of puffs to float me through the rest of the day.

I'd been saving money to buy a car when a friend came in and said he'd seen a cool motorcycle for sale close by. We went over to the house, and it turned out to be owned by the brother of the prettiest girl in my class, so I had to buy it. It was a burgundy Kawasaki 400 triple, with three chrome exhaust pipes. It was big and beautiful. I paid him $700 and carefully drove it back to the gas station. I'd had mini bikes growing up but never a real street bike. It took me about a week to get used to it because it was very powerful and super-fast, cruising perfectly between 80-100 mph. At that speed you had to pretend you were invisible because no one saw you coming. Also, you constantly had to play dodge with other vehicles because at those speeds they were essentially parked cars.

I couldn't wait to drive my Kow to the beach. Ocean City, Maryland is exactly three hours from Potomac across the Chesapeake Bay Bridge. My sister was living there and kept a nonstop party going featuring girls, pizza, beer, and bongs.

POINT OF CONTACT (POC)

So I had the Kow for about month before I got a chance to head to the beach. I wore jeans, a t-shirt, and black helmet with a clear pull-down visor. Wearing a helmet muffles a lot of sound and disguises the fact that your body is completely unprotected, giving a false sense of safety. It was a hot, sunny, day at the end of July, and I was off on my first beach ride. I was excited and completely on my own. I shot past Annapolis and got onto the Chesapeake Bay Bridge, which was the first bridge I'd ever crossed on a motorcycle. My front tire wiggled when I went over metal grills and that was disconcerting because I was on two wheels and up so high. I took it slowly and cautiously enough while still taking in the spectacular view of the bay.

Crossing the bridge is always symbolic of summer freedom and fun, and the beach party time to be enjoyed in just a couple of hours. Sometimes, when traffic backs up at several different bottlenecks along the way, all the single or multiple bikers slowly band into big motorcycle packs and travel on the shoulder or any other opening in the traffic jams. I was in a really good pack of about thirty bikes for about an hour averaging 80 mph. When I couldn't wait any longer to visit Mother Nature, I was bummed that I had to drop out of the pack.

Farmers say the corn is good when it's knee high by the Fourth of July and it was almost August, so it was good and tall to go into for a quick bathroom break. I pulled off onto the shoulder of the road and dropped my helmet. I made my way through the stalks of corn hearing the cars whizzing by on Route 50. It felt good to be off of the Kow and under a hot sun inside a cornfield. I decided that it would be a good time to take a few puffs off the doobie I had in my sock. I came out of the cornfield relaxed and stoned, put on my helmet, got on the bike, hit the kick start, and I was back on Route 50 doing 80 mph.

Traffic was really thin, which was a nice surprise. Most of the cops were in the small beach towns along the way rather than out there on the open road. I cranked it up to close to 100 mph where the bike seemed to be in its comfort zone—no wiggle, no vibration, and I cruised like that for a while. Finally, nothing was in front of me except a long open straightaway so I decided to take it up to 120 mph and see what that would feel like. An airplane can take off at 80 mph. I hit the throttle and the 350 pound bike didn't hesitate. My speed rapidly climbed until something I didn't factor in happened. A true hallmark of another nasty motorcycle crash death.

Flying down the road at 100 mph I hadn't realized that I had a forest on both sides of me the whole time. Just as I began to accelerate over 100 mph, I popped out of the forest to a massive, miles-wide and open soybean field on both sides with a really strong cross wind blowing across Route 50. It hit me hard, and I almost immediately went down on my right side. I was in the right lane, and it pushed me all the way to the edge of the median in the left lane. My heart in my throat, I overcompensated and almost pulled the bike down onto its left side. Everything went into slow motion, and I continued to go too far over on the left, then right, as I decelerated from over a hundred miles on hour. I held on tight, my life at stake, trying to calm my out of control bucking bronco. I was sure I was about to lay it down and just wanted to get my speed down as much as I could before that happened.

Finally, though I was an amateur and stoned, I must have done everything right. The bike slowed enough for me to regain my balance without touching the brakes, which would have been a disastrous and normal reaction. I started carefully down shifting to slow the bike even more, then pulled to the side of the road to stop and gratefully put my feet on the ground.

I felt like my heart had burst through my t-shirt, and I was proud my pants were still dry. I took off my helmet, turned off the bike, and climbed off. The hot breeze that had almost killed me now embraced me and was the only sound I could hear as I looked out at the huge soy bean field. I'm not sure how close I got to the pavement, but I think my knees and elbows almost touched.

Hanging out at sunset by the ocean with my sister and her friends a few hours later, drinking an ice cold beer never felt better.

53

The Price of Admission

I'd been to so many nightclubs in NYC to entertain clients after dinners at five-star restaurants that I had a routine. I'd give the doorman a fifty to be allowed to look around. If I liked it, I'd ask for the manager. Then, I'd give the manager maybe one, two, or three hundred dollars to get the best seat and service in the place. Half the time, I'd give the fifty just in order to go in and check out the club and crowd. Really good clubs often catered to different crowds on different nights, so I had to check each time.

One night, we pulled up to a club with a long line outside. I was riding shotgun in the front seat of the limousine with a security agent, while the VIPs were in the back. It was a little tight. I got out and right away the people in the line started shouting at me, thinking that I'd presumed I could bypass the line just because we were in a limousine. I knew right away that the shouting indicated this wasn't a crowd we wanted to be around. So I gave the doorman fifty and went in anyway while everyone waited in the limousine.

Sure enough, I walked around and knew the mix of people wasn't right. New Yorkers call them "bridge and tunnel people," meaning they're from outside the city. It was a no-go so I radioed the security guy to go to the next club, and I'd catch up in a minute. When I came out of the club the people in line started laughing at me and shouting, "Ha, ha, they left you! They took off and dumped you here!"

I smiled at them, coolly walked into the middle of the street, and clicked my radio twice. Within seconds, a speeding black sedan with a security guy in it raced up to me, almost screeching to a stop. I smiled again at the crowd as I got in and we took off. That felt sweet. I always kept my chase car out of view but within sight of us in case there was a problem. On my signal, they could swoop in as a surprise.

The clubs started to get repetitious, and I had a good friend in the know about special underground nightclubs in NYC. I always needed to be able to top the clubs we'd been going to if they became boring and my friend wanted to show me two that he'd been to. The first one was in the meat packing district located down a random dark alley with dumpsters in it.

I said, "I can't bring them here."

He said, "Just follow me." Then we walked down the alley.

Kitchen help hanging out in the alley ignored us. We walked up to and through a set of big, beat-up, double metal doors.. The place was dimly lit and looked as if we were going through the hallway storage area of a warehouse. We reached another set of double doors, and when my friend opened them I could only say, "Wow!"

It was a super-chic, hip nightclub completely unmarked and hidden. It was late in the day, but there were plenty of really beautiful model-like women and people in there. The music was ethereal and hip with a décor of beautiful woods and leathers. I asked what the name of the club was, and my friend said, "It changes." Like all the exclusive, in-the-know-clubs in NYC, this one got really good late at night with celebrities and models.

The second one he took me to was a club that moved around, he explained, and was only open three nights a week so you had to be on the inside to know about it at all and where it would be located. It was another after-hours club for models and celebrities. We pulled up to a random building around Tribeca with a guy on a motorcycle sitting by the door who didn't seem to be connected to the building at all, but he was in reality, the gatekeeper/bouncer. My friend tossed him a small box that he caught in midair then shoved straight into his jacket. He pulled open the metal door without ever getting off of his motorcycle.

This place was different from the first club and unique. It had black lights and aluminum foil covered walls with graffiti, a bar set up, and lots of random chairs and sofas with loud music. Not as nice as the first one but interesting and good enough for a change of scene.

When we left, I asked my friend what had been in the box he'd tossed to the doorman.

He replied nonchalantly, "Bullets."

54

Tunnel Vision

I was still in New York with my boss for King Hussein's address to the UN General Assembly. I'd been to the legendary John D. Rockefeller estate, Kykuit, the day before, where I saved the king from falling down when he tripped getting out of his helicopter.

We'd motorcaded over to the UN from the Waldorf in the morning and I really wanted to go in to listen to the king's speech. So I asked the USSS if I could leave my car unattended for a minute. He said to just leave my keys in the ignition in case they had to move it; otherwise it wasn't moving until the king came out. I had a security pin on and followed the crowds to the General Assembly right in past the security without anyone questioning me. I headed straight to the back so I'd be out of the way. I watched the room come to order, and the king finally came to the podium.

Near me, there was some type of large information or translation booth with two women in UN uniforms. One of the women who was a very attractive blonde and Dutch, I thought, started talking to me in between whatever she had to do. Jokingly, I told her I was a friend of the king and had come to listen to his speech. I told her we'd been at the Rockefeller estate the day before, and she seemed impressed. She was a few years older than me and extremely attractive, I thought again. She told me her name was Mia and she also did something for Salvador Dali when she wasn't working at the UN. I barely listened to the king because I was having fun chit chatting with Mia.

Finally, the king ended his speech to a large round of applause, and it was time for me to go. I gave her my phone number in D.C., and she gave me hers. I made my way back through the crowds to the motorcade and got to my car five minutes before my boss arrived to check up on everyone. He told me to see him when we got back to the hotel; he had something for me to do.

We were there for a while and then motorcaded through New York traffic back to the hotel. We were all lined up on the side of the Waldorf Towers that separates visiting heads of state from the regular Waldorf guests. I wandered into the hotel looking for my boss, knowing he wouldn't be hard to find since he was usually in the bar. I found him holding court with a few of the king's people. He handed me the keys to his Rolls Royce and told me to go back to the UN and pick up a general's wife and bring her back to the Waldorf. She'd recognize the car and would come up to me, he said, if I just parked out front.

I said okay, even though I really didn't know how to get back to the UN and then back again to the hotel. I didn't know NYC, and every time I was driving, I'd been in a motorcade. So I got the concierge to map it out for me, which seemed pretty simple, and headed back to the UN.

I parked in the big driveway of the UN and waited. I must have been there for half an hour when out came my translator friend, Mia. I tooted the horn, and she came over to me and sat in the Rolls. Her mind must have been spinning trying to figure out my deal. She asked me what I was doing, and I joked that I was waiting for her. I then thought, what the heck, I'd tell my boss I never saw the general's wife, and I offered Mia a ride home. She lived fairly close by, only a few blocks away from the UN, in midtown Manhattan, and she was thrilled since she'd never been in a Rolls Royce before. I couldn't believe I was hitting it off with such a beautiful girl, who chatted away in a pretty Dutch accent. Then she asked if I was free that night because she had an invitation and could bring guests to the re-opening of Studio 54. I couldn't believe my luck again. I'd always wanted to go there; it was the most famous nightclub of all time, exclusive to the jet set and movie stars. I didn't even know it had closed, but I was totally

POINT OF CONTACT (POC)

game no matter what the king was up to that night.

She said to come by her place at nine and come up for a drink. I told her I'd pick her up in a limousine since I knew there were extra limousines, and I could get one of the other guys to drive it. I went back to the hotel to tell my boss that I'd never found the general's wife and couldn't find him. I talked to  one of limo guys from D.C., and he told me we had a free night since he thought the king was hosting a dinner at the hotel, which was perfect. He was also game to help me with Mia. I didn't see my boss the rest of the day and gave the Rolls back to the hotel valet. I let all the guys know where it was if my boss was looking for it but no doubt he'd be going to the dinner, too.

I didn't have any good party clothes so I just wore a suit and an open shirt. My friend played it up big letting me ride in the back of the limo, opening and closing the door. I got over to Mia's apartment and was disappointed as there was a Dutch guy there who didn't like me or that I was there. Mia was so happy I'd come but didn't like what I was wearing. She actually had me change into some funky black nightclub shirt she had, which I was fine with. I was still in college and too young to even care or have any fashion sense so I just went with it. She showed me some Salvador Dali sculptures and paintings that she was representing scattered around her nice-sized apartment. Her Dutch boyfriend sneered at me the whole time asking me suspicious, condescending questions. I didn't respond to him most of the time, and Mia told him to stop to my relief. We went down and got into the limo. I saw Mia give her boyfriend a "so there" look.

When we pulled up in front of Studio 54, it was a total pandemonium. "I've heard that they pick and choose who they let in," I said. Mia wasn't worried and showed me the red invitation. The limousine definitely helped because as soon as she stepped out, the doormen knew her; he parted the crowd and we went right in. Wow! We were in. The music pumped right to my bones. There was glitter and people in costumes, or maybe that was the way they dressed. There was stadium seating with a dance floor and a big bar in the middle. I got us some drinks and the best part was that Mia's boyfriend was being such a jerk she told him to get lost, and I never saw him the rest of the night. I partied and danced with Mia for most of the night in that wild circus.

At one point when we were dancing, someone passed us something and they said "Smell this." We both had to sit down because it turned out to be amyl nitrite

163

some club thing that made your head spin for ten minutes. We both hated it. After that I explored parts of the club while Mia talked to her friends. At one point, I went all the way to the top of the stadium where I could look down on the whole place while the best classic disco music played nonstop.

There was hardly anyone near or at the top. I spotted a half-circle bar in the top right corner. There were three people sitting there when I walked up and got another vodka tonic. One person on either side of the half circle bar and one in the middle. They stopped talking as I got up to them to order my drink. On my left was Halston, the designer, on my right was Truman Capote, and across from me was Andy Warhol. They never said a word and didn't acknowledge me so I got my drink, played it cool, like I saw them all the time, and went back to tell Mia but I couldn't find her again in the crowd. I finally caught a cab back to the hotel at about four in the morning.

Fortunately, there wasn't much going on the next day, and my boss never asked me about the general's wife. The weather was nice, and I did get to walk around the city a little. I was looking forward to a good night's sleep when my boss called me fairly late and told me he wanted me to go back to Washington, D.C. that night! I couldn't believe it. I was exhausted from all the fun. I met him in the lobby, and he gave me the keys to a brand new blue Cadillac Sedan de Ville he'd bought for his son and wanted me to get it back before his son flew in from Switzerland. I asked the concierge again how I could get to the Lincoln Tunnel. I packed my bag, including Mia's shirt, and put on my jeans and a t-shirt. It was almost eleven at night.

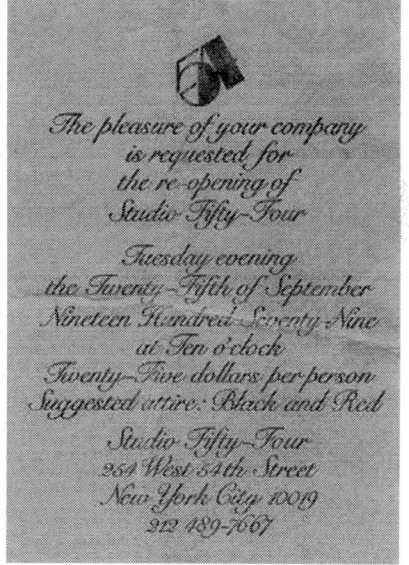

POINT OF CONTACT (POC)

The directions didn't seem too difficult so I drove across Manhattan and got confused by the signs for the entrance to the Lincoln Tunnel, completely missing it. Damn! I had to go around the block so I got in this line of cars that seemed to have missed the turn too. We got around one corner no big deal, then I made the next turn and saw that the line of cars I was in had to go through a huge crowd of people. Uh oh. What was going on? I made sure my doors were locked.

I was stuck with no way out. I had to follow the cars through the crowd. As I got closer I realized it was a sea of hookers, easily one hundred or more—and I was in their NYC pick up spot. It was complete frenzied chaos. They were making three or four cars disappear at a time. Finally I was close enough that they came charging at me and engulfed my car, screaming, fighting with each other, and yelling. They were rocking the car back and forth, pulling their tops down, pushing their breasts against the windows, kissing the windows, banging on the windows so hard I thought they would shatter, anything to get me to stop. It was like a massive cloud of nightmarish scary clowns of every shape and size, black, white, Latina, in mini-skirts, bikinis, sequins, high heels. I even saw some in wheelchairs.

I inched my way through, hoping nothing was happening to the brand new Cadillac until I finally popped out. I was pretty sure I held my breath the whole time. I swung around the block, cranked up some Led Zeppelin, and shot through the Lincoln Tunnel. I put NYC in my rear view mirror and made sure no one was still hanging on to the car.

55

Meant to Be

My friend, Scott, was getting married, and my group of friends decided to have a bachelor party for him in Miami. He wasn't a close friend, but my best friends knew him from school and had grown up with him. He was a clean cut, tall, weight lifter with curly reddish hair. He was a bit socially inept and a big health nut, but he could drink gallons of Heinekens. Just a bit eccentric, it seemed, and he had a secret.

I couldn't believe he was marrying a beautiful blonde girl who'd gone to Holton Arms, the high society, all-girls school in Washington, D.C., but all that really mattered to me was that the bachelor party sounded like a great time.

There were six of us; we stayed at the Fontainebleau Hotel on Miami Beach. This is the hotel where both James Bond's *Goldfinger* and *Scarface* were filmed so we fit right in. We were only down there for three nights so we wanted to get to partying right away. We hung around the first day, drinking and swimming in the huge pool with waterfalls. There were lots of hot girls in bikinis to admire all over the place.

Finally, one of us suggested we get some beers and check out the big hot tub off of the side of the pool. Personally, I don't like getting into hot tubs, or even bathtubs, but we were having a good time. As we approached, six nice looking girls in bikinis were getting into the hot tub with their cocktails so we asked if we could join them. They were completely up for our company and, as we found out, were staying at the Fontainebleau, also as part of a bachelorette party! We quickly hit it off as we paired up with them, believing we were going to get some action from these nice girls from New Jersey.

POINT OF CONTACT (POC)

The coincidences continued. They'd just arrived as well, and also just for three nights. It was meant to be. As we were chatting away I found a woman's watch on the side of the hot tub. It was a nice watch, not a Rolex or Cartier, but nice, so we passed it around and theorized that someone who'd used the tub before us had forgotten it there. We didn't care at all about the watch and jokingly insisted it was the future bride's watch; she played along and winked, agreeing that it was indeed her watch. We laughed and gave it to her.

We hung out for a while longer and wanted to go out with the girls that night but they already had plans. They said that the next night would be great and definitely by the pool the next day, although all of us would no doubt be hung over. We were so pleased with ourselves when we went out for a steak dinner. After dinner, our plan was to go to an upscale strip club that we'd heard about; one half was for women and the other half for men, with a bar in the middle. At the entrance, girls moved to the left and the guys to the right. A very clever concept.

Our side looked like a classy, comfortable, upscale sports bar with beautiful girls taking off their clothes to loud music. We had a bunch of drinks and, after a couple of hours, decided to call it a night. When we walked out of our side, the same girls from the hot tub walked out from their side. We couldn't believe our luck and the coincidence. We were all buzzed, our hormones jumping from what we'd just seen, and we were heading back to the same hotel! It was meant to be. We hooked back up with the girls we'd each hung out with in the hot tub. Things were cooking as we waited for our limos to take us all back to the hotel. We were having a blast; the stars were aligned, when suddenly a drunk Scott accused the bride of having stolen the watch from the hot tub. "Scott! Shut up, who cares!!" we all told him. Within seconds we were all sober, the girls had gathered around the future bride, and the Jersey came out!

"Fuck you assholes! Go fuck yourselves! Eat shit. Go to hell," they screamed at us. One of them even pointed to her crotch and said, "You could have had this tonight!!" There were two or three middle fingers aimed at us out the back window as they left in their limo. We all stared at each other, thinking the same thing, *What just happened!!???*

We were like deer caught in headlights and couldn't have seen that coming. We'd had the perfect storm set-up and it evaporated in seconds. It was like watching a car accident in slow motion. We could have killed Scott.

The next two days we'd see the girls around the pool and would either get icy glares or the middle finger. We returned to Washington and went to Scott's wedding. Six months later, we went to his funeral. He was secretly doing heroin and overdosed on New Year's Eve.

56

Someone to Watch Over Her

I was both thrilled and scared when I discovered that I was going to be a father. My daughter's birth mother did not want or have the energy to raise a child again so I ended up with full custody and completely on my own. I planned on learning my parenting skills in the last two months of the pregnancy. Unfortunately, there were complications, and my daughter showed up two months premature before I could learn anything. She went into the neonatal intensive care unit (NICU) for a couple of weeks, and I was in there during all the visiting hours, and at other times I took hospital courses for new parents. By the time my daughter came home, I was absolutely spent.

After a week home, I found myself, by a fluke, one night on my own with my newborn baby girl. No nannies, no girlfriend and no moms who knew how to take care of an infant. I had her by my bed in a bassinet, and I was both super-nervous at the responsibility and physically exhausted. She made all kinds of cooing noises in her bassinet as my body finally gave in to weeks of exhaustion, and I fell into my first deep, deep, sleep.

I was literally in a coma, and I'd been asleep for a couple of hours when I suddenly leapt up at the sound of someone dropping a big stack of china plates on my bathroom floor all the way on the other side of the room. I jumped out of bed, ran over, and flipped on the light. There was nothing on the floor. It was the oddest feeling because I was sure that the noise I'd heard had been a loud crashing sound.

I walked back to my bed and checked on the baby. She was quiet. That's good, I thought. Then I thought, Wait, she is way too quiet. I flipped on the light and rubbed her and nothing—she made no sound. I yanked the blanket off of her and started calling her name and nothing happened. I picked her up and she was completely limp and unconscious. I put her down and dialed 911!

I needed to stay calm to explain my emergency. I did and they sent the cavalry. I took my little, limp baby downstairs, all the time calling her name. I was in shock thinking that this couldn't be happening not now, not after everything it had taken to get her there. I didn't know if I should try mouth to mouth, or CPR, I didn't even know if she was breathing.

The rescue squad showed up in minutes and went to work on her right away laying her tiny body on the sofa and surrounding her. They were yelling her name, putting an oxygen mask over her face, pumping her tiny chest, as I stood there at two in the morning watching my baby pass away. After what seemed an eternity, she started to move ever so slightly, then barely opened one eye. They picked her up gently, put her in the ambulance, and we flew to the hospital with lights and sirens blaring.

I stayed with her as they put her little, fragile body through a battery of awful tests, including a spinal tap. It was horrible to watch, but a funeral would have been worse. I stayed up the rest of the night, adding to my exhaustion. When I finally went home for a few hours the next morning I realized, ironically, that it was Father's Day.

The doctors concluded that she'd had a near fatal event, on the verge of sudden infant death syndrome, and that she'd been within minutes of dying if I hadn't woken up when I did. To this day I can't explain the crashing plates, whether it was my daughter's guardian angel or my mother's spirit that woke me, but as exhausted as I was, it would have taken the sound of crashing, breaking china on a tile floor to wake me.

I still have nightmares about what might have happened if I hadn't awakened until the next morning. My baby stayed in the hospital for another three days before she came home with heart and breathing monitors, which we used for the next year. I'm now going on more than five years without sleep since that night!

Six months later, the whole family was together for my daughter's baptism in the beautiful Lady Chapel in the back of St. Patrick's Cathedral in New York City. It was December 19th and the best time of the year to be in the city. She was plump and adorable in her white christening dress and was calm throughout the ceremony.

While we were in St. Patrick's, a major blizzard hit New York. We had a limousine waiting for us and left St. Patrick's just in time, before the storm really got bad. I had her baptism party upstairs at the Russian Tea Room in the spectacular Bear Ballroom. It's a room out of a dream—with beautiful different colored, etched mirrored-walls and ceilings that are 25-feet high. There was a giant 9-foot rotating clear bear with gold fish swimming around inside of it. There was also a 15-foot tree sculpture with beautiful faux Fabergé eggs made of Venetian glass hanging from it. The place was over the top and a long way from that awful scary night.

It was such a surreal feeling to be standing there with my whole family at Christmas time in New York City with a blizzard swirling outside, toasting my beautiful, healthy daughter and the clumsy angel who'd dropped the plates.

57

Weaponized

I'd just finished an under the radar royal visit. The royal and his entourage had left the country, and everything had gone perfectly. A couple of the security guys wanted to take me out to dinner to thank me for working with them. We'd been staying at a hotel in Tyson's Corner, Virginia just outside Washington, D.C. One of them was Chris Caracci, an ex-Navy Seal Team Six member, one was ex-Special Forces, and one I'd just met that night who was a friend of the Seal. My new acquaintance was a big, barrel-chested guy with a shaved head, wearing a turtleneck and a sports coat. He was also some type of high ranking law enforcement officer from Maryland. Just a wild character. I knew from a certain look in all of their eyes that they were military wrecking balls, and well trained by the government too, although of course they didn't talk about it. I hit it off particularly well with Caracci who was really funny and entertaining. He made me an honorary Seal Team Six member and let me wear his SEAL insignia belt buckle (only for the dinner.)

We decided on a very upscale Chinese restaurant close to the hotel. I had one of the royal's limousines take us there and wait for us. We went in and there were hardly any people there so we took a table near the back. The four of us looked so different and out of place sitting together. I was in khakis and a polo shirt, Caracci was tall and athletic with a big Fu Manchu mustache, the Special Forces guy looked like a fire plug wound up tight, and we were all sitting with a loud, burly bald guy in a turtleneck. I wished I had a picture of all of us. Every time the burly guy leaned forward, something I couldn't identify popped out of his jacket. Finally, I had to ask him what he had in there, and he reached in and pulled out a long, thin knife that looked like it had a 1-foot blade. With a grin, he said that he always carried it, plus a few other things.

The waiter came over, and to my surprise Caracci ordered for all of us in fluent Mandarin or Cantonese Chinese. He even made the waiter laugh a couple of times. Even though he was no longer a Seal, he was sworn to secrecy and could never tell anyone where he'd been or what he'd done, for the rest of his life. I'd been wondering why an American would have a Fu Manchu mustache, and when he spoke fluent Chinese, I realized where he'd probably been assigned.

We were drinking beer, laughing, and having some appetizers when suddenly there was a commotion at the entrance of the restaurant. A few U.S. Secret Service agents came in and looked the place over with the manager. We looked at them and they looked at us, and I couldn't believe that they thought four such oddly different people were benign. I knew the guys I was sitting with were heavily armed because that's how they roll. They wear weapons the way regular people wear shoes or watches.

It was a presidential election year, and the race was now down to just a few candidates. The restaurant was practically empty when the Secret Service brought in the presidential candidate and his wife and had them sit, of all places, in a big empty restaurant, two tables away from us. Then the Secret Service agents made a wall of agents at the tables in front of all of us, including the presidential canditate's. We laughed because they'd put our table of heavily-armed, dangerous-looking people, except for me, inside their security bubble for the presidential candidate. I think even the presidential candidate picked up on it, as he nervously looked over at us a couple of times. The Secret Service agents were very young and probably just out of the Academy. They were oblivious to us as they ate their dinner.

My security guys thought it was over the top funny. An older, experienced Secret Service agent would have probably completely changed restaurants once he saw us. We took our time having dinner and before long, their whole entourage left with the presidential canditate giving us a nod good night. I found out later from my well-trained limousine driver that the presidential canditate had come out of the restaurant and asked him who I was and my driver had told him he didn't know, our standard operating procedure.

Caracci, with his ability to speak Chinese had made friends of the waiters and asked them to come over to our table as soon as the presidential canditate and the Secret Service left. To my amazement and theirs, the three guys started making a pile in the middle of the table of the knives they had hidden on themselves. When they were finished with the knives, they pulled out several different types of loaded pistols that they also had hidden on themselves, and put them on top of the knives. There were enough weapons on the table to start a small war. We were wide eyed looking at all of it, while the three security guys proudly leaned back in their chairs as if to say, "Hey, it's just Chinatown."

58

A World Cup Win

I had a European royal with his entourage staying at the Watergate Hotel. We started their visit mesmerized by the OJ Simpson / White Bronco chase, which we watched in one of the big suites. Then, out of left field, I was told they wanted to go to a World Cup soccer match at RFK stadium since their country was in a match while they were in town. This was out of my realm since it was soccer and nothing official, but of course, I figured it out because I had to.

Their embassy dropped off VIP tickets for all of us but that was it. Security was beyond max with the streets closed off and all kinds of warnings about getting in and near the stadium. I spoke to a good friend of mine who was a top detective in the Second District in Georgetown. We made a plan, and he took care of what I needed. Instead of using limousines, I arranged for a minibus that held twenty-one passengers to pick up my group of nine. I had the head of security get them into the minibus and meet me at an intersection near Capitol Hill. When they showed up, I was there waiting with two completely decked out off duty policemen on monster police Harley motorcycles, and the town car I came in. I jumped on the minibus and had the empty town car follow us to add to the charade.

The Harleys took off in front of us with lights and sirens. I don't know how many of the police were in on, it but it seemed like all of them. We zigzagged up streets in a totally fake motorcade, blasting through at least five barricades that were lifted by the police as we approached. It was such a rush watching the cops on their Harleys do their stuff right in front of us yet, neither official nor real. We flew into the motorcade area of the RFK stadium with gates and fences rapidly opening. Then I had everyone quickly pile out of the minibus and into the stadium through the VIP motorcade gate before anyone with a clipboard questioned us.

I hooked up with some friends who were at the game too, and had a bird's eye view of my group and security guys from the upper deck. I made a plan to meet the head of security after the match in a hallway near our exit. When it was all over and their team lost, it was pandemonium getting out of there. The security guy got mixed up and was in the wrong place so I had to find them and turn them around and get them through the crowds to the motorcade gate. When we got there, two stadium security guards were having trouble pushing the gate shut because so many people wanted to get out that way.

We arrived just as the gate was about to shut and someone in the group started yelling, "Open the gate! We have a prince coming through!" I gave him a look that said, "Shut the F up! No one is supposed to know!" The big cyclone fence was actually starting to squash the prince as they pushed it against him and the throngs of people. I grabbed the prince's hand and went airborne, smashing into the gate as it closed, knocking the two security people back, and springing open the gate. I pulled the prince through and held the gate to get the rest of the group through as the stadium security people tried to push me out of the way to shut it again. We got everyone on the bus and I told the bus driver to wait a second.

We didn't have our Harley escort anymore since the arrangement had been just for getting us to the stadium. Our good Irish bus driver told me that stadium security had come up to him several times to ask who he was driving since they were supposed to have three motorcades scheduled and instead there were four. He played dumb since he was in on the ruse. Finally one of the other motorcades began to pull out with lights and sirens. I told the bus driver to follow them out of the area, and it worked perfectly as we sailed right back through all of the blockaded streets.

The prince, who had been indifferent to me before, almost ignoring me, started greeting me and acknowledging my presence after that night. I thought I was out of the woods with the World Cup until we were in New York City about a week later. There was another match involving his country at Giants Stadium, and they wanted to go. The group had shrunk to just the prince and four of his inner circle, plus I had the security agent who had been on the whole trip. Just as I thought, they expected the same police motorcycle escort, which wouldn't work in New York, but I figured that I could at least arrange some type of VIP treatment at the stadium.

I was given the name of a State Department contact running the dignitary part for the World Cup. When I called him, he sounded frazzled and crazed and said he couldn't do anything for me because the prince didn't fall into the criteria he had for VIP treatment at the World Cup and he hung up. I was hitting a wall, and we were going to be pumpkins if I couldn't do something. Once again, I only had the VIP tickets and nothing else. The clock was ticking for us to leave. I went outside to make sure our stretch limousine was standing by, which it was. I then noticed there was a full monty motorcade standing by with an armored limousine, police cars, and lots of security. I went up to Jimmy, the doorman, and asked him who it was for. He told me it was for the Head of the World Cup and they are going to Giants Stadium. Bingo!

I was going to pull a rabbit out of a hat again, I thought. I talked to their lead agent, explained who we were, and that we were also going to the match. Could we get in his motorcade? I talked the talk, and walked the walk, finally convincing him to include us. He radioed someone inside the St. Regis who was with the Head of the World Cup and he agreed we could join his motorcade. I was so happy and so lucky!

I put our limousine into the motorcade only to have the prince and his group drag their tails coming out of the St. Regis with only seconds to spare before blast off. They were so close to missing our nonstop ride to Giants Stadium. I'd been yelling at the security agent to get them downstairs, on the edge of my seat, because I knew if they missed it, they would still expect the same treatment and there was only one rabbit in my hat. They appeared with seconds to spare diving into our limousine.

I rode in the front seat scrunched between the driver and the security agent. Flying around in a motorcade is completely different in New York City than the smooth streets of Washington, D.C. The limousine was bottoming out banging around so much that even glasses in the back broke. It was such a wild ride getting to Giants Stadium.

We arrived once again in the VIP motorcade fenced area in front of a group of New Jersey state troopers. I was so relieved that it was over. I'd be able to relax a little after I arranged our departure since the Head of World Cup was staying for a long time after the match. I waited for the New Jersey Governor, Christine Whitman, to pass me and go into the stadium before I went up to the head of the New Jersey state troopers standing there. I was definitely pushing my luck at this point when I asked him for a state trooper to escort us out of the area after the match so that we wouldn't get stuck in a traffic jam.

He was suspicious right away. He asked who I was and I told him, mentioning the State Department. Then he said, "Let me make a phone call." I thought, Uh oh, never mind! Not a phone call, since it was a big bluff.

POINT OF CONTACT (POC)

About seven really big and tall New Jersey state troopers in crisp imposing uniforms and saucer-shaped hats were closing in around me. At that moment, the head trooper looked up from the phone and said, "He doesn't know you or who you are." The troopers surrounding me actually leaned in on me, as I remained calm. I said, "Let me talk to whoever you are talking to," in an annoyed, commanding voice. Another bluff because I was really thinking, Gulp, yikes!!

I got on the phone and it was the crazed, pissed off State Department guy I'd spoken to from the hotel. He said, "You again! What is it now?" and I explained we'd come in with the Head of the World Cup, which made him back down a bit from being a barking dog. I said, "I only want an okay from you for a trooper to escort us out of the area after the match." He was frazzled and crazed, and said, "Okay, okay, put the head trooper back on." I put him back on the phone and he only said, "Yes, sir," and hung up. I got my trooper escort, and literally all the troopers surrounding me took two steps back. I thanked him and them, then sauntered into the stadium victorious.

59

The Prince and Chauffeur

During my college limousine job, my boss's son was going to spend a couple of months over the summer in Washington. He had gone to one of the most expensive schools in Europe, one that kings have attended. I was pretty sure he was asked to leave and was moving around Europe with his wealthy classmates. Now he was coming here, and I didn't know what to expect. I was thinking he'd be an over privileged, demanding snob. My boss asked each of us to take turns looking after him in order to keep him out of trouble. I was worried that if I didn't hit it off with him, I'd get fired.

He arrived and I finally met him at the bar of the Watergate Hotel with my boss's bodyguard, Carl. I couldn't believe the resemblance to his father in looks and mannerisms. It was as if his father had been cloned; it was so close. He was a very sharp dresser, wearing an Armani suit, silk shirt and tie, and Bally loafers. Just like his father, he also had a solid gold Presidential Rolex. He was really smooth, funny, charming and friendly. I liked him right away.

I was supposed to start looking after him the following week, which included finding things for him to do, so a week later, I picked him up in one of the limousines and we went to lunch at Clyde's in Georgetown. I wanted to get an idea of what he liked and wanted to do. Of course we were both on the same wavelength: girls, girls, and girls.

He was a decent-looking, Middle Eastern guy with lots of cash and lots of flash. The only problem was I only knew preppy girls who wouldn't be interested in him. So we ended up driving around D.C. talking and eventually ended up down on the Smithsonian mall. I took him to see the Air and Space Museum.

POINT OF CONTACT (POC)

The tourists around the museum seemed amazed that we got out of a limousine. That gave me a funny idea to try. I asked him if he was game for it and he totally was.

We got back to the limousine and this time he got in the back. He was always very well dressed so I thought our game should work like a charm. He was a little younger than me. I was only twenty-two at the time. We called it the prince and the chauffeur routine and we figured we'd experiment to see if it worked. All we did was drive around the mall, which is a big rectangle, around and around. When we saw a couple of nice girls, I'd pull over and make sure the girls saw us and the limousine. He stayed in the back and I walked up to the girls and told them I had a visiting prince who had noticed them, and asked if they would like to say hello since he wanted to talk to real American girls. He was so charming and played it to the hilt. They were in the limousine within minutes. Then within fifteen minutes, one of them would usually climb up front to sit with me.

It worked so well that we ended up with too many really, nice, small town girls from all over the country calling us after they left. They were all tourists and were gone in a couple of days after we met them, but they all went home wined and dined, with their wild prince story. After they left, we started over and went through the charade again.

The only place that looked like it belonged to a prince was one of his father's houses that had a big walled in compound with a swimming pool, just across the Potomac River in Virginia. I didn't know how to get there the first time since I'd never been there before so we made a plan. To reach the house, I had to turn in a series of lefts once I crossed the Roosevelt Bridge, so every time he said I was his "main man," I'd make a left. It worked perfectly.

We had so much fun, and I actually met my girlfriend, Charlene, doing this. She worked for a Delaware Congressman, and we'd scooped up her and her friend, while they were jogging around the mall. I spent the rest of the summer and fall with Charlene, who was really sweet and pretty. I was so relieved when my boss's son finally went back to Europe, and I didn't have to play the game anymore. We were young and it had been innocent fun. No one got hurt, but all of the girls we picked up wanted to marry the prince.

60

Banana Bikes

I had the best bachelor pad apartment in my twenties and thirties. I had been saving for a long time to buy it, and when I finally got it, I only had enough money left over to last six months in it. Somehow, I figured things out and kept it for twenty three years. A lot of living went on there—good times, bad times, and several romances. When I moved in, it was a brand new building located on Wisconsin Avenue in Glover Park, also known as upper Georgetown in Washington, D.C.

Whenever I tried to tell people where I lived, I'd give them landmarks. I'd say that it was below Calvert Street, by the Russian Embassy, by the Social Safeway, near the Holiday Inn, or if they still didn't know, I'd finally say, across the street from Good Guys. Anyone and everyone who lives in DC immediately said that they knew exactly where that was. Good Guys was probably the most infamous strip joint in D.C.

The whole five story building was made up of one bedroom apartments, and I was on the top floor in the front, with a balcony. My view was of the vice president's house, the Naval Observatory grounds, and the National Cathedral. The building also had a full roof deck with lounge chairs where you had a great view of the Fourth of July fireworks. Later on, I put my offices in the Georgetown office building, which was on the next block across the street. There was a sprinkling of people who had already moved in before me when I finally took possession of the place in May.

I couldn't believe I finally had my own place. I went in for the first time and everything was brand new, which was such a nice feeling. I then walked out onto the balcony and was glad the place was soundproofed because there was a bit of traffic noise. It was fun looking at the cars on Wisconsin Avenue, the people on the sidewalks, and the baseball game in the park next door. It was a hot summer day, and I was mesmerized by all the action. Then I got to watch one of the big green, white-topped helicopters take off right in front of me, rising up from the trees of the Vice President's compound. I thought, it can't get any cooler than this, and then a biker gang of about twenty really loud chopper motorcycles roared down the street.

They were going to Good Guys and stopped traffic while they backed all their motorcycles to the curb in a row. They were the real deal—grizzly men wearing leather jackets with the gang emblem with long hair, beards, and tattoos. They were right out of Central Casting and watching them was better than TV. They revved their bikes and milled around, taking over the sidewalk. I watched people cross the street so they didn't have to go near them. They were gathering as a group before going in and taking over Good Guys. The last few were parking when I saw something above me out of the corner of my eye flying toward them. Somebody on the roof deck had been watching them too and had flung a half-eaten banana at them.

It sailed past me, landing in the middle of the group and splattering. I was thinking that I couldn't believe someone would do that when suddenly they all looked up right at me! They began yelling all kinds of things at me, including death threats. My first day in my new apartment and that was how it started. I kept pointing up to the roof and denying it was me as a few of them tried to cross the street through the traffic to get to me. I retreated quickly back into my apartment in a panic, waiting for my door to get kicked in and to be tossed off of my balcony. I kept an eye on them from my bedroom window and, fortunately, dancing strippers appealed to them more than my flying lesson. I never found out who had thrown the banana at them from the roof but I didn't go back there for a week.

61

The Race

I had a quick, three-day French military VIP visit in Los Angeles that I had to arrange. When we were done in LA, we would go to New York, briefly, then I would put them on the Concorde back to Europe. I flew out to LA the day before the VIPs were scheduled to arrive to make sure all the meetings were set up, the rooms were ready at the Four Seasons Beverly Hills, and the limousines and drivers were up to par. I was using only one security agent who would meet the group in New York and get them on the Gulfstream IV to Van Nuys California. With a free night before they were coming in, I decided to call my friend, Tina, who worked in the movie business. She was happy to hear from me and asked whether I wanted to go to a party that night in the Valley with her and her friend. I was definitely up for it since I could sleep in the next morning since the jet wouldn't be in until the afternoon.

Tina was originally from Chicago and had worked for all the big studios at different times. I was never sure exactly what she did, but it seemed she had access to everything and use of a studio golf cart. She took me into Steven Spielberg's office once, which was built as an adobe village set. I saw he had the *Schindler's List* typewriter under glass which was amazing.

POINT OF CONTACT (POC)

Tina told me she was having dinner with her friend, and the party we were attending was for his secretary. She said to just wear jeans, nothing fancy, and she gave me the address of the restaurant. I decided I might as well pick her and her friends up in one of the VIP's limousines so I gave the address of the restaurant to the limousine driver, and he knew the place. As we got to the restaurant I could see the silhouette of two people waiting outside and knew one was Tina. We pulled up and they hopped in.

Tina introduced me to her friend Shaun, and gave the driver the address of the party. I thought Shaun looked a little familiar and then realized it was Shaun Cassidy, the singer who had been a teen idol and one of the Hardy Boys. I thought, how funny on my first night in LA. He's now a successful television writer and producer. I found him to be laid back and nice guy.

Tina used to be a comedy writer and kept us laughing and entertained until we got to the party. It was a small group of nice people and a typical birthday party. A relaxing evening before my marathon began. I had a good time hanging out with Tina, Shaun, and the other guests.

The next afternoon, I was suited up waiting at the General Aviation terminal in Van Nuys with three limousines. I gave the operations desk the tail number of the Gulfstream IV, and they told me it was inbound. They had a TV monitor of an area map which showed little cartoon jets and their tail numbers approaching the airport so you could check on how close your plane was to landing. When the jet got close enough I'd have the limousine go out onto the tarmac and wait so the cars could pull right up to the jet when the stairs came down.

I watched my little cartoon jet approach then it abruptly turned around and started flying away, doing giant circles around the area. Three times I thought they were coming in for a landing. I asked the desk controller what was going on. He looked at the pattern the jet was making then looked at me and said, "They're partying and don't want to land." He was serious! He'd seen it a few times, but it was new to me.

When they landed it was clear that he was right; they were pretty lit. The main passenger almost tripped down the stairs. The security guy looked at me and just shook his head, since he had been trapped on the Gulfstream. The next three days were a nightmare. They were an unreasonable, tough, and difficult group to deal with on everything. Finally, after what felt like a month, they were leaving for New York the next day in the early afternoon, and I was supposed to fly back on the Gulfstream with them. I looked at the times and realized I could beat them back to New York and get my first break from them by leaving on an earlier American Airlines flight. I booked a First Class ticket and made their departure the security agent's responsibility. He was equally frustrated with them but had to stay with them while I didn't.

The first glitch was a delay in takeoff. I had to be there with their limousines and hotel keys when their jet landed or I'd be in big trouble for not traveling with them. I already had the hotel rooms set up and the lead limousine driver picking up the keys while the other limousines were scheduled to wait at Teterboro. So I re-routed the last limousine to pick me up at JFK so I could go straight to Teterboro. I figured if somehow I didn't make it they could still fit into two limousines instead of three and they would at least have their room keys. The flight was smooth, and I had a couple of glasses of champagne, lunch, and watched *Legends of the Fall*. I couldn't relax, however, because I'd lost almost an hour before we took off, which took a big bite out of my time cushion.

My suitcase was going on the Gulfstream so when we landed I could hit the ground running. We finally landed at JFK but taxiing to the gate was torturous as I watched the minutes tick by. At last I was off of the flight and through security but couldn't find the limousine driver. I called their office just as he showed up. He'd been in the bathroom when my flight arrived. I told him there was no time to waste and that I needed to rush to Teterboro and that's when he realized that he'd forgotten where he parked. We walked up one or two rows of cars that he felt sure was where he'd parked when I told him to just set off the car alarm on his key chain. He was off by four rows!

He tried to start a conversation with me as I got in the back and I said, "We have to go! Drive as fast as you can, and we will talk all you want later." Traffic was medium heavy, and when we were about halfway there, he reached over with a small bag for me. I said, "What is that?" and he responded, "You wanted the room keys right!?" He said he'd been close to the hotel so he'd gone over and picked them up. I almost keeled over dead. Those keys should have been safely waiting at Teterboro in case I didn't make it. The reaction of the group when they arrived at the hotel and weren't able to go straight to their rooms would be volcanic. I really had to beat the jet now.

POINT OF CONTACT (POC)

I called the fixed based operator (FBO) facility and was told the group was on approach to land. The driver started telling me we weren't going to make it, an attitude I hate, because you're not late until you're late. I was just hoping they were having another party and would circle again to give me a few extra minutes. We kept getting hung up in traffic and I started directing the pessimistic driver to go left, go right, speed up, lookout! We finally made it to the security fence and intercom in overtime, but no one answered when the driver buzzed it. I could see the other two limousines getting ready to pull out, and I wasn't sure whether the party was in them or hadn't landed yet. Finally, the intercom responded, we gave them the tail number of our jet, and the gate opened.

I said, "Go go!" to the driver as we joined the other two limousines. As soon as I stepped out onto the tarmac and before I could say one word, the Gulfstream screamed past us and landed. I left a three hour cushion to get to Teterboro, and I'd made it with fifteen seconds to spare.

The group had been partying again on the jet but not as bad as when they landed in California. I got the same exasperated look from the security agent as I handed him his key and the main VIP's key. Then I gave out their individual room keys to their assigned rooms as each of them descended off the jet. The flight crew had loaded all the luggage in the limousines and as cool as if I'd been waiting for hours, I got in the front seat of the second limousine. We silently motorcaded into New York City as I thought, I won that race.

62

Inauguration Day in the Land of the Free

One of the greatest days of my college limousine job was the Inauguration of Ronald Reagan. I had my boss's dark blue Rolls Royce Silver Shadow, and I drove a wealthy couple, friends of the Reagans, who were from California. They'd come in on a private jet and were staying at the Watergate Hotel. It was such an exciting day not only because of the inauguration but because there were rumors that the hostages in Iran might be released after 444 days of captivity.

It was a typical cold January 20th in Washington, D.C. I took my passengers, who had VIP passes, up to Capitol Hill to watch the swearing in. Reagan was going to be the 40th president and the first to be sworn in on the west side of the Capitol building looking down the mall at the Washington Monument and Lincoln Memorial. There was a great deal of traffic and a lot of people trying to get as close to the Capitol as they could. I drove up New Jersey Avenue and was almost in front of the Hyatt when I spotted my friend Carl's limousine parked illegally on the sidewalk. Traffic was gridlocked and I told my passengers that this would be a good place to start walking. I drove the Rolls up onto the sidewalk too, and parked behind Carl's limousine. I told the people this was as close as I could get, even though it wasn't. I just wanted to hang out with Carl. It was an easy walk for them and would make it easy for them to find me after the ceremony.

My passengers were tan, wealthy, glamorous looking people. The wife wore a full-length, black mink coat and her husband had a tan, camel cashmere coat and a scarf. They were also very nice to me so I knew they were old money and accustomed to having chauffeurs.

POINT OF CONTACT (POC)

As soon as they disappeared, I headed right into the Hyatt to find Carl. The hotel muzak was playing Tony Orlando's "Tie A Yellow Ribbon Round the Old Oak Tree" for the billionth time. I looked around the lobby then headed straight to the bar where, of course, I found him. He was having a Bloody Mary even though it was only ten-thirty in the morning. I sat down next to him, and he was happy to see me and got me a Bloody Mary, too. We had a big TV in front of us so we could watch the Inauguration happening just up the street. Once again we'd found the best seats in the house for an event while all the other chauffeurs were either fighting traffic or stuck sitting in their limousines for hours.

Carl knew the bartender who gave us bar food and kept the Bloody Marys coming throughout the morning. We watched as the Reagans arrived at the White House and were greeted by outgoing President Carter and Mrs. Carter. That's when the first report appeared saying the hostages were going to be released after 444 days of captivity. The Algerians had helped to broker the hostage release and were supplying the jet to get them out of Tehran.

The hostage crisis had been a black cloud over President Carter, Washington, D.C., and the rest of the country. Ted Koppel had reported nightly on the crisis, emphasizing how many days the hostages had been in captivity and detailing the status of negotiations. People actually started marking personal events by saying this or that had happened to them on day 93 or 128, 297, 343.... "The Star-Spangled Banner" played at noon on all the radio stations every day, yellow ribbons were around every tree possible, and you couldn't get away from Tony Orlando's tedious song.

We were a little buzzed when what seemed like an exciting horse race began. We watched the Reagans leave the White House as the hostages were leaving their compound. The Reagans drove to the Capitol. The hostages were driven to the airport. The picture on the TV went to split screen. I wondered if this could finally be happening or was it a cruel Iranian trick and at the last second they wouldn't be freed? The Reagans reached the Capitol. The hostages reached the airport. The bar was silent. Everyone watched mesmerized by the unfolding events. The timing of the two events was so closely choreographed, it was incredible.

The Reagans took their seats. The hostages boarded the Algerian 727. You could hear a pin drop in the bar. The hostages began to taxi to the runway as everyone held their breath. Ronald Reagan was sworn in as the 40th president of the United States. The jet taxied to the end of the runway. George Bush was then sworn in as Vice President. The jet stopped at the end of the runway and didn't move as President Reagan took the podium to give his very moving Inaugural speech, never mentioning the hostage crisis. And still the jet didn't take off. It just sat there. It had to be another cruel trick. They weren't going leave.

Reagan continued his very rousing speech as the sun began to come out after such a gray gloomy morning. As soon as President Reagan finished his speech, the jet suddenly began to move, then started to roll down the runway, faster and faster, gathering momentum, then rocketing into the air. The hostages were wheels up, and the crowd went wild! There was cheering and hollering and back-slapping all over the hotel and outside. Wow! It was finally over after 444 days of keeping the U.S. on the edge of war, either with Iran or Tony Orlando.

The Iranians must have been scared of Reagan, and they'd sure put egg on Jimmy Carter's face, I thought. I'd stopped drinking my Bloody Mary before Carl since he was a big guy, and I couldn't get too buzzed. I had to drive the people back to their hotel for lunch and then a long night of staying with them for the Inaugural Ball. I was glad they were leaving the next morning because I'd still be paid for the whole day and wanted to hang out with my friends.

The ceremony ended, and the Reagans went into the Capitol. The crowd began to break up so it was time to go back to the Rolls and wait for my passengers to return. Carl was driving one of the event organizers who had gone to the Reagan lunch, so he didn't have to leave for a while. Everyone had big smiles on their faces as I left the hotel and went outside.

Normally there's a festive atmosphere around an Inauguration but this was different. I had on my long, dark blue overcoat, and when I went outside, it felt like spring it had warmed up so much. The sun just added to the magical day of there being a new president and freeing of the hostages. People were euphoric, ecstatic, as if their favorite team had just won the Super Bowl. Smiling people carrying their heavy winter coats paraded by as if they were at a big party. Finally, my people popped out of the crowd carrying their coats. They were very happy with the swearing in and at how the day had turned out. They wanted to skip the parade, which was good news for me, so I took them back to the Watergate where they told me some friends were picking them up for lunch. They didn't need me until seven that night to go to a couple of the Inaugural Balls, including one for the top donors to the Republican Party.

After I dropped them off, I put my overcoat in the trunk, took my jacket off, and rolled down the windows since it was so warm. I headed for a friend's house where people were always coming and going. I drove up Independence Avenue with people still streaming away from the Capitol. I couldn't believe I was listening to the news about the hostages being released. Everywhere you looked, people were smiling, relieved that it was a new beginning for America. I kept getting caught at red lights on the way, and I stopped at one by the Air and Space museum. A plain car pulled up next to me with its windows down listening to the same news station I had on. I had my arm out the window as I

POINT OF CONTACT (POC)

glanced over at the person in the front passenger seat in the car next to mine. Both car radios made it sound like they were in stereo. He looked over at me, and we both smiled at each other. I realized that it was Walter Cronkite, who I had just been listening to in the bar reporting all the events of the day. We gave each other a small goodbye wave when the light turned green.

My friends and I hung out and watched most of the Inaugural Parade on TV. It was just total jubilation. The unexpected weather was such a nice surprise, too. Eventually, I had to get back to the Watergate for the long night. My passengers went to a couple of the eight Inaugural Balls and a big donor party. These were really tricky getting in and out of because of all the limousines, police, and Secret Service. Plus the president was coming and going. So it took skill dropping the people off, then finding them again at some random time when they came out.

I had to say they looked dashing, which I told them, and they liked hearing it. That's the other fun part of being in the middle of everything; you get to speak to, as well as see, all the famous politicians, celebrities, and wealthy people up close.

There was a great fireworks show on the Mall that night that punctuated this incredible historic day. We'd gotten back to the hotel at almost two-thirty in the morning, which made for a really long day that had started with Bloody Marys. They wanted me to pick them up at 8 a.m. so they could take off in their jet by 8:30 a.m., and they apologized about the early time. I told them it was fine, just part of the job, and that I'd see them at eight. I realized that by the time I got home, went to bed, woke up, got ready and back there I'd only get a couple of hours of sleep. So I decided to pull an all-nighter and sleep after they left.

I walked around the circular driveway of the Watergate Hotel but it had gotten really cold again so I got back in

the Rolls trying to doze off but couldn't. Finally, I decided to drive around D.C. I cruised M Street and the quiet back streets of Georgetown listening to music, then I thought I'd do the Inaugural route starting at the White House. I drove along Pennsylvania Avenue and stopped in front of the Presidential reviewing stand in front of the White House. I got out of the car and walked up to it admiring the beautiful Presidential Seal above and the angled pastel blue ceiling thrusting upward. There was a huge bulletproof glass boxed area in the middle where the Reagans, their family and friends had sat watching the parade. It was the middle of the night, and no one bothered me or cared that I was there. Then it really started getting cold.

I jumped back in the Rolls and cranked the heat and the music and continued down Pennsylvania Avenue to the Capitol. I owned the city, I was the only one awake and everything was still. It was kind of a serene feeling after all the excitement of the day to be driving around in the middle of the night listening to music, the only car on the road. I saw that the National Christmas tree had been lit to honor the hostages, which was a big surprise since it was a month after Christmas. I drove up the Senate side, and across the Capitol parking lot at the foot of its grand east side steps and stopped for a few minutes listening to music. Then I drove out and down Independence Avenue. I still had a few hours to wait so I went past the Botanical Gardens and around the two circles at the base of the west side of the Capitol. I decided to pull over and park at the bottom of the west side steps since I was tired and bored.

The Peace Monument was inside this circle. I got out to get some cold air and to try to stay awake. It was very cold, which was so weird after the spring weather earlier that day. I casually walked over to the Peace Monument in the circle and looked up at the life-size female figures of Grief, History, and Victory. Below them was baby Mars and baby Neptune with the inscription *They died so their country might live.*

As I was looking up, a snowflake came down, then another, and then it started lightly snowing. I pulled my collar up and walked back to the Rolls. I decided to walk up some of the Capitol steps and maybe get a better view of the Inaugural podium. I started walking up the steps with the snow gently coming down, which was really pretty as I drew closer to the Capitol Building. It was probably around 4:30 a.m., and there was absolutely no one around. It was very quiet as it snowed. I had a good view of the swearing in stand and Presidential Seal surrounded by bulletproof glass. I then figured I might as well walk up to the top so I could see it better. I got to the top and now could see the podium that President Reagan stood at to be sworn in as president and give his speech. I couldn't believe I was so close to it.

POINT OF CONTACT (POC)

I looked at it for a little while and thought, let me get closer. I did this a couple of times without any Capitol police stopping me until I found myself standing at the podium. I had my hands on both sides of it surrounded by the bulletproof glass and the snow coming down. I was standing and holding on to the actual podium President Reagan had. It was surreal to think I was standing at what had been the center of the universe less than twenty-four hours ago with thousands of people surrounding this spot.

I stood there for more than twenty minutes, thinking how cool it was to be standing there. Then I started to think how tired I was and how tired I was of driving limousines. I was tired of life in the fast lane and not just literally. I needed to stop driving and go back and finish college once and for all. I didn't want to be in the front seat anymore and the best way to the backseat of a limousine was to get my degree or maybe even become president of the United States, which made me smile to myself because of where I was standing.

Then out of the darkness to my left I heard, "Hey, you, what are you doing?!" Here we go, I thought, as a Capitol policeman rapidly approached. I didn't feel like dealing with him. He came right up to me and told me I shouldn't be up there. I told him that I was driving some people, and I had to get up too early to go home, then pointed to the Rolls Royce. I was well dressed and driving a Rolls, so he realized I wasn't a threat or problem. I said, "It was a great day, wasn't it?" to try and defuse any trouble I might be in, and he agreed, but said I should get going. I told him goodnight and casually walked down the steps still smiling to myself about what I'd just done.

Looking back I realize how naive the world was then. It was a time in which I could go to the front of the White House or the Capitol in the middle of the night, and nobody bothered me. Today, if I tried that, I'd be swarmed, tackled, and arrested by either the Secret Service or Capitol police instantly.

I went back to the Watergate Hotel, and to my relief, my passengers came out on time, and it was a quick ride to their private jet at Butler Aviation. They were very generous, and the wife actually gave me a kiss on the cheek. I couldn't have asked for nicer people to drive for the Inauguration. I shot back into Washington to drop off the Rolls and go home to sleep for a week. The snow had changed to a misty rain as I passed a dirty box truck parked near the Watergate. In big letters, someone had scrawled in the dirt on its back door: USA 52, IRAN 0.

63

Graduation Party

I went to a public high school for my senior year at Winston Churchill in Potomac Maryland, which supposedly, was the model for *Beverly Hills 90210*. Darren Star, the creator, definitely went there after I graduated in 1976, because when I was there, the kids and the school were completely out of control, unlike in the show. Most of the students were from wealthy families and had no regard for rules or authority. It had to be a nightmare for the teachers and the police. A tough new assistant principle got control of the situation after we graduated and got the school back on track.

After our graduation ceremony, a girl whose parents were out of town had an open party at her house near the school. This was typical of the out of control parties we went to throughout the year—they always ended with tear gas and riot police, we were that bad. Everything started out fine, with the usual kegs of beer, bong hits, and classic rock and roll music as cars began to accumulate up and down the streets. I went with my sister and our neighbor, Randy, who drove, since he always had a car. We quickly hooked up with our friends and began toasting ourselves with beer for actually graduating.

The police hated our class and school for these parties and our antics. Their police cars had a single bubble, easy to unclip, that covered the red police lights on the car roofs. Everyone collected the big clear plastic bubbles as trophies that proved you'd gotten close enough to a police car to snatch one. After graduation, some of us put them all together and let the police know where to find them. I think there were more than fifteen just from me and my friends.

Finally, at the peak of the graduation party, after almost our entire class had shown up, the police arrived. There were people everywhere, all over other people's houses and lawns up and down the street near the main party. The music blasting from the party house could be heard blocks away. The usual events began to unfold as the police, in riot gear, began lining up along the street and all the kids lined up across from them with everyone shouting. It was loud, raucous, great fun and super entertaining, except this time, something was different. Someone in the back of the crowd tossed a bottle at the police and all hell broke loose. The police started firing tear gas at us, and everyone went crazy, running around screaming.

It was literally a riot and normally would have just been funny and wild, except that this time the police had had it with us. We didn't realize it at the time, but only a couple of months before, Robbie Angell, a member of our class who had dropped out, had robbed a bank, lured two policemen into the woods and killed them, each with a single shotgun blast to the head. We were teenagers, completely oblivious to the new emotional charge the police had now. They'd brought paddy wagons and began grabbing kids and arresting them, which they'd never done before. There was gas and smoke and kids running in every direction as the cops grabbed anyone within reach. I lost my friend and sister in the melee, and my eyes were starting to burn when I was suddenly grabbed by a cop from behind. I never saw his face as he grabbed my hair with his right hand and shoved my left arm up my back. Damn, I thought, he had me.

I'd never been caught before, and my parents were going to be really upset, I thought, as he pushed me down the street through the crowd of screaming kids and tear gas toward the waiting paddy wagon. As he was shoving me down the street, I saw my sister being pulled into a police car by another officer. She saw me and started yelling at me to help her. I knew I was in trouble but when my parents found out that my innocent sister, who wasn't supposed to be there, was involved as well, they'd be furious with me for getting her into trouble.

The policeman had an iron grip on my hair, and my left arm was twisted up my back to the point of dislocation. Thinking about facing my parents, I got a huge adrenaline rush and took a fast, hard swing at the cop holding on to me with my free right arm. I'd been lifting weights all year and was pretty strong. I hit him as hard as I could, landing a wild punch right on top of the badge on his chest. I must have knocked the wind out of him because he instantly let go.

I've always felt bad about hitting an officer because even though we had fun playing cat and mouse with the police, I always liked and respected them. It was just an instinctive reaction to a moment of panic. I immediately took off running toward my sister and never looked back to see if the cop I'd hit was chasing me. I was running at full blast as I passed my sister and grabbed her hand, yanking her away from the policeman who was pulling her into his car.

We ran as fast as we could, laughing and zigzagging as we dodged screaming kids running every which way through the police and plumes of tear gas. We reached the end of the street and jumped over a 4-foot hedge and hid, watching the wild action through the bottom of the hedge. What a getaway we'd just pulled off! I was surprised my cop had given up so easily—although it was lucky for me. The really funny part about this was that we were at the end of the street, at least ten houses away from where the party had been held behind a four-foot hedge and yet, passed out drunk on the ground next to us was Randy, our ride home.

64

Shielded from Harm

My mother wanted to take my younger sister and me on a vacation. My father had passed away a couple of years before, and she wanted to recreate the kind of trip we'd taken growing up. The three of us were very close and had the same sense of humor. We were the "Trifecta."

We decided to go to Maui, Hawaii for two weeks where some friends of ours were going to be at the same time. We stayed at a resort by Black Rock on Kaanapali Beach. We met our friends—Cindy, who used to live on Maui, John, and Cindy's daughter—who were staying on a sailboat close by.

Cindy was sweet and pretty. A minor, but funny fact about Cindy, is that she was comedian Lewis Black's prom date in high school. We were having a great time; my mom met some people who were from Bellerose, where she'd grown up in New York. She hung out, had lunch, and played cards with them every day. Whenever I checked in with her, she was laughing because the husband was really funny. We went scuba diving a few times, and one day at a place by Black Rock, the current was so strong, we had to pull ourselves along the bottom to get through it, encountering a huge moray eel as big as I was that came out of an old pipe laying on the bottom.

People kept telling us to check out Haleakala, which means "house of the sun." It was a dormant volcano about an hour and a half from us. So after looking at the possibilities, Cindy, John, my sister, and I signed up for a trip to be driven to the top to watch the sunrise and then we'd put on helmets and get on little stingray bikes—the kind I'd had when I was a kid. These bikes had no gears so the trip back down would be as fast as you could coast downhill without having to pedal. It sounded fun except for the part about having to be picked up by a van at 4:30 a.m.

We were driven up to the rim of the volcano so we could see the sunrise but, unfortunately, a near hurricane strength tropical storm made it impossible. The trip had been a long zigzag up the side of the volcano that took quite a while. The tour company asked us if we wanted to cancel, but they had rain gear and no way was I going to get up that early again on vacation. Almost all of us wanted to ride back down regardless of the weather and the rest just rode in the van.

We suited up in bright yellow rain suits and blue motorcycle helmets. The visibility was getting really bad even though the sun had come up at this point. The crater could hold the island of Manhattan yet standing there at the top, we could only see a couple of hundred feet because of the clouds and rain. We went to the edge of the crater to pose for a picture on the sacred spot where we were told that, supposedly, the Hawaiians used to sacrifice people by tossing them in. Then I picked out bike #13 for fun. There were about ten of us all together and a wild hippie guide who was our leader named Wild Bill.

We took off, and it was such a rush to just fly down the side of a volcano battered by the wind and rain. I tried to pedal a couple of times but it was pointless since the pedals just spun around, we were going so fast. We had to be careful not to fly off the road since our whole ride was basically on the side of a cliff that is all razor sharp lava. The guide was funny and wacky, yelling out both stories and caution at different points as we sailed down. The incredible thing was that he would turn completely around or do tricks to entertain us. We found out a few months later that he was killed when he sailed off the road doing this exact thing. At one point, we flew in and out of a huge eucalyptus forest and the aroma engulfed us as if we'd just ridden through a giant cough drop.

Slowly, one by one, bikers dropped out, giving in to the torrential rain, and getting into the van following us down. Finally, #13 lived up to its reputation and my back tire blew out, which made my heart skip a beat, but I managed to get the bike stopped pretty quickly. Everyone wanted me to give up but there were only a couple of miles to go, and I was determined. I got another bike out of the trailer and finished. What a rush!

POINT OF CONTACT (POC)

On the ride back to the hotel in the torrential wind and rain, I got a great idea, that we should go back on a clear day first to see the crater and the spectacular view from up there. Secondly, to make the trip back down with a ten speed bike in order to quadruple our speed. My friend John was up for it. A couple of days later, we saw that the weather was going to be perfect for the next week. We picked a day and found a place to rent nice, ten speed bikes in Lahaina. In the bike shop were big warnings signs and the contract made it clear that we were forbidden to take the bikes up Haleakala for the purpose we had in mind.

Of course, we rented the bikes with helmets and went straight to the top of Haleakala. It was definitely worth the second look. We were 10,000 feet up and could see the Manhattan-size crater perfectly. It looked like the surface of another planet out of a science fiction novel. The edge of the cliff we had crept up to for our group picture, without being able to see the bottom before, was now a clear 2000-foot drop. That's almost four Washington monuments (555-feet). We could look out to the ocean and were above big, white puffy clouds, clouds that we'd ride through on the way down.

The air was crisp, clean, and cooler than you'd expect, but we were prepared and had brought sweaters.

We checked our bikes carefully so we could avoid blow outs this time, and Cindy agreed to pace us in her rental car to tell us how fast we were going. She also had the Heinekens. The first time down was a rush, and now we were going to triple or quadruple our speed. The fact that it was absolutely dangerous added significantly to the rush factor. We took off with John in the lead, and the gears made all the difference. We blazed down the volcano. Cindy later told us she was scared to drive as fast as we were going downhill so we left her far behind. We descended into clouds and were immediately submerged in dusk, as if on the moors of Scotland, and the wet fog of the cloud, then we burst out into sunlight, drenched. We whizzed through the eucalyptus cough drop forest. I've never gone so fast on a bicycle.

About two thirds of the way down, John started slowing down and pulled off to a scenic overlook. We both got off of our bikes and waited for Cindy. She couldn't believe how fast we were going, and she said she'd last clocked us at 42 mph but was too scared to keep up. John opened a few Heinekens, and we sat on the overlook wall and drank them in the hot sun. We were getting ready to finish the ride when John said he had to pee. We were out in the open, and the only private place to do it was below the wall. There was an area of thick long grass growing over the edge of a nearby deep crevasse of razor sharp lava. John wanted to pee in the crevasse. I didn't really have to go, but that sounded pretty cool. I told him to wait up and I would go too.

Robert H. Remmert

We slowly walked up to the crevasse. When we were about two feet away from the edge, I yelled out and stopped John. I was frozen. I had just put my foot down and stepped on nothing at all. Half of my foot was on the edge of the crevasse and the other half was over the edge. The long grass had grown two feet over and past the real edge. One more step and it would have been like falling through a trap door to a horrific end.

Hawaiian folklore says the Grandmother of Maui lives in the volcano and she certainly was looking out for us that day. When I got back to Washington, D.C. and looked at my pictures there was one weird one. It was the group shot where we'd posed at the edge of the crater during the dawn storm.

There is a perfectly shaped, ghostly shield, hanging directly over my head.

65

Saudi Arabian Customs

I was in Saudi Arabia, staying at an American compound about a year before 9/11. I received an invitation to have dinner at a very high ranking prince's palace and was told that a car would pick me up. I was picked up by one of the prince's deputies who was funny and friendly and had gone to college in the U.S. He spoke perfect English and said he couldn't wait to get back to America and American girls.

Some areas we drove through were open, barren, rocky desert and others more urban. It was hard to see much since a lot of places were dimly lit or not lit at all. We reached the prince's palace in Riyadh and right away, I realized the whole place was surrounded by a tall marble wall. I was very impressed since he had a massive wall around his palace made of it, and marble costs a fortune. We were let into what seemed like a beautiful European courtyard through its large guarded gates. There were tropical plants, cobblestones, and statues, and some staff wandered around. I was led up some steps and through the palace doors to a very large foyer with polished floors and high ceilings.

The prince came out of a large reception room and greeted me as he escorted me back into the room. I had met him several times in the United States so it was really interesting to meet him in his home. I had to take my shoes off before I entered the reception room and found funny the variety of footwear by the door, everything from old worn sandals to military boots, to very expensive Italian or British type shoes.

The prince was wearing a long *dishdasha*, which is the long white pajama-like garment the Saudis wear under their flowing black or white robes. There were several people scattered around the large square room with low, banquette seating and cushions lining the walls. The prince sat in the middle of the main banquette and had me sit next to him. He had a big, flat screen TV on the wall, and he was constantly channel surfing with his remote. The other people ranged from a couple more princes, military types, Bedouin camel herders in their native garb, and me. There was a Middle Eastern version of a butler who kept serving everyone, including myself, either tea or fruit juice. It was fun to watch him because he served everyone flawlessly but never turned his back on the prince, so he had to walk backwards quickly half the time. All you had to do was shake your shooter sized tea cup ever so slightly and he came right over.

The prince took turns conversing with each of us about whatever he thought we were interested in. He spoke mostly in Arabic to the other people, and when he spoke to me, I could see some curious looks in the way the older Bedouins looked at me. I was looking forward to dinner since I'd not had lunch, and I realized I was getting kind of buzzed on the tea and sweet drinks—a kind of caffeine sugar high, which was a pleasant feeling.

There were a couple of random photographs on the wall but no artwork and I realized there weren't any windows anywhere either, no doubt because of the heat in the summer. The palace was a bunker and reminded me of the National Gallery of Art building in D.C. I'd been sitting there for almost an hour and a half when dinner was finally announced. I followed the prince and knew that if I copied whatever he did, I'd be fine.

There were about twelve people all together as we walked to the large dining room with big crystal chandeliers. Just before we got there, we stopped outside the dining room, and everyone went into a large room with twenty solid gold sinks and fixtures, no other plumbing. It wasn't a bathroom; it was strictly for washing your hands. I knew that at times Arabs eat with their hands and to never use my left hand but I wasn't sure if we would tonight, not that it would have made a difference to me.

When I walked into the large dining room, there weren't any windows again and a very long table with a couple of big candelabras and huge crystal chandeliers. There were large platters of chicken, fish, lamb, and rice, as well as other dishes I didn't recognize, and knives and forks. I waited for the prince to sit down at the head of the table and then he motioned for me to sit at his right—the seat of honor. Across from me were the two other princes who were either his brothers or cousins.

Everyone else sat at the far end of the table leaving the four of us alone to chat. There was a server who brought the platters around. We did speak a little bit about Washington issues, but the occasion seemed to be more about eating,

POINT OF CONTACT (POC)

which I realized when the dinner ended abruptly about twenty minutes after we sat down. Everyone got up and performed the same hand washing ritual again on their way out. That's when I realized that the whole socializing part of the evening had taken place when we sat in the reception room. It seemed like dinner was about eating, not socializing, unlike in the U.S.

The prince and the other two princes wished me well and goodnight in the foyer. I then was escorted out by the prince's deputy who had brought me.

The evening had turned out to be more relaxed and informal than I'd expected, much to my relief, since I was really a fish out of water. The princes were all very nice and spoke perfect English, and I thought were as interested in my life as I was in theirs. When we walked out the front door of the palace, there were three identical Mercedes 600s side by side, aimed at the front gate, ready to go. The drivers' doors were open, engines running, and attendants held the doors open and ready for the princes' departures. Even though it was late, they were going out. I was told that when it really gets hot, around 130 degrees, they reverse day and night, sleeping in the daytime and staying out all night. The car for me also waited, running with its doors open. We drove out of the palace listening to hypnotic Arabic music into the dark Saudi Arabian night.

66

Celebrating My Birthday with Lincoln

On my 28th birthday, a few of my closest friends, and my younger sister, met me at Austin Grill, a Tex Mex restaurant in Glover Park in Washington, D.C. We had a lot of margaritas and laughs at dinner before leaving to go bar hopping in Georgetown. I had lined up a black limousine to drive us around after dinner.

We started at the Third Edition and stayed there for a while. My friend, who was making too much money for his age, kept ordering bottles of Dom Perignon. He was a one-person circus, entertaining to watch. He drank champagne out of his girlfriend's shoe just to freak us all out; it was so funny. We went to a few other bars and somehow, at 2:30 a.m., all of us ended up sitting on the steps of the Lincoln Memorial drinking Dom Perignon. We decided we were probably sitting about where Martin Luther King made his "I have a dream" speech, so we made a toast to him. We sat there and kept an eye out for Park Rangers or police, but it was a quiet October night in D.C. Luckily, we never encountered either.

So many historical moments and protests had taken place right where we were hanging out, as well as the filming of countless movies. We were the only ones around, looking down the reflecting pool at the Washington Monument with Lincoln sitting behind us. We stood up and wandered into the Lincoln Memorial. We scattered around while some of the buzzed girls read the inscription of the Gettysburg Address out loud. Someone else started reading Lincoln's inaugural address from another wall as I admired Lincoln's statue.

I took in the small velvet rope surrounding the statue and the 10-foot base Lincoln was sitting on. I got everyone together and ran my idea by them. Let's

POINT OF CONTACT (POC)

all sit on Lincoln's lap and have someone take our picture. We walked up to the base of the statue to see if we could climb it. It was easily ten feet just to reach Lincoln's feet but we decided we could do it. We spread out to check in and around the entrance for police. We all then ran and jumped over the velvet rope, pushed one of the group up onto the statue and he helped pull the next one of us up and the next. We did it until all the guys were up there and the girls took a few pictures.

I have to say it was an incredible feeling to be up there with Lincoln himself. We were having a good time and meant no harm or disrespect. I think Lincoln would have gotten a laugh out of it. We carefully scrambled off of the statue and took our time walking down the steps, taking in the night as we watched the Park Police question our limousine driver. Four score and too many birthdays ago....

67

All-Day Duty

I was in the middle of a dignitary trip and staying at the Four Seasons in Beverly Hills when I realized I had the whole afternoon off. The main VIP and entourage would be at a secure facility until that evening. So I called a friend who worked for a top movie producer, and she invited me over to MGM Studios for a tour and lunch. I called one of the security agents, who was also an active undercover policeman, to see if he wanted to go too.

I'd rented a brand new convertible Mercedes 500 to blend in while in California. It was still early so we headed over to the Beverly Hills Hotel and hung out for a while drinking coffee in the Polo Lounge. We were dressed California casual in t-shirts, jeans, and sports coats. It felt good to be out of a suit and especially out of a tie.

The studios were close by. We met up with my friend, Tina, who had us park right in front of the MGM building—a large, black glass, curved building with a circular driveway and the MGM logo on top. She took us around to the big studio buildings where filming was in progress. It was just as you might imagine: camera equipment being moved around, actors in costumes, golf carts shooting by us, and occasionally, a big movie star who waved hello to

POINT OF CONTACT (POC)

us. I asked why any major actor would wave to people who were clearly tourists, and Tina said, "Because I'm giving you a tour. You look like rich guys from Indiana or Kansas who want to get into the movie biz. They think that by waving or saying hello, you might be inclined to cast them in your movie. Of course, if you did get involved in a movie deal you might get fleeced." She laughed.

We peeked into an enormous building where a spooky interior of a castle was being built for a Dracula film. Then Tina said, "Hey, you'll like this," and took us to the legendary commissary for lunch. We sat down in a large, open room which filled up quickly since it was break time from filming. As I looked around, I realized we were the only non-celebrities in the entire place. Some of the biggest movie stars and directors were either holding court with their crew or making moves on young starlets. People just looked at us, wondering if we were up-and-coming stars, directors, or pigeons ready for plucking.

We had a fun lunch and lots of laughs while star gazing. It was so interesting that no one bothered anyone; if these same actors had been outside at a restaurant, they'd be swarmed by paparazzi. It actually seemed like a high school lunch room where the cool kids, jocks, and nerds each had their spots.

All of the big stars were relaxed without worry of harassment. Tina walked us out, saying hello to a few people. She said we should head to Malibu and the beach at that point, since it was a classic California day. We shot out toward the beach, driving with the top down along the coast, until we found a beach bar. The security agent couldn't get over how cool it was going to the studios and getting a glimpse behind the scenes. "This must be how a movie star's day feels," I said. We walked to the back deck looking out over the beach and ocean.

Since it was late in the afternoon, no one was in the bar so we leaned against the back railing and had a couple of Coronas. The sky was blue, seagulls flew overhead, and the breeze was fresh off the ocean. The security agent kept saying that it was the best day of his life and that he couldn't wait to tell everyone back home all about it. He must have said the same thing two or three times when all of a sudden we heard the sound of seagulls fighting up on the roof behind us and then a weird rolling sound. I looked at the agent and a beer bottle flew past our heads missing us by inches. Holy shit! Someone must have been drinking up there and had left a bottle that almost sent one of us to the hospital. We looked at each other, thinking, Whoa did that just happen? That was almost the yang to a yin kind of a day.

We decided maybe it was time to get back to the Four Seasons, so we shot back to the hotel as the sun was setting. Pulling in, we handed the Mercedes keys to the valet who took the car away immediately. As we started to walk into the hotel, we heard a commotion in the driveway and turned around in unison to see our motorcade and VIP entourage arriving back at the hotel. The main VIP, crew, and my security people, all nodded or said hello as we marched into the hotel together—a spontaneous and fortuitous moment of timing that seemed professionally choreographed.

From the look of things, we'd been standing at attention all day, just waiting for their arrival.

68

The Queen Mother

During my college limousine job in Washington, D.C., I was sent to join a small motorcade for Queen Sirikit of Thailand. The embassy just needed an extra limousine for a few hours while the queen went shopping. I met them at their hotel and we motorcaded to Mazza Galleria in Chevy Chase—a small, exclusive mall with a Neiman Marcus as the anchor store.

There was the usual State Department security, a couple of black embassy cars, but the queen was in a light-colored Cadillac Seville, which was unusual. The queen's driver was, I thought, probably usually the ambassador's driver except when someone like the queen was in town. It seemed likely since he was well dressed and not in a dark suit like the other embassy drivers. He had a really long, white scarf around his neck that he kept throwing around. This actually was typical of the way embassy drivers dress since the ambassador drivers at embassies usually can wear whatever they want while the lower ranking have to wear dark suits and ties.

The queen, her entourage, and some of the diplomatic security went into the mall. We were going to be there for a while and I saw the queen's driver go into the mall as well. I asked one of the security agents if I could go in and he said yes. "Just don't start shopping and get back as soon as you can." The other embassy drivers just hung out by the entrance while security kept an eye on the parked motorcade.

There was a McDonald's downstairs so I thought I'd get a burger and soda. I ran into the queen's driver and asked if he wanted anything and he said no. When I was done I came back up, and the queen's driver was sitting on a bench so I went over to him to chat. I asked how long he'd been with the embassy and he said a long time. He was thin, with minor pockmarks on his face and he was a little hyper but interesting. He asked me a few questions about myself, and we ended up strolling around the mall, occasionally catching glimpses of the queen shopping. Any time we were spotted, the group smiled and acknowledged the ambassador's driver. We made small talk until it was time to leave and then motorcaded back to the hotel where I was finished and free to go. The queen and everyone went in and I saw the ambassador's driver going in, too. I stopped him and told him it had been nice to meet him and that I'd see him around D.C. sometime. He kind of smiled and said he had to go inside the hotel because he had to catch up to his mother.

69
Twentieth High School Reunion

I had an incredible 20th Winston Churchill High School reunion because I wasn't there. Instead, I'd been invited up to Ringing Point, the Seal Harbor Maine home of David Rockefeller for the first time. I flew up with my girlfriend, my best friend, and his wife. It was just the four of us and Mr. Rockefeller having martinis and feasting on lobsters in his intimate Maine home. I looked around his cozy living room, at the fireplace, the piano, and the incredible paintings, as I listened to Mr. Rockefeller. I took a sip of my martini, looked at my beautiful girlfriend, and thought that if there was ever a moment to think "if they could see me now," this was it.

70

The Hidden City

I was the guest of a very high-ranking government official in Oman, staying at the spectacular Al Bustan Palace Hotel, which looks out on the Gulf of Oman. Unfortunately, my host was called away on a trip with the Sultan just before I arrived, so on the first day I toured around Muscat in a six-door Mercedes with his son and two eldest daughters who were the equivalent of royals in Oman. I was friends with all of them since I knew them from Washington, D.C., where they also had a home. They were in their late teens/early twenties, were fun to be with, and spoke perfect English with a good sense of humor. Customs were a little more relaxed in Oman compared to Saudi Arabia. Here the men wore a simple ankle-length, collarless, long sleeved gown called a *dishdasha*. On their heads they wore the *muzzar* which is a turban made of tightly-folded, colored fabric. They could also wear the traditional *khanjar*, an ornate, curved dagger, distinctive to Oman. The women wore very colorful outfits of long, flowing, embroidered dresses and headdresses. Unlike in Saudi Arabia where the only color is either black or white, here they wore colorful clothing and you could also see a woman's face.

We went to their palace, which was spectacular, sitting high up on a cliff in a neighborhood of palaces just outside

Muscat, the capitol. There was a small village of staff that lived near the entrance on the grounds, as well as guards at the main gate. There were kids running around everywhere and I found out that my host's brother and his wife had been killed in a car accident, after which my host had taken in his brother's six kids as his own. They were having so much fun together playing on the long front lawn as we arrived.

There were small cannons on either side of the entrance to the palace and front doors more than 20-feet high. The palace was huge and open. The foyer had several large reception rooms with colored pillows around the walls where you could be invited to sit on a beautiful carpet. I found it unusual that in one of the reception rooms one wall had all kinds of machine guns on display. Then I realized that one room was for the men, one was for the women, and one was for the kids. Everything was beautiful, modern Middle Eastern architecture.

Next was a huge open area. When you looked up, you could see five or six floors ringed by large balconies. I was told that there were two or three full apartments on each floor for the kids to occupy when they eventually had families of their own. We

walked out the back to a massive patio on the rugged cliff overlooking the Gulf of Oman. There were two large houses to the right of the palace one for my host's brother, and one for an American who managed all of the affairs for the family. Next to that was a garage full of every make of car you could think of.

Both my host's brother and the American, like the rest of the family, were very friendly and gracious. I noticed a massive tower with huge, dark, mirrored windows on the side of the palace that dropped six or seven stories down to the beach below. I asked what that was and they told me it was the private offices of their father who was away. One floor was a full disco, but the kids were never allowed in the tower.

I had something to eat with them, then ended up on the front lawn with all of the kids throwing balls, playing tag, and tossing Frisbees. My host's children took me around Muscat the next day and showed me the Sultan's palace and a restricted active fort that they had access to. I thought how great it was to get to see the capital from behind the scenes like this. The following day, my host arranged for a government Toyota Land Cruiser with a driver and an escort from his office to show me Nizwa and other cities out in the desert.

The Land Cruiser had special government license plates that helped at some checkpoints and places throughout the day. The car had a refrigerator built in between the front seats stocked with water, sodas, and Heinekens. Being out in the desert all day looking at camels, forts, and lots of *wadis*, which is the term for an oasis, we almost emptied the refrigerator except for the beer. I figure I could have one when I got back to the hotel in case it would offend the escort or driver.

I was surprised that the country had no visible water issues and so many *wadis* featuring beautiful palm and date trees. The terrain was rugged everywhere we went and we seemed to always be surrounded by beautiful mountains shooting straight up from the flat desert along the coast. We visited several old forts and towns in *wadis*, where they still make handmade rifles and swords. I was pretty much ready to head back to the hotel after a long day of being in the desert when my escort said he wanted to show me one more thing. We were at the foot of a very tall rugged mountain that went up at an angle instead of straight up. I thought they wanted to show me the view from the top since there wasn't anything up there that I could see. We zigzagged up the mountain for about a half an hour and were almost at the top when I saw a huge crack open up across the mountain ridge. It was an optical illusion from the base of the mountain since you couldn't see it until you were right on top of it. There was a place we could safely park. I slowly got out of the Land Cruiser and couldn't believe what I was seeing. It was like something out of an Indiana Jones movie. An entire hidden village descended into the darkness of this crevasse.

Some of the villagers came out to the truck and saw the government license plate. They were in awe of me since I wasn't an Omani, yet I'd arrived in a government vehicle. The funny thing is, I was wearing a white Britches brand shirt with their logo featuring two warthogs and a shield. All the villagers wanted to touch it thinking it was some kind of royal crest. The

driver told me there were hundreds of people living here. They were mostly women and children from what I could see, and they were all smiles as they followed us around. We walked in and out of caves and under waterfalls on narrow dirt paths that had to be a thousand years old. The path kept snaking and disappeared down into the crevasse. We were above the tops of date trees then we were under them, and they just disappeared down into the crevasse, too. I could see village cave homes lit up by oil lamps deeper down the path.

The waterfalls, date trees, and hidden city were one of the coolest things I've ever seen. Villagers kept trying to invite us into their cave homes, which I wanted to do, but my escort didn't want any part of it.

We made our way back up the path through carved stone arches, past the numerous cave homes, waterfalls, and date trees, back to the Land Cruiser. My host's children met me back at the hotel, and we hung out on the beach until it got dark. Then I had to pack up to leave this Arabian paradise the next morning.

71

In the Money: the Best Summer Job a Guy Could Have

One of my best summers was spent living at the Playboy Club in Atlantic City. As I was heading into my senior year of college, I knew the limousine company I'd worked for the whole time I was in school was collapsing. My boss had a bad gambling habit, which ultimately led him to sell 500% of his company, borrow from loan sharks, and finally embezzle three million dollars from a D.C. bank. He had pretty much stopped running the company and spent all his time at the Playboy Casino gambling—a situation the casino, at least, was very happy about. He was a "whale" in casino lingo, living large in their finest suites with Carl, who was his bodyguard, his accountant, Dean, and his attorney.

Because of his addiction, he didn't care about the restaurants, shows, or most of the time, the bunnies. He just had to gamble. Everything was comped by the casino as long as he kept gambling. I got in on the whole thing when my boss had me bring his lawyer up from D.C. one day. Carl took me around, told me just to stay, and got me a comped room. I only saw my boss from a distance as we partied. Carl had my girlfriend, who worked for a Delaware congressman, come up along with his own fiancé, who worked at the Capitol. He called her the Queen of C-Span, she was on there so much.

POINT OF CONTACT (POC)

We had huge expensive dinners at Chat Noir (Black Cat), the main restaurant, and the best table in the house for the shows. We were so close to the stage that once when they turned the lights off then back on, I had a huge Bengal tiger about a foot away from me. They had motorcycles in round cages, magicians, singers, and dancers. We'd order two or three bottles at a time of Dom Perignon or Perrier Jouet, all with little red Playboy stamps on them. We'd compete and have the hotel photographer take our pictures with as many bunnies as we could fit in the picture. The casino charged $35 per bunny in each photo. We descended on the gift shop and cleaned it out. All we had to do was sign purchases to our boss. I felt like Ray Liotta in *Goodfellas*. It got so crazy.

The boss finally found out I was staying there, but he didn't care since the casino was picking up the tab as long as he was gambling. I went home a few times for clothes, or to pick up money for him, or to take money from him to the office. I took turns with Carl carrying packs of ten thousand dollars each and we had designated times to be at either a roulette or baccarat table to deliver the money to him. He'd gamble a little in the afternoon then a lot at night. Virtually every time I approached his table, I could hear the gasps of people watching him gamble.

He was wild, making huge bets that either vanished in seconds or multiplied. He didn't care that he was putting on a big show in his super expensive suits, silk shirts, ties, and Gucci loafers. The management would rope him off by himself, and when the dealer spread out all the cash there'd be more gasps. He might as well have been in a zoo from the amount of people watching him. He'd give

me up to $500 in chips a day to gamble with, depending on his luck, but I just tossed them in a drawer. He could lose big or win big by the hour. He drank Chivas Regal nonstop but never got drunk. I thought, why work, when I can live my boyhood fantasy surrounded by obliging red hot Playboy bunnies, high on the hog at the beach all summer?

I was now riding in the back of limousines going out to other casinos or taking quick round trips to D.C. with cold bottles of Dom Perignon. Occasionally, my boss would leave for a little while in the Playboy helicopter to go back to D.C., then come back flush with cash from wherever he had it hidden. That meant we had to leave until he came back since we weren't gambling. The hotel was right on the boardwalk and the beach and we'd go out from time to time, for a change of scenery.

Our rooms looked out over the ocean, and my girlfriend loved to jog on the boardwalk or hang out on the beach. My boss had all kinds of people coming and going, visiting him, or there for him to try to get more gambling money from them. Near the end of the summer, he must have seen the writing on the wall. The bank's money was running out, he'd already sold 500% of his company, I was told, and he'd tapped out all his sources, so he decided to have one huge, blow out party at the casino's expense.

Carl and I arranged more than thirty rooms in the hotel for the weekend for everyone back at the office and some of the limousine drivers. Hardly anyone was left to even answer the phones. There even was a grandmother who drove one of the limousines for our company and she came, too. My boss just let everyone loose on the hotel. Nothing was organized except for the rooms. My boss was staying in the Asia Suite near the end of summer, which was surreal to go into and became the communal meeting place.

Out of the blue, someone pulled out a bag of magic mushrooms and practically everyone took them, including my boss. It was a riot. We roamed the casino, restaurants, shows, and gift shop in packs. We drained the hotel of all of its steak, lobster, shrimp, Dom Perignon, and Perrier Jouet. It was the wildest weekend imaginable and an incomparable end to the greatest college job ever.

Not long after that, the FBI descended and arrested my boss, his lawyer, his accountant, a few other people, and raided both the office and my boss' homes. Carl got off as a witness and they never knew about me, not that I'd done anything wrong.

My boss was finally sentenced to fifteen years in Club Fed (Allenwood Penitentiary,) but ended up serving only three years. The funny thing is that the FBI never recovered any of the money he'd embezzled. So after my ex-boss got out, he tried everything in his power to buy back one of his former houses that had been seized. He did supposedly have a couple of new walls built there during that last blowout summer....

72

Memories of El Salvador

When I was a little kid, we lived in San Salvador for five years. El Salvador and living there are my first memories. My father was working on all of the bridges for the Pan American Highway at the time. We had a beautiful home with a large pool that sat up high, overlooking the countryside. There was a big coffee finca (farm) next door, and the Chinese ambassador lived next to that. Our home had seven maids and a gardener who all lived there too in order to take care of the place, as well as the four of us, my brother and sisters, two boys and two girls.

My parents were young and life was good for them there. These years were probably some of the happiest of their lives. El Salvador was sleepy, safe, and peaceful back then.

In 2005, my stepfather's daughter was temporarily living there doing some humanitarian medical mission work. My stepfather decided he wanted to visit his daughter and take my ailing mother and my younger sister who had been born there. I didn't like the idea at all. I checked with a friend in the CIA and another with the State Department, and they both said not to go because it had become very dangerous. Unfortunately, my stepfather was completely oblivious and ignorant about these dangers. My mother and sister would both rather have stayed home. As a blonde, my sister would stick out in a country

where most of the inhabitants had black hair, but she had to go because she was worried about my mother.

I tried to talk them out of going, but my stepfather dug in his heels. I had some work things going on as well as a California trip at about the same time so I wasn't sure whether I could go. But I also wasn't invited.

The day before they left I had a family dinner, and they outlined their schedule and where they were staying at the San Salvador Hilton. My sister was nervous and not happy about going and I felt bad for both of them. They left and I realized I had to go in case anything happened to them. So I rearranged my schedule, bought a first class ticket on TACA, booked the Hilton, and left the following morning.

My State Department associate gave me the lay of the land regarding what to do and see. The road between the airport and hotel was the most dangerous, depending on the time of day. That was where all the robberies and murders occurred because the criminals knew their victims would have suitcases. My contact said to never, ever travel at night. I'd done things like this before but just wasn't in the mood and was a bit uneasy, especially when, as it turned out, I was the only gringo on the plane.

I'd packed two suitcases, one for El Salvador and one for Los Angeles; the latter I left by my door at home because as soon as got back I had to turn around to leave the next morning for LA. I had to go back to D.C. so my LA suitcase wouldn't get stolen instead of flying right to LA from El Salvador. It was an easy flight down and I was surprised at how small San Salvador was as a city. It also looked like it was on the side of a huge volcano. Getting my bag and going through the airport was fine but I knew as soon as the airport exit door opened, it would be a chaotic throng of Salvadorians. It was worse pandemonium than I'd expected, and I had to really push my way through the crowd.

I started to get concerned when I couldn't find my ride and realized no one knew I was there. I pushed my way to a driver standing next to a nice van holding a sign for someone who was going to another hotel. I told him I would give him $40 to take me to the Hilton. He instantly dropped his sign on the ground and told me to get in. I got out of the chaos and was flying down the highway in seconds, much to my relief. I was back, I thought, looking out the window at the beautiful scenery flying by.

It was hot and sunny just as I wanted El Salvador to be. We reached the hotel without a problem, fortunately. As I got out of the van a small motorcade with a bullet proof Suburban and some heavily armed men arrived. I watched as they let out a nicely dressed woman who went into the hotel. At first I thought it was a politician but realized it was just a normal wealthy lady afraid of being

POINT OF CONTACT (POC)

kidnapped. I checked in and got a room on the same floor as my mother and sister and dropped off my bag.

They'd said they were going to spend the first afternoon at the Mayan Club near the hotel. I asked how close it was then got a taxi there. The place looked nice with lots of tropical plants and trees, lizards, as well as carved Mayan statues all around the walkways. I passed a bar on my left on the way to the pool, hoping they were there so I could surprise them. There were hardly any people at all there, but I saw my stepfather watching his daughter playing tennis so I knew I was in the right place. Sure enough, I saw my mother sitting at a table and my sister on a lounge by the pool. I turned around and went right back to the bar, ordered a *Suprema* a Salvador beer then lit a nice Cuban cigar. I put on my sunglasses then casually walked up to them with my *Suprema* in one hand puffing on my Cuban cigar.

I almost got all the way to them before they realized it was me because it just wasn't registering that I was there in San Salvador. They were as happy and thrilled as I was that I'd come and found them so easily. I told them I was also at the Hilton, which we laughed about as my stepfather came up to us with his daughter. He was surprised too, of course, but also annoyed to see me. We had a nice lunch by the pool. They told me they'd gone by our old house and my stepsister tried to ask the owners through the intercom if they could see the house in her limited Spanish. They only answered "no," so they'd gone on to the Mayan Club. My mother said we could drive by it on the way back to the hotel so I could see the outside. We all jammed into my stepsister's little jeep.

When we got there, it was surreal to see the entrance again after so many years and the big stone wall that climbed 50-feet to the side yard and pool. The name of the house was *El Manatial* which meant "The Spring," as in water, but the sign that had hung on the gate was gone. We pulled into the driveway to turn around when I said, "Let me try the intercom. I speak Spanish pretty well. I'm not one hundred percent fluent, but I know enough that I can carry on a conversation. There was a camera on us and I buzzed the owner again and he seemed annoyed the same people were back. I spoke to him in Spanish for a few moments and then the big metal gates slowly opened. He'd told me our car should stay to the right, which seemed odd at first until we started driving up and realized the house had been cut in half to make two homes.

My mother and sister were impressed with my Spanish and so glad I'd showed up since now we were all about to see our old home. I remembered the place instantly from a lifetime ago. The owner had come down the stairs and greeted us. He was in his late sixties and didn't speak any English. He remembered our family name since the house had belonged to his parents and it was they who had rented it to our family. We went into the house where we met his son and wife and granddaughter. He told his son to go get something and bring it to us outside. My frail mother said that her Parkinson's was beginning to take its toll. She seemed in a trance looking around, no doubt reliving memories of my father, a bunch of kids running around, parties, and mariachi bands. I held her hand the whole time as we walked around. I remembered one of my fondest memories of my mother dancing around each of us singing, "Que Sera Sera" as we sat mesmerized by her.

The man explained that he and his brother's families live there now and had built a wall to divide the house into two homes. I held on tight to my mother's hand as we went into the backyard to the pool. I couldn't believe that the pool was gone. They'd filled it in to make the yard bigger. I'd learned to swim in that pool and had had so many good times splashing around in it with my friends. But the pool had vanished, just like all the years since we lived there had vanished. My mother recognized two massively tall trees in the yard  that she'd planted when they were only 3-feet tall. I didn't realize it as I looked around but I think my mother was really in total shock. As if she'd gone through a worm hole and ended up standing in the place of the happiest times of her life again, but as an old woman.

The son came out holding the big *El Manatial* sign over his head that had hung on our front gate when we lived there. They had saved it and when my mother saw it she began to cry. I let go of her hand and put my arm around her. I was so glad I'd made the effort to go to El Salvador and was able get us into our old home for one last time.

My mother passed away three years later, and I'm sure she is once again hosting her parties at *El Manatial* with a bunch of toddlers running around her as she sings, "Que Sera, Sera" to them.

73

Thai Chicken

It was my last day in Phuket, Thailand, where I'd met two of my friends for a vacation. I was headed back to the States the next day while they were staying longer, so when they wanted to go into town to party, I decided to spend my last day chilling out on the beach. We were staying at a bit of a bohemian resort that had been built among a village of fishermen and their families. The pristine, white sand beach and sparkling bay were still undiscovered by the big resorts and as exotic as you could imagine. Huge palm and coconut trees lined the beach, blowing gently in the light tropical breeze.

As I walked down to the ocean, two women in traditional clothes offered me an hour-long massage on a thatched mat under the palm trees for $5. I thought it would be the perfect thing to do after I checked out the beach. There were very few tourists; the area was primarily filled with locals living their daily lives—some people were burning tree branches and old coconuts as others were fixing nets or boats.

There were some interesting old Thai boats anchored among a few western sailboats. The water was crystal clear, and the waves lapped gently on the shore. I took a long walk on the beach, relaxing and admiring the exotic beauty of the place and appreciating the local people who walked by and smiled without harassing you. My friend had bought some opium in the Golden Triangle and left it in the hotel safe, so I decided I would smoke a little and get a massage under the trees.

Those few days I spent in Thailand on that trip were the only time I'd ever smoked opium because it's highly addictive and it's really, really, good. Whatever buttons it pushes are so pleasurable you never want the experience to end. I called it the velvet roller coaster because the moment you closed your eyes your mind took off, and you enjoyed the most pleasant and happy thoughts you could ever have. The other amazing thing about it was that when your eyes were open, you weren't high at all; you were completely in control. So after a pit stop to the room, I visited the massage ladies and lay on the palm mat in my bathing suit under the trees.

One lady was working on my back and shoulders and the other on my feet and legs while I went off on my velvet roller coaster ride. It was about as close to heaven as it gets. When they finished after an hour, I had them start over again, and when they finished after the second hour, I had them start over yet again. They laughed and carried on. Near the end of the last massage I smelled some roasting chicken. Hungry, I got up like I was made of rubber and thanked the ladies who were expecting $15. I gave them $40. They were thrilled, and I walked off to find something to eat.

As I headed back toward the hotel, I saw a local man cooking a chicken in front of his shanty, which must have been what I'd smelled. I walked over to where he sat on a fallen palm tree next to some coconuts, to see if I could buy his chicken. He couldn't speak English so I showed him about $6 worth of baht, the Thai currency and he nodded enthusiastically. I felt bad because I thought the chicken was probably his or his family's lunch, so using hand gestures, I showed him I only wanted the legs and thighs and he could keep the rest.

He was very happy with our deal and pointed to a wooden bench facing the ocean under the trees for me to wait. A little while later, he brought over my chicken legs and thighs nicely cooked. I was shocked and amazed when he delivered them and gave him $10 instead of $6 for the extra surprise. The feet and claws were still on the cooked chicken legs, which were delicious.

74

Broccoli Goes to the Movies

I had a friend in the DC public relations business who gave me two fundraiser tickets to the James Bond *Living Daylights* premiere in Washington, D.C. She told me to get there early because it would be a mob scene. There would be a red carpet for movers and shakers and possibly some celebrities. I'd just bought two new limousines but had no one to drive them and a brand new girlfriend to impress. I read the tickets, noting the time to be there, the group benefiting from the charity fundraiser, the name of the movie, and that the movie producer's name was Broccoli, which I thought was funny. So I asked Derrick, the parking lot attendant at my office building, if he would drive us and he agreed. All he had to do was drive up Wisconsin Avenue, drop us off at the movie theater, wait for us, then drive straight back down Wisconsin Avenue into Georgetown. Easy peasy. We had regular tickets, not VIP ones, and would have to wait to get into the movie until the VIPs were in.

We were a little early getting to the theater so we drove past and then I had Derrick make a U-turn to get in front. I could see a long line of more than one hundred or more people behind the velvet ropes next to the red carpet. I figured that was the mob we'd have to join so, instead, I told Derrick to pull up directly in front of the theater, right at the red carpet, and not to move, not to get out, and not to go near the mob of people.

My girlfriend asked what I was up to, and I said I wasn't too sure, I was just going to see what happened. I didn't open the door, we just sat there behind the tinted windows. It took almost a minute until a girl came running out of the theater with a clipboard and a headset. As she got to the limousine, I slowly opened the door and said hello. Right away, she asked who we were and without missing a beat, I said, "Broccoli." She practically fell over trying to assist us, even helping us out of the limousine. She then whisked us into the theater, past all the people trapped behind the velvet rope. She explained how the evening was going to flow and said we could sit anywhere we wanted. We followed her to a private elevator that took us down to our seats. My girlfriend just looked at me and shook her head smiling. We walked in and laughed because we were practically the first ones there. I said, "I hope the clipboard girl doesn't single me out to make a speech as producer of the movie." Gulp!

We sat midway on the aisle and within ten minutes people were pouring in. I recognized a lot of politicians, some celebrities, and the usual Washington high society. Halfway through the movie I needed to go to the men's room. I took care of business quickly then waited in the back of the theater with a couple of other people for the right break in the action to get back to my seat. I was there for a few minutes and realized I was standing next to John F. Kennedy Jr. who was watching the movie from there. I quickly got back to my seat. I did feel a little sheepish when the lights came on, hoping there wasn't an angry girl with a clip board waiting for me.

75

It Wasn't Me: A Brush with the Law Between Brussels and Paris

I caught a night train from Brussels to Paris. Just before I left the station, my cousin gave me a little hash and a small stone pipe for the ride. I had my own compartment, which was roomy and comfortable with velvet covered seats that turned into beds. Since it was late and less than a two-hour trip, I decided to smoke the hash. The train was quiet so I went down the hall to the bathroom to smoke. For some reason, the window was sealed so I took a couple puffs then hid the pipe behind the mirror.

The small bathroom was full of sweet smelling hash smoke that I figured would go away after a while and hardly anyone was on the train. So when I opened the door to leave, to my surprise a uniformed policeman was waiting to use the bathroom. I had to brush against him quickly since it was so narrow and I'm sure I reeked of hash. I didn't look at, or say anything to him, and shot back to my compartment, hoping he wasn't in pursuit since he had to go to the bathroom first.

I opened and closed my sliding compartment door, closed the curtains, then I went right to the window, opened it, and pitched the remaining hash into the night. I sat down and turned out all the lights. I looked out the window at the passing night scenery on the way into Paris as the hash crept over me. I had nothing on me to get arrested if the train cop did anything.

About twenty minutes later, my door exploded open, all the lights went on, and the cop and another uniformed cop, along with three plain clothes cops, burst into my compartment. They had me stand up and give them my passport. They asked if that was my pipe in the bathroom. I denied ever seeing it, saying the bathroom had smelled that way when I went in. They had me empty all my pockets and went through my luggage. The interesting thing is they looked at all the key hiding places a drug smuggler would use in a train compartment—the ones that they knew so well. I was calm and relaxed since I was stoned and had nothing illegal with me anymore.

The cop accused me again of smoking and said he knew that he'd found my pipe. I just denied that it was mine once again and said the smell was there when I went into the bathroom. Frustrated that they hadn't found anything, they left my suitcase and compartment in shambles as they retreated knowing of course, that it was me.

I got up, closed the curtains, turned off the lights, and went back to listening to Enya. Yikes!

76

Breaking (In) Bad

I'd been living and working in Washington, D.C. for more than ten years and knew, no matter where you lived, you were vulnerable to crime. It's the nature of a city. I'd been in my fifth floor apartment in Glover Park for about eight years when our 79-unit building was systematically burglarized. The police and management couldn't figure out how the burglars were getting in, and it didn't matter which floor you lived on, the burglaries were on random floors. My office was across the street in the Georgetown Office Building and I moved back and forth between my apartment and office throughout the day but never saw anything suspicious.

    I was getting ready to go to San Diego for a few days with a college buddy, Ryan, in order to meet his brother Drew who was living there. I went to my apartment and started putting clothes and few things I was going to take out on my bed. I was in a business suit and it was the middle of the afternoon when I heard an odd noise on my balcony. I looked around the corner to see the hose from the roof deck hanging down onto my balcony.

    At first, I thought it was the building maintenance guy, but then wondered why he would let the hose dangle over the edge of the roof? Then I saw some feet and someone using it to climb down. I watched from around the corner as a guy descended onto my balcony using the hose as a rope. I recognized him as someone I thought lived in the building. I picked up my bedroom phone and called the building maintenance guy and told him to get up to my apartment right away. I had police friends who had advised me to put a broomstick behind my sliding door because those doors could be jiggled open and that was probably how the burglars were getting in. The broomstick prevented the door from opening even if the lock was popped. Those buddies also used to say that it was better to explain yourself to twelve people than to be carried by six, so I also had a Colt .45 pistol, although it was illegal in D.C.

I watched this guy trying to get my sliding glass door open, realizing this was the burglar. So as he was messing with the door, I walked up to it and tapped on the glass with my pistol. He jumped back in total surprise with his hands up. It was so cool! I never took the gun off him while removing the broomstick, unlocking the door, and making him come into my apartment. The entire time I was spouting movie clichés like, "One wrong move and I'll make you look like Swiss cheese."

I told him I knew him from the building and now knew he was the burglar, a fact which he denied up and down. He said that he'd been locked out of his apartment and was just going to cut through my apartment. It was such a ridiculous story. The guy actually had nice clothes on, but he was a bean pole with unusually long arms and legs. The building guy knocked on my door, and I told the burglar again that I'd blow his head off if he moved. So without him realizing it, I put the gun in a drawer in the kitchen because I didn't want my building guy to know I had one, and opened the door.

I explained the situation to the building guy but said I didn't want to get involved. He recognized the thief as well. The burglar kept denying it up and down, claiming it was a big misunderstanding. The building guy didn't want to deal with him either so I told the burglar that if another apartment was burglarized, or if he ever came back to my place, it would be his last time. Then I told him to get out, and he left by way of my front door.

I showed the building guy the hose on my balcony the thief had used to climb down. He left and I went back to packing. Before I left the apartment again, I double checked to see that my broomstick was back in place behind the sliding door. I flew out to San Diego with Ryan and stayed at the Omni where we could see all of the Navy ships and submarines coming and going. Ryan's brother showed up on a huge, silver Kawasaki Voyager XII 1200 with a giant windshield and built-in speakers blasting music. If it fell over, it would take two or three people to lift it up.

We rented a convertible Chrysler to ride around in, California style. The rental papers had all kinds of warnings that prohibited us from taking the car into Mexico for any reason, so we partied and hung out around San Diego. At one point, we had drinks at the famous Hotel Del Coronado where Ryan and Drew's grandparents had gotten married. That's when we decided to go to Ensenada, Mexico the next day.

POINT OF CONTACT (POC)

We decided to take both the car and the motorcycle, with each of us taking turns on the big bike. I rode in the car with Ryan, and Drew rode the Kawasaki across the Mexican border. Then I planned to take the bike once we got through Tijuana. The big fence separating the U.S. from Mexico was impressive and stretched as far as you could see, but as a deterrent to unauthorized border crossings it had to be a joke to the Mexicans. Every couple of hundred feet, we could see little cantinas with supplies next to them, supplies you might need sneaking into the U.S. There were ladders next to each cantina that people were probably charged a fee to use, in order to climb over the fence.

We made our way through the bustling border city. There were all kinds of smells, traffic, shanties, smoke, people, and buildings in all types of condition. We finally made it to the outskirts and it was my turn to ride the beast of a Kawasaki. All we had to do was ride along the Pacific through Rosarita then to Ensenada, about an hour away. Once I got comfortable on the bike, I cranked it up to a 120 mph where it was in its comfort zone, and shot down the highway looking out over the waters of the Pacific. My friends kept up pretty well. I had to slow down when we went through Rosarita, as it was a small, busy beach city and a tourist trap. Then I blasted off again until we reached Ensenada.

We picked out Hussong's Cantina right on the beach and spent a lazy afternoon eating Mexican food, drinking beer, doing shots of tequila, and talking to senoritas. We were there a long time but decided to head back so we wouldn't have to go through Tijuana at night, which would be dangerous. Ryan rode the Kawasaki all the way back to San Diego and I rode with Drew in the convertible, but along the way, we decided to stop in Rosarita to see if we could buy 1/4 sticks of dynamite that I'd heard about.

We found the dynamite easily in one of the drugstores along the strip. We each got two big fat red sticks, just like in the cartoons. We started walking back to the car and the motorcycle when my friend heard someone calling his name. Amazingly, it was three girls from our hometown of Potomac, MD.

They were cute, horsey girls, Carol, Kitten, and Holley, and it was so bizarre to run into them in flyspeck Mexico at that very moment. We all laughed about how bizarre it was to run into them. Unfortunately, we were on our way to San

Diego, and they were on their way to Ensenada, which was disappointing because they were all fun and cool to hang out with.

I decided we should get a picture quickly before we left, so we leaned against their car while cars were whizzing by in front of us. Ryan held two sticks of dynamite on one end, with the girls in the middle, and I stood on the other end. Drew was about to take the picture when a car came so close to us I could hear the side mirror whap into the sticks of dynamite my friend was holding. He went white and my heart skipped a beat, but they didn't explode and the girls were oblivious to the danger.

We said goodbye and promised we would party with them when we got back home, then took off. Before we got to Tijuana, we pulled off of the road at a place high up, looking over the Pacific. There wasn't anyone below us and only an occasional passing car so I did a Clint Eastwood with a small cigar; I lit the fuse of one big red stick and tossed it over the edge, then followed with the other sticks. The explosions were loud and fun, scattering gravel and dust, making a big mushroom cloud each time. We crossed back into California without a problem and spent the next day hanging out in La Jolla before catching a red eye back to D.C.

When we got back to Dulles, it was pouring down rain and evidently it had rained the whole time I was away. I decided I'd stop by my mother's house on the way back since I hadn't seen her in a while. She was having breakfast with my sister who had stayed over. I sat down and had some coffee with them but I could tell that something had happened. I asked what was up, was everything okay? They said, "Are you ready for this?"

I said, "I guess so. *What!*??"

While I'd been away, my mother and sister had gotten a few phone calls asking if I was okay because the callers thought I was dead—including the D.C. police. My mother and sister both knew I was in California and said so, but the same burglar I'd caught, had come back to my apartment, and unable to get in, had attempted to go to another apartment from my balcony, where he slipped and fell to his death. His body had been left on the sidewalk for a long time until the authorities could confirm the dead person wasn't me.

They later found a vacant apartment in the building the burglar had been living in with everyone's stolen stuff. The police said that because of his long and lean build he was like Spider-Man, going from balcony to balcony. It turned out he used to live in the building and was from a wealthy New York family who had cut him off because of drug problems. It was a tragic end for him and haunting return home for me.

77

Fine Wine

It was the end of an almost three-week trip around the U.S. with a dignitary and his entourage. I was at the St. Regis in New York City shutting everything down—the rooms, the luggage and the hotel bill. The lead security agent went with the group of about six people to have a final lunch at a well-known Italian restaurant. During the trip, one of the group, whom I'd been with before, told me that he was separated from his wife. I told him that I was sorry to hear that and he smiled and said, "Yes. We are separated by the Atlantic Ocean." He was the comedian of the group.

After everything was finished at the hotel, I went to JFK and checked them and their luggage in at their airline. This was easy to do before 9/11 and impossible to do now unless people are on a private jet. They showed up and seemed pretty buzzed but happy to be going home. I was relieved because I was starting to lose steam. They left satisfied that the trip had gone really well. On the ride back into NYC, I asked the security guy what had happened at lunch because they all seemed so lit. He then pulled out an empty bottle of Chateau Lafite Rothschild from the 1920s. I said, "What is that about?" He said they'd had a big Italian lunch and had drunk three, $1,000 bottles of wine. The restaurant had had this bottle on display at the entrance to the restaurant and after they'd had the first three bottles they decided they wanted the now empty bottle he was holding. He said the owner had tears in his eyes as he opened it. Their last and fourth bottle of wine should have been their first bottle since they probably couldn't taste it anymore. That last bottle was $8,000, he told me.

78
9/11

The last time I saw the twin towers of the World Trade Center in New York City was on June 12, 2001. I'd flown up from Washington, D.C. that morning with David Rockefeller and his personal assistant on Mr. Rockefeller's Falcon jet. As I was getting onboard, the pilot asked if I was okay flying in helicopters. I said sure, but thought it was an odd question since I was boarding a jet.

It was Mr. Rockefeller's 86th birthday, and I gave him a Charvet tie on the short flight up to New York, but as we descended, I looked out the window and saw only ocean and beaches. I asked where we were and discovered that we were landing in Islip Long Island where the jet was going in for service. We would be taking the helicopter into the city. How fun, I thought.

The jet came to a stop, the door opened, and the helicopter was right in front of us, its engine already roaring and the blades rotating full blast. We simply slipped off of the jet, got into the helicopter, and took off. The cabin was fairly quiet for a helicopter, with two comfortable bench seats facing each other. You couldn't see the cockpit, just the tops of the pilots' heads through a small opening. We flew low and fast across Long Island to the city. I was mesmerized, looking out the window while Mr. Rockefeller read the New York Times. Then New York City rose ahead of us like a mountain range and we seemed to be racing straight at the United Nations, then we veered slightly and landed at the East 60th Street Heliport. Mr. Rockefeller went to his office in Room 5600 at Rockefeller Center, and I decided to fly up to White Plains with his assistant then drive back into the city with him for fun.

POINT OF CONTACT (POC)

We took off, skimming the East River then rising like an elevator to almost roof level of the World Trade Center. We flew by the towers slowly, and I admired them in the early morning light. Eerie now, thinking how doomed they were, and that they would vanish a few months from that day.

Later on that summer day, I joined the office staff for a surprise birthday party in Central Park for Mr. Rockefeller.

The moment the first plane hit, I was in my apartment in Glover Park just above Georgetown in Washington, D.C. I was taking my time that morning, watching a movie on HBO and relaxing because I didn't have to meet David Rockefeller until 2:00 p.m. I'd sold my last company on January 1, 2001 to a corporation that had offices internationally and they'd based me out of Alexandria, Virginia near National Airport and the Pentagon. They'd given me a nice token office but, in reality, I didn't have much to do. I thought I'd go to the office and hang out until I had to meet Mr. Rockefeller. If I'd been watching a regular channel, instead of the movie, I never would have left my apartment. My government associates, and the people I'd been professionally involved with the year before in Saudi Arabia, had been warning me that there would be a terrorist attack soon.

I had a convertible black Porsche and, since it was a spectacular day, I put my top down and pulled out of my building with the radio off. There was a Starbucks next door with an outdoor patio facing Wisconsin Avenue, and I thought people sitting there looked stressed and silent. Normally, a few people would be laughing or smiling or having animated conversations as they drank their morning coffee. I didn't turn on the radio until I headed down Wisconsin Avenue to 34th Street so I could cross the Key Bridge.

The first thing I heard was that a second plane had hit the twin towers in NYC. I slowed down and turned up the radio, listening intently as I continued past all the old homes of Georgetown. This is it, I thought, this is the big one.

I had a quick flash of the fun night I'd had with my cousins at Windows on the World restaurant on the 107th floor of the North Tower and the crazy limousine ride afterwards. We'd gotten there before sunset and had a great booth facing north so we could see all the way up Manhattan. Ironically, it felt like we were having dinner in an airplane. Now I knew why everyone had looked so strange walking around as I started crossing the Key Bridge. I called my sister who worked for the management company at Washington Harbor. I knew that if an attack was happening in NYC it could happen here in D.C and told her that. Like everyone else, we were incredulous that something like this was happening at all. She told me what it looked like on TV since I still had no idea.

Washington Harbor is right on the Potomac River; it's a large complex of restaurants, offices, and condos. My sister asked me where I was and I told her that I was speeding down the George Washington Parkway near National Airport. As you near the Pentagon on the GW Parkway, you get glimpses of the iconic building. Everything was normal as I passed, except that at that exact moment my phone cut out. The jet had just slammed into the Pentagon on my right. I didn't know it or feel it, but it was bizarre later thinking that I'd been driving parallel to the American Airlines jet with all of those terrified people heading in the same direction at the same moment.

By the time I reached my office, newscasters were reporting the crash. My sister said she'd kept trying to call me and had gone outside to see a giant plume of black smoke growing bigger and bigger, seemingly from the spot where I'd just told her I was. Twenty tense minutes later, to her relief, I called her from a landline, since cell phones were useless now. She said it just figured I'd be right there when it happened and scare her. She couldn't leave since she was with management and had to help evacuate the harbor.

I knew David Rockefeller wouldn't be coming now, and I was stuck on the wrong side of the river with roads that would become instant parking lots. I closed the door of my office since there was such commotion in the building, made myself comfortable, and stayed all day, which was unusual. I followed the attacks and towers collapsing on my computer. I made phone calls most of the day to check in with everyone who mattered. Deafening F-16 jets were rocketing low all over the place, rattling my windows and making white circles in the sky. Finally, around 4:30 p.m., I decided I might as well try to get home.

GW Parkway would be gridlocked since it's only two lanes so I figured I'd go via West Glebe Road and catch I-395 into D.C. Since everyone was trying to get out of D.C., I'd go in. Traffic was worse than I thought; everyone inched along. I had my top down and people had their windows down since it was still a warm, crystal blue sky day. It took more than two hours to get up to the I-395 on ramp. It was almost 6:30 p.m., and it normally would have been a ten minute drive.

When I had the ramp in sight, I saw a police car with flashing lights blocking it. That would now send me into a labyrinth of jammed roads, gaining an inch at a time in my bullet Porsche, probably until the next day. When I started inching past the police car blocking the on ramp and heading into oblivion, I couldn't

POINT OF CONTACT (POC)

believe my luck and timing. I watched the policeman casually walk around his police car, get in, and drive away at that exact moment! Before anyone could get in my way, I shot up the ramp.

The Porsche I had had a tiptronic transmission which means I shifted gears with my thumbs on the steering wheel. I switched the radio from the news and pushed in a CD as I blasted through all the gears and shot out onto I-395. It was spooky and surreal. There was absolutely no one behind me—I could see for miles—and absolutely no one in front of me, and I was on one of the busiest highways in D.C. I was alone as I revved up to 100 mph, since the police wouldn't bother with a speeder on a day like this. For a moment, I spaced out on what had happened earlier as I blew by the Army Navy Country Club. I was simply relieved to be free of the traffic and was reveling in having the whole highway to myself. Then I came to the bend in the highway just before Crystal City, and my breath was taken away. I began to tear up. I immediately downshifted as fast as I could go, coming to almost a skidding stop in my lane.

On my left was the Pentagon, still a raging inferno even this late in the day. Yellow, orange, and red flames were still shooting high above its roof, coming from the collapse black hole that was once busy offices. I had a side view of the damage and flames. I could see that either side of the hole had blackened a huge part of the beige building. I never even noticed fire trucks or people on the ground; I was so hypnotized by the fire and smoke. I was so used to driving by, indifferent to the building, and now, today, it was jarring to see it so massively, dramatically, damaged. Then I realized the wind was blowing east, carrying the thick jet black smoke right across the highway instead of straight up. It was right in front of me and I would have to drive through it. It looked like a solid black wall against a deep blue sky about 40-feet high, snaking to the east. Cars began to appear in my rear view mirror. I cranked up the CD and took off, blasting through my gears. I held my breath as I hit the black wall with zero visibility, and in a second, I was on the other side looking at the Washington Monument. The smell, which stayed with me for a minute, was an acrid, burning, electrical smell. I'd expected a fuel or burning wood smell but it wasn't either. I made it home, checked in with my loved ones and stayed glued to the TV for the next three days. I remember how nice and polite people were to each other for the next week, which faded away eventually. It was too bad it took something like 9/11 to bring that out in everyone.

I found out much later that I'd missed Mohamed Atta, the ring leader of the hijackings, by two weeks when I'd left Portland, Maine. It's not a huge airport. I was going to D.C. and, as the world now knows, he went to New York.

79

Saying Good bye

I had one of the sweetest, kindest, and most beautiful mothers. She had movie-star looks and I used to joke that if you looked up "mother" in the dictionary her picture would be there. So when she developed Parkinson's disease, it was heartbreaking watching her wither away. She'd smiled her whole life, and that didn't change, even then. No matter how difficult her struggle became, she had a warm smile on her face.

My mother had lived for the last thirty years in Potomac, Maryland, and she loved to go to Great Falls Park nearby, in order to walk along the rushing water and waterfalls of the Potomac River. The disease had made her tiny and frail and stolen her outer beauty so she also didn't look in the mirror anymore and could no longer speak, but she was lucid right up to the end. My older sister had died fourteen years earlier and we hadn't seen my estranged older brother in thirteen years. My younger sister was spending all her time helping care for my mother along with a really sweet caretaker, Mirian, from Ghana.

After five years of this horrible disease, we knew Mom's death was fairly close, so we took her to Great Falls Park one last time. We had a lightweight wheelchair for her, and my sister, Mirian, and I wheeled her on the bumpy, graveled C&O

towpath to the boardwalk that led out to the falls.

It was a beautiful, crisp spring day and the falls, as always, were spectacular. We even stood our mom up so she could take them in, and she was so happy. As we started to leave, it was so sad to know that this was the last time we'd all be there together, and I didn't want to go. By the time we got back onto the bumpy towpath heading back to the car there weren't any people around, just one lone fisherman fishing in the canal. We didn't pay much attention to him and slowly made our way up the path toward the parking lot, about a hundred yards away.

We'd already walked two locks and stopped to look at one of them, when suddenly, out of nowhere, the fisherman appeared right next to us. It was startling as, when we'd last seen him, he was maybe sixty yards away and now,

instantly, he was standing only a couple of feet from us. He leaned over to show my mother a beautiful silver fish he'd caught. What happened next was surreal, yet we all experienced it.

The way the April sun shone from behind him gave him an ethereal glow. He spoke directly to my mother, telling her that the best to be was still coming, and that she didn't need to worry because everything was actually fine. He continued saying things like that, speaking directly, and only, to her. We were hypnotized by his presence, almost in a trance. My mother had a huge, peaceful smile on her face gazing up at him from her wheelchair.

He had a groomed, dark brown beard, a beautiful fisherman's hat, a red and black plaid shirt, a thick, tan leather belt which held a woven fish basket, tweed pants and black boots. In his hand he held a long, dark wooden fishing pole. He looked like he had just walked out of L.L. Bean. I'd never seen him there before, and I never saw him after that.

When he stopped speaking the trance was broken. We thanked him for taking the time to visit with us and said how much we appreciated it. I'm not very religious but religious enough in my opinion, so a few quiet minutes later I asked, "Did we just meet an angel or even Jesus!?" We all agreed it seemed like that, so we decided we had. The encounter was bizarre, surreal, and ethereal, and made my mother's and our day.

A few days later I sat sobbing with my mother, my best friend, on her deathbed. I was alone with her for the moment. It was another beautiful spring day, and she was surrounded by pictures from meaningful times in her life and beautiful tulips from my farm. We had the TV tuned to easy listening music when "Que Sera Sera" by Doris Day came on. I couldn't believe the timing since my mother had often sung it to me when I was a little boy, asking what I'd be when I grew up.

My mother was alert but couldn't speak or open her eyes so I did my best to sing along, completely choked up and crying. It was our final time alone together. If you've ever heard of the phenomenon "death rattle," you know it's a terrible sound made as the person dying breathes, that indicates death is imminent. That sound now came from my mom. We surrounded her in her bed, all crying our eyes out, and my sister leaned close to her face and asked Mom to kiss her. My mom had zero energy and hadn't moved in hours yet she did. I immediately asked my mom to kiss me too, leaned very close to her face, and she kissed me too!

The priest had given my mom last rites and was praying for her as she passed. I sensed my mom's heartbeat, slowed and slowed and slowed, then stopped. She was gone; a beautiful human, flower, bird, sunrise...

After she'd left the house for the last time, we went out to the back patio surrounded by the trees and flowers she loved, and we all drank a toast to her from a bottle of Dom Perignon I'd brought. Nothing would ever be the same. I was now an orphan.

The day of her funeral, I wanted to be alone for the ride from my farm to the Congressional Country Club where everyone would rendezvous to begin the whole funeral process for my mother. I put in "Nocturne" by Secret Garden, and drove the winding country roads to get to River Road and the club. I needed to get everything I had bottled up out before I had to deal with people. I thought about never being able to see or talk to my mother or make her laugh again. Tears streamed down my cheeks, and I let out what was trapped inside, making some

POINT OF CONTACT (POC)

primeval wails and sounds that I'd never made before or since. It was primitive and came from deep inside of me, yet far away—incredibly mournful sounds similar to a wolf howling at the moon. I was going to my mother's funeral.

The funeral was a blur.

My older sister had died fourteen years earlier. She'd been cremated and had wanted her ashes spread at Caneel Bay on St. John, U.S. Virgin Island, where we'd had the most fun summers growing up. My mom had made an attempt several years earlier to spread her ashes, but couldn't bring herself to do it and brought the ashes back to the house where they'd been sitting for years. My younger sister and I decided that two weeks after the funeral we'd go to Caneel Bay in the Virgin Islands and take a break from going through the drama/trauma of the past year, relax, and finally spread our sister's ashes. A former girlfriend who'd become a good friend of ours, Audrey, joined us.

I was really surprised and happy how, when the airline realized we were carrying ashes, they were so respectful of the small, brown paper-covered box, and gave us VIP treatment all the way.

The only way to get to St. John is by boat from the larger island of St. Thomas. It was an incredible feeling arriving at the dock for the first time since we were teenagers. Our father had had construction projects around there, so it had been a great excuse for awesome summer vacations. There were so many great memories: my first make out sessions with a frisky girl from Kansas, many deep sea fishing trips with my father, and scuba diving at night after a couple of Planter's Punches.

Caneel Bay was built by Laurence Rockefeller and gives you a real feeling of island living, no TVs, no phones, and no air conditioning, which, fortunately, was the only thing they'd changed in all those years since we'd been there. There are seven beaches on the resort, but Caneel Bay, Turtle Bay, and Hawknest Bay were always our favorites. We got a couple of rooms right on the beach at Hawknest Bay. Hawknest is full of sea life especially sea turtles and features rugged scenery. The whole resort has a very low profile and impact on its environment, so you really get an authentic feeling—almost as if you've been shipwrecked on a tropical island.

We decided we'd spread our sister's ashes at sunset on Mother's Day, which was about five days away. Audrey arrived, which made it more fun than just hanging out with my sister. She was sure she'd sat next to Kenny Chesney on the plane since he has three houses on St. John. It was very cute how she kept bringing it up. She has three kids now and was considering divorcing her husband, but made a huge effort to keep this secret rendezvous.

In the meantime, I took the box with my sister's ashes in it, drew a bikini on it, put her in a chair with a straw hat and seashell, and she sat on the beach with us. She went out on the beach with us every day like that until Mother's Day. That day, my sister, Audrey, and I got casually dressed up and walked over to Caneel Bay. We picked out a spot to spread the ashes. I didn't ask for permission to do it because that's a quick way to get a "no." I tore off the brown paper covering the box, a little apprehensive about what I might see. There was a white box with my sister's ashes in a clear plastic bag. The water was calm, and the sun was setting as I gently poured them over the water, watching them sink into Caneel Bay and disappear. It was an intensely somber moment. I saw flashes, like mental snapshots, of my beautiful older sister throughout her life. My younger sister and Audrey were quietly sobbing as they threw some flowers on the spot. I got tears in my eyes but was more relieved than sad that we had finally released my sister where she wanted to be.

A couple of small waves came in unexpectedly from the calm water, and I still believe that was my sister thanking us and saying goodbye. That night we partied high atop the resort's mystical 18th Century sugar mill ruins that looked out over the Caribbean to the lights of St. Thomas. It's a dark, cool place and to quote the hotel "tropical breezes drift in to a setting that is simply intoxicating." The Sugar Mill was lit up by mood lighting and tiki torches with mellow island, Sinatra, and acoustic music. We were the only ones there that night except for the manager, Frank, who was so cool; he let us stay almost until dawn. I don't know how many bottles of wine we had that night but we listened to music, we danced, we drank, we laughed, and we cried in the ruins of the sugar mill.

80

New School: A Survival Strategy

My father had an international company that had us moving almost every two years. We always joked that we grew up in the nose of jets with flight attendants as babysitters. My parents were both born in New York of German-Irish-English decent, but I was born in Bangkok, Thailand, which requires an explanation on almost every application I have to file.

It seemed as if I was always starting a new school, which required a survival strategy, and eventually I devised one that worked really well. I was always sent to private schools since we were in all parts of the world. My classmates were the children of the privileged class of that country or city—kids who were very entitled and spoiled. To survive, I'd first observe the dynamics of the class to figure out who was the smartest and who was the most popular. It was easy to figure out who was the biggest. I'd then slowly make friends with the friend or even the friend of the friend, of the smartest kid, the most popular kid, and the biggest kid. By this indirect approach, I'd eventually become friends with the smartest, the most popular, and the biggest kids. This would fast track me for good grades, a social life, and physical protection because the student bodies of private schools prey on the weak and outsiders, so for me, time was of the essence.

81

Table for Three (Two Rock Stars and Me)

I arrived early as the leader of another three-week visit to the United States by a royal dignitary and his entourage. I was going to use my favorite hotel in New York City, the St. Regis, to start the trip. I had everything in place: a Gulfstream IV on standby at Teterboro, the best hotels across the country, security, limousines, and lots of cash. When I arrived at the hotel, it was in the middle of the afternoon, very quiet, so, dressed casually in slacks and a polo shirt, I decided to go into the King Cole bar to get a quick lunch.

As I approached, I noticed a big guy sitting outside the bar by himself reading a magazine. He looked up at me for a second as I stood in the doorway for a moment looking at the Maxfield Parrish mural over the bar. I took a deep breath knowing the three-week marathon was about to begin. Here we go, I thought, another mystery trip with a prince arriving on the Concorde tomorrow and the whole thing has to go perfectly. The lead security agent was coming in that night and we'd go over the details with steaks and martinis. The maître d' came up to me and said, "Welcome back. Good to see you. Please sit anywhere." I ordered a Bloody Mary and sat at a small table for two facing the left side of the room with the mural and bar on my right.

I thought the bar was empty but the maître d' had blocked my view of two people sitting in the corner that my table faced. I didn't look at them when I became aware of their presence, just studied the menu and decided on my usual lobster sandwich. My Bloody Mary came and I took a sip and finally looked over at my bar companions. They stopped their conversation and looked at me. I gave a quick smile and looked away. I'm not star struck since I've been around famous people since my twenties but I was still thinking, Wow! It was two of the biggest rock stars in the world—Elton John and Billy Joel. Then I remembered they were on tour together and realized that the big guy outside had to be the bodyguard.

I had my lunch, thinking to myself how awkward and uncomfortable my position was. Of all the places to sit. I'd never have picked this table if I'd known anyone was sitting there, but the staff had set it up so quickly that the commotion of moving would have been worse. Of course it was difficult to eat with them directly in front of me. I casually had my lunch and left before Rocket Man and Piano Man finished.

82

The Fourteenth Street Bridge

It was January 13, 1982, and there was a huge blizzard in the Washington, D.C. area. I was at the University of Maryland finalizing my last semester class registration for a spring graduation. I'd commuted to college from Potomac with my friend Mike who would graduate in the spring too, if all went well. It was a little complicated registering because we had to pile on an extra class each to have enough credits to graduate. During the day, running from building to building in the snow, we heard that an Air Florida jet had crashed on takeoff from National Airport into the 14th Street Bridge. We thought how awful that was, also knowing the commute home would be a nightmare because of the blizzard.

    We finally finished and met up at his Honda Prelude, which was really good in the snow, and got into the long line of cars inching off campus to Route 1. It was bumper to bumper, with deep snow gullies in the road making it possible to follow the car in front of you. We smoked a little doobie to pass the time, listening to music and the news about the plane crash. We'd been inching along for over an hour and had almost gotten to the beltway when Mike realized he'd forgotten to turn in a key class registration. There was no way anything would be open in the next couple of days and registration would be closed at the end of that day. We had no choice but to go back after all that inching along! Otherwise, he wouldn't be able graduate in the spring.

    Once we turned around, it was a pretty quick ride back to campus because everyone was heading away from campus and no one was going in. It actually only took us about fifteen minutes, though the snow was really coming down. Mike's little Honda with front wheel drive just zipped around in the snow without a problem. We got to the building and I waited in his car while he ran in to drop off his last class registration. When he got back, I had an idea. Instead of getting back into bumper to bumper traffic, why not go into D.C. and have dinner and drinks at Rumors on M Street until the storm and traffic died down, then go home?

We drove easily into D.C., down Route 1, passing miles and miles of jammed up cars in traffic on the other side trying to get home. We stayed for a few hours, had a good dinner, listened to music, hit on some girls, and had drinks as the snow came down. It was such a better plan than hours in the car, and we'd probably get home about the same time anyway.

We were getting ready to leave when we thought, since we were already downtown, we'd see how close we could get to the plane crash. It didn't take long going down to Constitution Avenue, around the Lincoln Memorial and across the Memorial Bridge to the George Washington Parkway. The snow had ended, and D.C. was a ghost town with hardly any cars on the roads.

We figured we would try to park at the Waves and Gulls Monument's small parking lot and walk up to the bridge. We were lucky that the parking lot was plowed out and there was one other car there. We were a little buzzed as we trudged through the knee deep snow up to the bridge. Even though it is called the 14th Street Bridge, it's actually two bridges for incoming and outgoing traffic. Air Florida had hit the incoming bridge. We could see bright lights and heard the sound of generators. We had no idea what we'd see as we climbed up the snowbank. When we got up and on the bridge there was only one man and woman already there. There was some minor activity on the other bridge where the generator lights were blasting. If it hadn't been for the generator sound, it would have been very quiet and spooky still.

We realized the lights were shining on flattened cars the jet had landed on. They had been covered with tarps since the people were still in them. Those people hadn't had a chance since they were stuck in bumper to bumper traffic. The guard rails were gone on that section of both sides of the bridge. The fast moving Potomac River below rarely freezes at all but it was frozen solid. As we walked up to the edge of our bridge to look down, the sight was surreal.

The ice had shattered where the plane had crashed into the river, then refroze. There was a really long, sheared off section from the top of the jet that had flipped over and was facing upright in front of us. The whole ceiling, revealing a section of almost twenty five seats, the seat lights, call buttons, exit signs and all the overhead cabinets, were exposed, some of the cabinets open, some closed. There were things that I wasn't sure of as well as many clothes and personal items were strewn all over and frozen in the ice. The police had put green glow sticks all around the debris which were frozen in the ice too.

There was a stillness around the huge, frozen, shattered hole in the ice. We turned quiet and somber looking down, knowing that there were sixty or seventy people still strapped in their seats under the ice who met a horrific and terrifying end to their lives. I'd seen the aftermath of plenty of plane crashes around the Caribbean but nothing as big or haunting as this. I don't know why we went there that night, but what we saw was so disturbing, we never talked about it again.

83

Mermaid Tales

I've lived in historic Annapolis on and off since college and moved back when my daughter was four. One of our favorite pastimes was to take meandering walks through the Naval Academy at least once a week. It's a beautiful campus full of impressive buildings that could have been designed by Disney, since they were that spectacular. We loved to watch the plebes and upper class midshipmen going back and forth to classes, training boats on the water, and exciting to occasionally witness the Herndon Climb and the Blue Angels.

My daughter loved mermaids, and we had all kinds, big and small, including a glass one hanging from our chandelier. One of her favorites, however, was her Barbie Mermaid, which had a detachable, sparkly pink tail. One day she wanted to bring Barbie Mermaid on our Naval Academy walk. We wandered around past the training boats in the Santee Basin, each with an inspiring name: *Bold, Victorious, Courage, Honor, Invincible*—on our way to Triton Light, which houses a glass ball containing water from all twenty two of the world's seas. It's located on the Naval Academy grounds where the Severn River meets Spa Creek, flowing on out to the Chesapeake Bay.

All along our walk, my daughter danced and spun around with her Barbie Mermaid as happy as could be. Upon reaching Triton Point, I sat on one of the few benches enjoying great views of passing boats and cool breezes as my daughter ran around the seawall. She loved to take the tail off of the mermaid, play with it, toss it around, then put it back on Barbie. So she was jumping around, tossing the tail in the air and chasing it, when suddenly it bounced and dropped right into the deep water off the point. She stood frozen in shock, unable to comprehend that it had just disappeared. Seeing what had happened, I leaped up hoping against hope that it was floating, but no, it had gone straight to the bottom. I made some attempts to retrieve it to console my daughter who at this point had burst into tears and was really upset. This was a tragedy of catastrophic proportions. I rocked her on one of the benches telling her that maybe the fish would find it and give it to a bird and the bird would drop it back on land for her to find again. "Don't worry," I promised her. "You'll see the Barbie Mermaid's tail again. I knew of course, that I'd have to buy another Barbie Mermaid just for the tail because only the original tail would be acceptable, not a replacement doll.

Sure enough, my daughter mentioned the lost mermaid tail almost every day over the ensuing weeks, always searching for it, always hoping that by some miracle, it would turn up.

In the meantime whenever I could, I checked toy stores for this particular Barbie. It had been a gift so I had no clue what store it had come from. After two months of searching, and at least a dozen futile trips to toy stores, I found it at Target. I felt like a champion and knew my daughter would be thrilled. I also knew my fish and bird story would come true. So the next day, I put my plan in motion, pocketing the mermaid tail before we left the house. We took our leisurely walk through the Academy and finally got to Triton Point where she started searching for her mermaid tail as usual.

When she wasn't looking, I dropped it by the USS Maine Mast Memorial near the Triton beacon, then steered her over to it, acting like I didn't see it. She flipped out when she found it, jumping up and down, overjoyed that she'd gotten her Barbie Mermaid tail back. She was simply over the moon happy.

"The fish really found it and gave it to a bird, just like you said, Daddy," she exclaimed. Delighted with my sleight of hand, I sat down on a bench and watched the sailboats as she ran up and down the seawall with her mermaid tail, yipping and singing. I was feeling like a really good dad, a creative dad, as she suddenly came running up to me, calling, "Watch this!"

To my horror I realized she was about to fling the tail back into the water. I leaped up just in time to restrain her. "Why were you going to throw it back in the water?" I asked, truly bewildered.

She was all proud smiles. "Don't worry, Daddy!" she assured me with new confidence. "The fish will bring it back!"

84

VIPs Converge

I had an interesting moment one evening while standing in the middle of the lobby of the Four Seasons in Washington, D.C. I was staying at the hotel looking after a royal in the presidential suite and his entourage. As I was waiting for the prince to come down so we could go out to dinner, President Clinton walked through the lobby. I also worked for him at that time, handling White House motorcades for heads of state visits. I was also good friends with one of his lead Secret Service agents, and we acknowledged each other and smiled. My friend was busy since everyone comes up to President Clinton and we all had our game faces on and were in work mode. As I turned to look for the prince, the King of Spain, Juan Carlos, walked through the hotel lobby. My company was also looking after him through the Spanish Embassy. Everyone vanished into the hotel, and the prince came down and we left for dinner. That was some rarefied air for a moment and another typical day.

85

After You: Good Manners Save the Day

I was on vacation in Antigua and staying at the Halcyon resort, one of only a sprinkling of resorts on an almost mile long beach. The island seemed to be less developed than most of the others I'd been to in the Caribbean and so it had a good island feel. The resort had a complimentary ski boat and captain on standby that guests could use whenever they wanted to ski. So every morning before breakfast, I'd go waterskiing, which was a nice way to wake up.

Each morning, half asleep, I'd stumble onto the beach, wade out to the ski boat, put on my skis, and off I'd go to the far end of the bay and back again, jumping the wake, going back and forth, checking out the beautiful island scenery. One round trip was enough since every muscle in my body couldn't take anymore; it was great fun.

I did this every morning at about the same time for around six days, and I never had to wait because hardly anyone else made use of the boat. By the seventh day, the boat captain was happily accustomed to seeing me each morning, but on this day I arrived at the exact same time as a Frenchman who wanted to ski as well. He said, "It's no problem, you can go first," but I figured he'd probably just arrived and I'd been plenty of times, so I politely declined and invited him to go first.

POINT OF CONTACT (POC)

Sitting on a beautiful beach for half an hour wasn't even remotely an inconvenience. I plunked down in the sand and watched the Frenchman wade out to the boat. The captain tossed the skis to him, he struggled but got them on, and then the captain tossed him the ski rope as well. They were about to take off when the Frenchman absolutely went berserk, insane, acting as if he was being attacked by a school of sharks. He was screaming and shrieking in French, but it was obvious to anyone listening that he was in pain. His flailing around in the water was so bad that I leaped up, but I couldn't see what was attacking him. He finally got his skis off and came flying out of the water. His face was contorted in pure agony as he collapsed on the beach in front of me looking like he'd been whipped or burned all over his chest, stomach, and neck. Long, red welts were getting redder by the second. He was starting to whimper when he suddenly jumped up and ran back toward the resort in order to get medical attention.

I looked at the boat captain who was using one of skis to show me a big spaghetti mess of clear tentacles he'd just pulled up. It was some type of ferocious Caribbean jelly fish that had wrapped itself around the Frenchman. I was really glad I'd been polite that morning and I gave the captain a casual salute. "Maybe tomorrow," I said, turning to walk back to the hotel.

86

Chance Encounters

I worked for years with the British Embassy in Washington, D.C., personally involved in jobs from time to time when a Prime Minster or any of the royals arrived at Andrews Air Force Base. My organization facilitated the visits of Queen Elizabeth, Prince Charles, Princess Diana, Princes Andrew and Edward, assorted lesser known royals, and lastly, Prince William and Kate when they came to California.

On this occasion, we were meeting Prime Minister Tony Blair. All high level dignitaries come into Washington through Andrews Air Force Base (AAFB) because it's both secure and private. The weather had surprised everyone, and it was a beautiful, Indian summer day. Our routine was to set up the motorcade with U.S. Secret Service on the tarmac in front of the small main terminal and control tower and then go to the Distinguished Visitors Lounge. The Distinguished Visitors (DV) Lounge is on the side of the terminal where VIP delegations wait for arrivals. This is also the area where the president, vice president, and secretary of state arrive and depart. Air Force One is kept around the corner. The lounge isn't big, and it's full of puffy brown leather sofas, chairs, phones, and a bar for coffee and water. There are huge windows looking out onto the tarmac to watch any arriving or departing jet. The tarmac itself is massive and littered with different types of Air Force aircraft as well as parked foreign aircraft. Fighter jets scream in and out all day long.

I'd driven my black Suburban, and it normally takes a while driving from D.C. out Suitland Parkway to get to Andrews. I'd then get in the motorcade alone in my Suburban for the police lights and sirens rocket ride back to D.C.,

POINT OF CONTACT (POC)

blasting good rock motorcade music the whole way. I'd peel off after the first stop, which on this day, was the White House.

Everything is strictly timed and scheduled when dealing with high level officials. Tony Blair arrived a half hour early and we were supposed to go straight to the White House. So instead, the motorcade picked up the prime minister (PM) and his entourage at his jet. The Secret Service then decided to park on the side of the DV lounge and wait there for thirty minutes to get us back on schedule. It was such a nice day that the PM had his jacket off and was wearing a light blue shirt. The PM, the ambassador, and British entourage hung outside by the motorcade chatting it up in the road. I decided I might as well visit the men's room since we were just hanging around for a bit. I walked back into the DV lounge and could see it was filling with an India delegation, which meant their PM would be arriving soon.

The men's room was so tiny that it could barely hold two people at a time, and it was located down a short, very narrow hallway. What I liked was the great goodie basket by the sink for travelers. When I finished nature's call, I picked through the basket but didn't see anything I needed. As soon as I opened the door, I almost crashed into someone coming in and he had to back up. The first thing that registered in my mind was that the man was wearing the same color shirt Tony Blair was wearing. It was Tony Blair! He gave me a polite smile as we squeezed by each other. It was a surprise encounter and awkward, but better than ending up in the tiny spaceship bathroom with him.

I always enjoyed looking after and being around high level government officials and dignitaries, but preferred, personally, to be invisible. I never went out of my way to interact with them directly. Clearly, sometimes, it just couldn't be helped.

87

Paris by Night

After college, I flew to Paris with two girls from Potomac. I was friends with one and couldn't stand the other. Fortunately, I wouldn't be with them long because I was going on to Brussels to meet my cousin. We stayed in the cool Latin Quarter of Paris at a small boutique hotel. Jetlagged, we wandered around Paris the first day and checked out Notre Dame. We went back and took naps before we went out to a nearby cafe for dinner and drinks. We stayed out late since our body clocks were still upside down. The girls finally decided to go back to the hotel but I was buzzed and wanted to cruise around Paris at night.

    I found a taxi and got lucky. The driver was a nice French guy named Didier who spoke English. I had him give me a tour of all the monuments, and we became fast friends. I ended up riding in the front with him and we laughed about all kinds of things. At about 3 a.m., I wanted to end the night at the Eiffel Tower. He took me there and asked if I'd like something to enhance looking at the tower. I knew right away what he was talking about as he handed me a joint and some matches. Awesome, I thought!

    He waited in the taxi as I walked under the Eiffel Tower and lit up. It was a bit chilly, but very quiet and still, as I stood directly under the massive web of steel girders, puffing on my doobie. No one was around, and fortunately, not even the French police. I stood on the crunchy pea gravel looking straight up the tower, surrounded by the four massive steel legs and I owned it for the fifteen minutes I was there. It was a surreal feeling since I'd just been home in Potomac the day before. It started to get cold and a light fog rolled in so I called it a night. I thanked Didier for making that moment and had him meet us the

POINT OF CONTACT (POC)

next day. The girls ended up having a blast with him, even having lunch with his family on the barge he lived on while I had to take care of a favor. He really showed us a great time the few days we were there and made the trip. I was so glad I'd decided to stay out that night, especially since it was Paris.

88

A Deer in the Headlights

I had a very high level, older HRH prince in Boston for a month along with six security agents. He was in the presidential suite of a five-star hotel, and his group had all of the rooms on that floor. I received a message in Washington, D.C. that the prince wanted to see me before he left so I flew to Boston and met with him privately in his suite.

He sat in a big chair in a full white Arabian robe with gold fringe and a white *gutra* headdress. He was very old and didn't speak English, but he had his doctor translate for our brief meeting. He then gave me a gold Gucci watch, which was really flashy. I thanked him and said I would see him at the airport. Going to the airport for an arrival or a departure always shows a sign of respect.

The doctor escorted me out, and when I was about to leave, he handed me a thick white envelope which, of course, was packed with hundred dollar bills. One thing the doctor said to me before I left was a bit odd. He said he didn't know how people could live for less than a million dollars a month!

I spent the rest of the afternoon on Boston Commons with an old girlfriend from D.C. who I hadn't seen in a while. When it finally got dark, I headed out to Logan Airport to the private aviation terminal. I had the tail number and was not surprised to see that it was a DC 10 which is a very large aircraft. I walked out to the plane and climbed the stairs. The crew and the beautiful Moroccan flight attendants could have cared less that I was wandering around the jet.

The whole center of the plane was a beautiful lounge with etched peacocks in glass and plush built-in sofas and chairs, all with seat belts. Built-in televisions everywhere you looked. If I didn't know I was on a jet I would have thought I was in someone's elegant home.

I walked toward the back where there were some plain bedrooms with bunk beds, then to the back of the plane which was about ten rows of first class seats for staff. It struck me as funny seeing first class seats in the back of the plane, instead of the front. Then I headed up toward the cockpit. I walked through the big lounge with the peacock etchings and entered a large master bedroom to the right of the jet entrance. One of the gorgeous flight attendants was sitting in there putting her make up on and barely gave me a glance.

I always liked to check out the cockpits since I've ridden in so many for takeoffs and landings. So I was really amazed at this one because there weren't any cockpit doors or wall, it was just wide open. There was a long, plush, built-in sofa facing it so you could sit and watch the pilots fly the jet anytime during the flight. What a great idea.

I went back to the lounge and sat there for about an hour looking at different Middle Eastern magazines with female body parts blacked out. One of the flight attendants brought me a ginger ale, but a martini would have been better. I'd forgotten it was Halloween night, so Boston would be a little wild, but my plan was to have dinner with the security agents, then fly home that night. I walked up to the door of the jet waiting for the limousines to arrive. It was getting to be a windy, misty rainy night when they finally pulled up to the bottom of the jet.

I got down the stairs before the limousines stopped and opened the door for the prince. I shook his hand quickly, and let him get onboard and out of the weather. I was sure he was anxious to get home after a month. I had one of the limousines take me to Capital Grill for dinner where everyone celebrated the end of the visit with big steaks and wine. There were people in costumes everywhere, which made it a bit surreal. I left them there because they were going to Salem after dinner to look for witches on Halloween. I finally caught my flight back to D.C. because it's not where you go to sleep but where you wake up that counts.

I got home around 1 a.m. and no one was awake. So I took off my jacket, loosened my tie, got a Heineken, and sat outside on my front porch. The house faced the road but was hidden by brush and trees. I was about halfway through my beer when a car came speeding down the road and I heard a *thaaaawaak!!* and the sound of crushed metal and broken glass. I sat up to listen as the car stopped for a second then hit the gas and took off. They'd hit a deer.

I put my beer down and walked down to my gate to see how bad it was. There was a street light there but I still couldn't see the deer. I could hear some rustling and then the deer charged out of nowhere and almost nailed me with its antlers. Both its front legs were broken but it was launching itself around with its back legs. It was frantic and freaked out and hurt very badly. I went back into the house and called the police since the deer jumping around on the road could send the next car into a tree.

I finished my beer and went back to the road where the deer was now in a gully flailing about. The policeman arrived and turned on his lights. I showed him the deer and he went and got his shotgun. I stood there as he shot it three times without much change. I asked what he was shooting with and he told me birdshot! On a 200 pound buck! I said, "You're torturing it! Use your pistol!" and he told me he had to account for his bullets.

I said, "Well, account for one and put him down!" Next time I'm staying in Boston....

89

Shark Bait

There was a big group of family and friends in Acapulco. Someone had a connection, and we were able to borrow a 60-foot motor yacht with a crew for the afternoon. It was a big deal for my girlfriend to go because she needed all kinds of permission to leave the country since she was fluent in Russian and worked for the NSA. It was also my first badly needed break after starting my first company. So we were trying to have the best time we could that week.

The yacht took us to La Roqueta Island, about thirty minutes out in Acapulco Bay. We had lots of food, tequila, beer, and music, and we were also having a great time diving off of the highest part of the yacht. Locals in rickety ski boats would come by to see if anyone wanted to go water skiing. Finally, my sister, her friend Adam, and I decided go for a spin. My sister got into the locals' boat in her bikini, and Adam and I got into the water to ski at the same time.

Now there are a lot of stories of unreported and reported shark attacks around Acapulco Bay. Mostly the attacks are from tiger sharks—sharks that are big and eat anything and that are attracted to garbage in the water. So the name of the game was to ski without falling into the water.

We took off, and everything was going great. We whizzed around, the two of us going back and forth over the wake, my sister waving to us from the ski boat. We were skiing for only six or seven minutes, when the boat suddenly made some sputtering noises then broke down. Adam and I both slowly sank into the water.

I looked around and we were dead center in the inlet where the tiger sharks were known to come in from the ocean into Acapulco Bay. We were too far from shore to swim and about a quarter of a mile from the yacht. We sat there floating in our life jackets like sitting ducks, watching them working on the engine. We had to let go of the ski ropes because they were starting to drag us but if we'd realized the boat wasn't going to start again, we would have pulled ourselves into the ski boat.

The ski boat drifted away from us quickly carrying my distressed sister in a bikini with two Mexican guys. We realized it was taking too long and we were going to have to save ourselves by swimming all the way back to the yacht. We tried waving at the yacht, but they were too far away to realize we were in trouble. We thought about abandoning our skis, but figured at least they gave us something to use against a shark, which of course was completely false security.

We pushed the skis along in front of us. Adam kept joking, making one of his skis look like a shark fin sliding along next to him, which I didn't think was funny, so I kept him behind me. We crept along in the water toward the yacht not wanting to even make a ripple. Meanwhile everyone on the yacht was partying and oblivious to our life and death situation.

It was the longest, scariest swim I've ever done in my life, knowing my feet and legs were dangling just waiting to be attacked by razor sharp teeth. It took almost forty five minutes of high anxiety to get back to safety. We were back onboard the yacht for about ten minutes, trying to figure out how to rescue my sister, when the ski boat came speeding up. We gave the guys their skis back and after a few tequila shots, I started to calm down.

I didn't go back in the water the rest of the day and stayed close to my girlfriend as I admired my still-attached feet.

90

Night Owls

I had a dignitary group I was looking after which liked to stay out late. We were staying, as usual, at the St. Regis Hotel in NYC, and we would go to all the best nightclubs. They only drank Cristal Champagne, which normally costs $200 a bottle, but was very expensive at the clubs. Some places were so exclusive that they charged $1,000 for us just to sit down. Sometimes, even after paying that, the group would leave after only half an hour.

    The trip had just started, and we'd been out very late as usual. We returned to the St. Regis around 4:30 a.m. but couldn't get near the hotel because it was surrounded by flashing lights and fire engines. We had the limousine drop us off as close as possible since there were pools of water and fire hoses criss-crossed like spaghetti all over 55th Street. There were eight of us, including one security agent, stepping over the hoses and around the fire engines. We were, of course, concerned that the St. Regis was on fire. We were all dressed in our expensive suits and when we reached the hotel, the front steps were covered with unhappy hotel guests in white bathrobes. We went in through the revolving doors into the lobby. More sleepy, unhappy people sat leaning against the walls in their white bathrobes. I saw captains of industry, movie stars, diplomats, and wealthy people sitting all over the lobby floors. The hotel definitely smelled like smoke and in the middle of the lobby was a group of very tall Irish firemen.

    We stepped over and around people to get to the King Cole bar where we actually got a few chairs for the main VIP and a couple of his entourage. We were the only ones dressed and got some looks since it was clear we'd just returned to the hotel after a night on the town. I wandered around to see if I could find a hotel staffer who was "on my payroll." While I was doing this, our security agent got into a small argument with a famous movie star who was taking pictures of us and he tried, rightfully, to stop her. They weren't letting anyone up to their rooms and it was going to be a while before they would.

    I finally found one of my people who said that he could get us back to our rooms right away while everyone else had to wait. He told me that the fire was next door at Bijan on Fifth Avenue and not at the hotel, but all the smoke had made its way over to the St. Regis. I told him to wait for us, and I got our group out of the King Cole bar. We had to step back over everyone in their bathrobes again and made our way through a combination of different routes across the ballroom on the top floor, with its vaulted cloud-painted ceilings and gilt covered chandeliers, then down to our rooms. It definitely paid off being a night owl that night and gave the group an excuse to stay out late for the next several nights in case there was another fire.

91

Here Comes the Bride

After my friend's wedding at the National Cathedral, which is as prestigious as it gets in Washington, D.C., I attended the reception, held at the Woodrow Wilson House—the former president's home at one point. The party went on as usual—catching up with old friends, witnessing the bride and groom dance, the cutting of the wedding cake. Eventually, the groom got pretty trashed and needed help getting up to the changing room on the third floor in order to prepare to head off for the honeymoon. We were all standing outside the door to the changing room, a couple of the groomsmen and me, saying goodbye to him. He then drunkenly flung open the door and the bride was standing in front of us, topless, half out of her wedding dress. We were frozen, and she was frozen, but the groom didn't have a clue. Without ever turning around, he simply kept talking to us. His poor bride screamed, mortified, and dove behind the bed. They divorced a few years later.

92

Cadillacs

I was working at my college limousine job when I got a request to drive Mr. DeFazio, who was one of my regular clients. It was at the height of a presidential campaign and the Iran hostage crisis. Mr. DeFazio was from the Midwest, a very wealthy self-made businessman. He had his own jet and came and went from Washington, D.C. once or twice a month for a few hours each visit. He was down to earth, friendly, and knew I was working my way through college. So in a fatherly manner, he was always above-and-beyond generous with me.

On this particular trip, he was coming in for a small private donor fundraiser dinner for a very well-known presidential candidate at a home off of Foxhall Road. I picked him up at his jet at Butler Aviation, the private jet terminal, and we chatted on the short ride to the home. There was a Secret Service checkpoint at the entrance to the estate where Mr. DeFazio checked in and then I drove him down the driveway to the main house. There were Secret Service walking around, a parked motorcade, and some other limousines there. Mr. DeFazio said he'd see me when it was over and went into the mansion.

This was great since I needed to catch up on my studying. I asked one of the Secret Service agents where I could park, and he pointed toward the side of the mansion. He then told me there was food in the kitchen for staff. Those were magic words to a perpetually hungry college student.

I parked and walked in the side door of a large kitchen with a big table. Some Secret Service agents had just finished eating and were getting up. The uniformed staff were busy coming and going with drinks and hors d'oeuvres for the pre-dinner cocktail party as the kitchen staff prepared the dinner. I went up

POINT OF CONTACT (POC)

to a sweet-looking, little black lady who was probably in her seventies. She was wearing a white uniform and seemed to be orchestrating much of the activity. She was apparently some type of governess or head housekeeper, and I asked her if I could have something to eat.

She couldn't have been nicer and immediately took me by the arm and prepared me a plate, asking me to select what I liked. I liked it all. She was really funny too, calling me all these endearing words like "sweetie" and "honey." Then she got me a knife and fork and said, "Follow me." We walked right past the kitchen table where I should have been eating and out the swinging kitchen door to a huge open rectangular room. A Secret Service agent stood at a hallway entrance and behind him I could hear the whole cocktail party going on. The huge, elegant room didn't have much furniture in it and the lady led me to a large sofa and handed me my plate. She went back into the kitchen to get me a Coke, and as I looked over at the Secret Service agent at the far end of the room, he just gave me a blank stare, then looked away.

The governess came out with my Coke, and I asked her whether or not I should be in the kitchen. It seemed totally weird to be eating alone on the sofa in this huge room. She said, "No, honey. You just sit there and enjoy your dinner. It's fine."

Something wasn't right so I figured I better eat quickly and get back to the safety of my limousine. I could hear everything from the lively cocktail party including some very famous voices and that of the presidential candidate.

I was halfway through eating when suddenly the cocktail party ended, and it was clear the guests were getting ready to move into the dining room. I didn't know the house and was hoping I wouldn't see anyone as they went to dinner. Before I could move, however, I could hear them heading toward the big room I was in. I started to put my plate on the table next to me when the presidential candidate emerged. Right away, I thought, "Uh oh!" He locked onto me immediately and leaned over to the Secret Service agent to ask who I was, and the agent just shook his head. I could tell the candidate was furious at the sight of me sitting there. He looked like he was going charge over to confront me but the group started coming out and blocked his path.

He directed all the guests around the corner and into the dining room, never taking his eyes off of me. They were burning holes through me, he was so mad. That's when I stood up and thought, time to go. Mr. DeFazio waved and said hello to me in his typical manner like it was no big deal as he headed into the dining room. That was a small relief for half a second but I still wanted to run. By luck, the candidate's niece came out of the cocktail party just then, and the candidate told her to go over and chase me out. Fortunately, I'd driven her around for three days a couple of months before so she knew me. She asked me what I was doing in there, and I told her I was driving Mr. DeFazio and that I wanted to be in the kitchen but had been led out there by the governess. She was very nice about it and said that I better get back in the kitchen, which I was more than happy to do. As I walked back, I could see her explaining what had happened to the candidate who gave me one last angry glare as they disappeared into the dining room. Yikes, I thought, as I sat down safely at the kitchen table to finish my dinner with all the kitchen activity swirling around me.

When I was done, I started to get up to thank the little governess when she took my arm and said, "Come with me, honey," and headed back toward swinging doors into the living room.

I stopped and said, "No! No! No! I can't go back out there. I think the candidate was really mad I was sitting on the sofa," and she said, once again, "Don't worry, sweetie, they're all in the dining room. They won't see you. Do you want to see some special family photos while I pick up all the glasses?"

She assured me I wouldn't be seen so I went back out with her across the huge living room, passing the Secret Service agent again. She led me by the hand, giving him an unspoken look that could have been interpreted as, "I know, I know." He gave me a look that could have been interpreted as, "You're pushing your luck" while shaking his head.

She took me into a cozy elegant room where the cocktail party had been held. The room was covered in fascinating family pictures and memorabilia that the public has never seen. I was looking at some pictures as the little governess was putting the cocktail glasses on her tray when I realized she was doing Cadillacs. A Cadillac is drinking a half-empty drink somebody else has left behind. I stopped and watched as she downed one after another, no matter what it was. It was funny and cute and explained a lot.

I insisted on carrying the tray back to the kitchen for her since she'd been so nice to me. Once safely back in the kitchen, I took the tray over to the sink as the phone rang. She twirled around and answered it. It was a soon to be famous movie star, and she chatted with him for a moment as if they were old friends. He was calling for the niece. The governess was about to go and tell the niece she had a phone call but tried to give the phone to me so I could talk to the famous movie star. Instantly I raised my hands.

"No! No! No! I have got to go," I said and thanked her for being so nice. I quickly exited the mansion and climbed back into the safety of my limousine and my books.

93

The Five Elements

In Chinese philosophy, the number 5 represents the five elements: water, fire, earth, wood, and metal. So on May 5, 2005, at 5:00 pm, I flew from Washington, D.C. to New York City on a Gulfstream IV. I had a glass of Cristal Champagne on the flight up, and went to 55th and 5th Avenue with five people.

Nothing unusual happened.